HUSBANDS, WIVES, AND LOVERS

THE GUILFORD FAMILY THERAPY SERIES
Alan S. Gurman, *Editor*

Recent volumes

HUSBANDS, WIVES, AND LOVERS: THE EMOTIONAL SYSTEM
OF THE EXTRAMARITAL AFFAIR
David J. Moultrup

MEN IN THERAPY: THE CHALLENGE OF CHANGE
Richard L. Meth and Robert S. Pasick with Barry Gordon,
Jo Ann Allen, Larry B. Feldman, and Sylvia Gordon

FAMILY SYSTEMS IN MEDICINE
Christian N. Ramsey, Jr., *Editor*

NEGOTIATING PARENT–ADOLESCENT CONFLICT:
A BEHAVIORAL–FAMILY SYSTEMS APPROACH
Arthur L. Robin and Sharon L. Foster

FAMILY TRANSITIONS: CONTINUITY AND CHANGE OVER
THE LIFE CYCLE
Celia Jaes Falicov, *Editor*

FAMILIES AND LARGER SYSTEMS: A FAMILY THERAPIST'S GUIDE
THROUGH THE LABYRINTH
Evan Imber-Black

AFFECTIVE DISORDERS AND THE FAMILY:
ASSESSMENT AND TREATMENT
John F. Clarkin, Gretchen Haas, and Ira D. Glick, *Editors*

HANDBOOK OF FAMILY THERAPY TRAINING AND SUPERVISION
Howard A. Liddle, Douglas C. Breunlin, and Richard C. Schwartz, *Editors*

MARITAL THERAPY: AN INTEGRATIVE APPROACH
William C. Nichols

FAMILY THERAPY SOURCEBOOK
Fred P. Piercy, Douglas H. Sprenkle, and Associates

SYSTEMIC FAMILY THERAPY: AN INTEGRATIVE APPROACH
William C. Nichols and Craig A. Everett

HUSBANDS, WIVES, AND LOVERS

The Emotional System of the Extramarital Affair

DAVID J. MOULTRUP

THE GUILFORD PRESS
New York   London

To Donna, Elise, and Cara

© 1990 David J. Moultrup
Published by The Guilford Press
A Division of Guilford Publications, Inc.
72 Spring Street, New York, NY 10012

Printed in the United States of America

This book is printed on acid-free paper.

Last digit is print number: 9 8 7 6 5 4 3 2 1

Library of Congress Cataloging-in-Publication Data

Moultrup, David J.
    Husbands, wives, and lovers: the emotional system of the extramarital affair / David J. Moultrup.
        p.   cm. — (The Guilford family therapy series)
    Includes bibliographical references.
    ISBN 0-89862-105-4
    1. Marital psychotherapy.   2. Family psychotherapy.   3. Adultery—Psychological aspects.   I. Title.   II. Series.
    [DNLM: 1. Family Therapy.   2. Marital Therapy.   3. Sex Behavior.
WM 430.5.F2 M927h]
RC488.5.M69   1990
616.89′156—dc20
DNLM/DLC
for Library of Congress   89-71492
                                                                                    CIP

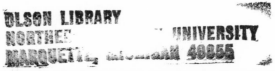

Preface

There are three stories that may help set the stage for this book. The first is about an encounter with a lawyer, who inquired as to the subject of the book. When I responded, "extramarital affairs," he turned deep crimson from head to toe and asked if this would be the type of book people carry in a brown paper bag on the bus. I don't think he believed or even understood me when I answered in the negative.

The second anecdote serves as a complement to the lawyer story. A radio station producer called and asked if I would do an on-the-air interview about my work with affairs. After I agreed, we proceeded to plan a time and then began to discuss the material to be covered. Shortly into that discussion, the producer interrupted and said with undisguised disappointment, "Oh, this is very serious work you're doing!" When I answered in the affirmative, the producer indicated that the material was not what the station had intended and that it would not be useful to do the interview after all.

The third story has been recapitulated countless times, usually within the first few minutes of conversation with someone new to the project. The dialogue inevitably turns to questions about how and why I decided to do a book on this subject. This line of questioning usually is expanded, with humorous overtones, to whether any field work was needed for the book. These humorous overtones probably relate to the anxiety, curiosity, and ambivalence that surround the topic.

This book is an outgrowth of presentations given at the annual meeting of the American Association for Marriage and Family Therapy. Those presentations were, in turn, developed as a forum for illuminating the complexities of applying theory to practice. Affairs were chosen as the focal point because I had an abundance of clinical material from which to draw, because relatively little had been developed in the field regarding the subject, and because affairs are an intrinsically compelling subject. Since the subject of the application of theory can be rather dry, I wanted a subject that was sufficiently interesting to counteract that deficiency.

There are three interrelated main themes in the book. The first is the emotional meaning and function of extramarital affairs in a family system. Perhaps in developing this, the anxiety noted above can be somewhat dissipated. The second theme is a necessary building block for the first. It involves the development of a broad but coherent image of an emotional system. It is unlikely that this is actually possible in any one presentation. The intention is simply that the images in this book make a modest addition to the overall understanding of systems. The third theme relates to psychotherapeutic treatment. The goal here is to articulate one model of the application of theory to practice.

This book will be demanding for a number of reasons. Aside from the content, which at times may call for some reflection, the English language poses certain inveterate problems for the communication of ideas. The most frequent problem here is gender-related. There are four characters who appear constantly, the involved spouse, the noninvolved spouse, the lover, and the therapist. Any of these four roles can be occupied by a male or female. This creates the linguistic problem of needing to express many ideas in the form of he/she and his/hers to establish gender equality.

Since this can be cumbersome to read, only one gender is expressed in any one sentence. Most of the time, the masculine gender is used to refer to the therapist, simply because I am male. Other references to the three people in the primary triangle are assigned a gender only for ease of reading and carry no further implications of statistical probability or dynamics. The burden of gender equality has been handed over to the reader in the interest of parsimonious yet correct grammar. It will be the reader's responsibility to know when both genders need to be understood to be included in a concept or statement.

A book is such a consuming project that it is quite impossible to produce one without considerable input and support. The group of people who have made the most valuable and courageous contribution are the people who have involved me in their personal ordeals as they struggled with the crisis of an affair. In their attempts to make sense of their experience, they have developed many of the ideas found throughout the book. They will remain anonymous but are sincerely thanked for their role in this book.

There are several specific people who should be mentioned. I want to begin by thanking my wife, Donna, whose presence in this book is significant. In addition to bearing the burden of household chores for the three years this book was in gestation, she was invaluable as an ongoing source of support and reflection during the process of conception and writing—and irreplaceable during the editing process. Most importantly, the love and caring in our relationship gives me a perspective on emotional systems which undoubtedly has permeated the fabric of this presentation. In that same vein, my parents, John and Therese, merit a warm note of gratitude for their place in my life and contribution to this book.

Several others have had a direct impact on this book, and deserve heartfelt thanks. Virginia Long, ACSW, offered an important editorial review of the book. Prior to that, she provided me with supervision in my first professional position and was my link to Murray Bowen, M.D., whose work is a cornerstone of this presentation. Carl Brotman, M.D., offered helpful insight from the perspective of a practicing psychoanalyst, teacher, and sensitive clinician. My music teacher, Billy Novick, whose musical contributions can be found in folk music, jazz, and movie scores, had an indirect but critical role in Chapter 4. My brother, Gary, provided crucial computer supervision, making the technical production possible.

This book would not be a reality without the support and direction of the editors at The Guilford Press. Seymour Weingarten and Alan Gurman are routinely acknowledged, but they should be honored as a very special team. They have a marvelous ability to provide support along with critical assessment of works in progress. I want to thank them for their contribution to the book, for the opportunity to work with them, and for the opportunity to contribute to The Guilford Family Therapy Series.

David J. Moultrup

Contents

CHAPTER 1

An Affair
Is Not an Affair,
Is Not an Affair

Edward sat across from me with a peculiar mixture of characteristics. His finely tailored business suit, complete with white shirt and tie, went well with his soft-spoken, articulate manner. Barely past the age of thirty, Edward had succeeded in rising to the top of his division and had assumed a leadership position in his company. His high level of competence had been recognized and rewarded on the job.

But on this warm summer day, the composure and self-confidence that were Edward's strength on the job were nowhere to be found. Edward was distraught. His confusion, anxiety, and depression could be seen in the strain in his face, his stiff posture, and his nervous, abrupt movements. He was so ineffective at work that he had canceled several meetings and made room in his busy schedule for an appointment with me.

Edward proceeded to describe the situation that was the cause of his agitation. He said he was caught in a situation he didn't understand, didn't like, and would not be able to tolerate for very long. He had become infatuated with a woman who was one of his subordinates. And she had become infatuated with him. He acknowledged that she was very attractive but emphasized that he was taken with her spontaneity, her wit, and her romantic creativity. He thoroughly enjoyed his time with her and found her a marvelous conversationalist. He also admitted that he had become sexually involved with her. Edward emphasized strongly, and sincerely, that the sex was not the focus of, or the primary benefit from, his relationship with her.

There was, of course, a complication. Edward was married. He didn't understand why he had become so involved with this woman, because he would have assumed that he had a good marriage before all this happened. Indeed, he emphasized his wife's good points. She was very attractive, warm, supportive, and an excellent mother to their son. Now, however, he was faced with the possibility of leaving her and disrupting the family. The more he considered that possibility, the more confused and distraught he became. He was left feeling torn between two different women, and two different lives. Despite the fact that his brief involvement with his co-worker over the past several months had been exciting and enjoyable, his confused feelings had become intolerable. He needed to escape from the feelings that were tormenting him.

The Therapist's Dilemma

Edward poses several problems for the therapist. On a very basic level, there is the problem of what to call Edward and how to label his crisis. Although both of these questions can be somewhat ignored or glossed over during the intensity of the interview, the answers will sooner or later have an impact on the therapist's perspective of Edward. This perspective, in turn, will have an impact on the treatment that is developed. The questions must be answered if the treatment is to be effective.

Once past these initial concerns, there are more problems confronting the therapist. First, how does one understand this type of crisis?

Why did it happen?

What does it mean for the client?

What type of psychotherapeutic treatment is called for?

Answering these questions is quite complex. The complexity is a function of the multiple levels of experience inherent in the situation. These multiple levels of experience can be seen as different levels of a complicated emotional system, all of which interact as part of the emotional system of the extramarital affair. The levels of systems that are pertinent to Edward, and the treatment questions, can be organized from the most specific to the least specific.

The Individual. Edward as an individual presents a certain set of features that can be developed from the vantage point of Edward as one individual. These include, but are not limited to, psychological defense mechanisms, affect, traits, cognitive style, and physiology.

The Nuclear Family. This level of the emotional system includes the interactional and relationship dynamics pertinent to Edward's immediate family.

The Extended Family. Looking past the immediate family, the extended family, including Edward's family of origin, his wife's family of origin, and various extended family members, has an impact that needs to be defined and understood.

The Immediate Social Network. Edward lives and works in regular contact with a group of people. This is a more peripheral level of the emotional system, but one that can be significant in the balance of the system.

The Therapist. The therapist becomes part of the overall emotional system when Edward begins the therapy. Not only does one individual get added to the emotional system, but the intangible influence of the emotional system of the therapist becomes included as well.

The Professional Community. One additional level of the system brought into the equation by the therapist, frequently unconsidered and unacknowledged, is the emotional system of the professional community. Therapists congregate into various subgroups, frequently defined as a function of such concerns as philosophical beliefs and geographical accessibility. This level of the system can have a profound effect on the therapist's answer to the questions. This, then, will influence Edward's therapy experience and his more immediate emotional system.

The Broad Social System. This level of the system has perhaps the most distant and most intangible impact but is noteworthy nonetheless. Mass media, including dramatic presentations, magazines, music, and popular literature, have been intrigued with traumatic experiences similar to Edward's. There have been countless reenactments of this type of experience, all offering a slightly different perspective on the meaning and implications. To the extent that there is some contact between Edward and this level of the system, it too has an impact on his individual emotional system.

Developing a model that can account for these multiple levels of the emotional system is a problem when considering Edward's trauma. When his experience is compared to other experiences that would seem to be somewhat similar in nature, the answers become increasingly difficult. Each different experience would seem to demand slightly different words, explanations, and approaches.

A Diverse Sampling of Experiences

June

June became involved with her lover almost seven years before entering therapy. Indeed, she did not really enter therapy to discuss her affair but rather to explore problems she was having with her work situation. Her lover was someone she had met through her involvement with Alcoholics Anonymous. She felt entitled to the relationship and was clearly disconnected from both her husband and her lover. She held her husband in contempt. She disparaged his lack of career success, his overinvolvement with their children, and his slovenly personal habits.

But she was equally wary of her lover. She freely admitted that she couldn't marry him and expressed concern when he made reference to leaving his wife for her. She saw him as being possessive, chauvinistic, and not trustworthy. She primarily enjoyed the places he would take her and the gifts he would give her. At the time of entering therapy, she was considering leaving both men.

Jake

Jake was in his mid-forties when he came to see me. He had been in therapy on and off with several different people for almost ten years. He related a chaotic history, including chronic one-night stands with women he would pick up in bars, homosexual involvements, and severe conflict with his wife. She also was involved regularly in affairs with other men. He was the evening shift supervisor at a local plant and was able to slip out of work unnoticed and pursue his activities. Jake was not exactly interested in changing his lifestyle, although he was interested in a more peaceful existence with his wife. Jake left therapy after several sessions, pessimistic that any changes could be made.

Lois

Lois's story is different from any of the other three. A mother of three children, Lois was in her late thirties when she found herself attracted to the husband of Helen, her best friend. She and her husband frequently saw the other couple. They went on outings with the two families and casually dropped in to visit each other on almost a daily basis. When she and Don, who was Helen's husband, began taking the same evening class at the local community college, they began to have more time to talk with each other. Lois began to feel that she could talk to Don more easily and with more satisfaction than she could talk to Glenn, her husband.

They found that their mutual involvement in the class gave them a strong common interest not shared by either spouse. They also found that they each felt dissatisfaction with their marriage. The bond that they felt with each other led fairly rapidly to sexual involvement. Lois felt tremendously ambivalent about it. She enjoyed the comfort, satisfaction, and closeness it provided but did not like the feeling of being disloyal to her husband, Glenn. Lois emphasized, much like Edward in the first example, that the sexual element of her relationship with Don was less significant to her than the closeness she felt when talking with him.

Sally

Sally's story has a certain commonality with the others but adds another twist that highlights the complexity involved in the multiple levels of the emotional system. Sally had taken a new job that entailed quite a bit of travel. One of her trips brought her close to Bill, a former neighbor. They spent a weekend together. She, too, emphasized the fact that the sexual element of the weekend, though enjoyable, was not as important as being with someone who was warmer and more understanding than her husband.

Sally's story loses its simplicity quickly. Sally's husband, Larry, had a chronic disease and had been partially disabled for several years. In addition to the chronic disease, he had slowly increased his level of alcohol intake. He was at the stage at which other people, including Sally, thought he had a drinking problem, although he still denied it. He had been out of work for several years, leaving Sally as the only provider for the two of them and their three girls.

Several years earlier, when Larry was first struggling with his disease, Bill had been around to help both Sally and Larry adjust to the illness. At that time Larry had been concerned about needs Sally might have that he would not be able to fulfill. In that spirit, he had arranged a sexual encounter between Sally and Bill. All three people were quite positive about the experience initially. But different reactions led to different conclusions in the wake of the incident. Sally was more pleased and enthusiastic than Larry had anticipated. Although he still was not exactly jealous of the sexual encounter, the emotional rapport that he sensed between Sally and Bill left him unsettled. He was spared the problem of taking any decisive action on his concerns since Bill was transferred out of the area soon thereafter.

When Larry discovered that Sally had been with Bill on her business trip, he was livid. Sally felt compelled to deny having any sexual contact, hoping that would placate him. Larry accused her of abandonment, and both of them saw her as an "adulteress," in spite of her feeble denial of sex.

The Language Problem

The language used to describe the experiences in these vignettes is as diverse, and justifiably so, as the range of experiences. The labels weave into the tapestry of the emotional system by way of subtle inferences regarding the type of experience, the motivation for the experience, and attitudes toward the experience. In addition to extramarital affair, terms such as extramarital sex, infidelity, cheating, adultery, one-night stand, fling, dalliance, indiscretion, screwing around, philandering, love triangle, swinging, swapping, and co-marital sex have been used to refer to experiences that have some basic similarity to those developed above.

The problem, of course, is that the similarity may only be minimal. As is evident from the small sample of experiences already described, the range of behaviors, experiences, and dynamics that can be categorized as some type of extramarital relationship is considerable. The language does reflect this diversity, though often with confusing connotations. For example, philandering and screwing around can connote chronic or frequent extramarital involvement, whereas a fling or an indiscretion can connote a one-time occurrence, as does the more specific term of a one-night stand. Each label also can have overtones of motivation and propriety. For example, sowing wild oats has an almost benign suggestion of an innocent, developmental experience, whereas cheating suggests a type of malicious, inappropriate act. The multiple possibilities for interpretations and inferences in the language result in a clear need for accountability and precision in using the various labels.

The diversity in language, combined with the complexity inherent in the multiple levels of systems, creates a fertile ground for the development of the meaning of these relationships. The challenge is to avoid the misunderstandings possible with the inappropriate application of language and concepts and to develop a generalizable model.

The Sex Factor

In the last vignette, Sally's feeble attempt to deny any sexual contact is a critical illustration of the prevailing perception regarding extramarital relationships. Sexual involvement is, time after time, the primary focus for concern. If there is no sexual involvement, the relationship is not seen as a problem in the same way as if there were sexual involvement. This probably is a vestige of attitudes conveyed by the biblical commandment of the Judeo-Christian heritage, "Thou shalt not commit adultery." Adultery was defined as sexual relations with someone other than a spouse, thus establishing a clear and strong expectation for a sexually monogamous relationship.

To the extent that the commandment reflects certain very human characteristics as much as it actually shapes them, there is a more basic premise for the preoccupation with the sexual possibilities of extramarital relationships. There is a common perception that physical impulses are more compelling, and thus more likely to be acted on, than are emotional needs. In other words, the commandment is ostensibly founded on the assumption that people will act on sexual attraction to others unless they are commanded to do otherwise. This assumption seems to have become so common that it is taken to be "the truth."

This supposed truth, however, is in sharp distinction to the confused protestations of several of the protagonists in the vignettes above, and countless unnamed others. When people first try to explain that sex was not the primary benefit of their extramarital relationship, they frequently are struggling with a type of cognitive dissonance, a discrepancy between their assessment of their emotional involvement and their images of what they think is expected. It is as if they are not sure they can even believe themselves! Perhaps, they think, they are fooling themselves. Perhaps they should be honest and confess that they needed sex. But in many if not most instances, that simply does not fit with their experience.

This confusion about the relative importance of sex is not limited to the confusion of a "philandering villain" grappling with anxiety and depression. Sex is inextricably linked to the notion of an extramarital relationship, and it is woven into a general confusion about sexual attraction and sexual needs versus emotional attraction and emotional needs. Since emotional needs can't be correlated to hormone levels or physical gratification, there is a tendency to discount them entirely, or give them less import than the physical impulse. In fact, clinical evidence consistently indicates that even when there is sexual involvement, the emotional and dynamic underpinning of that relationship is more critical in the etiology and maintenance of the relationship than the simple physical act.

An affair is an emotional solution to an emotional dilemma, not a behavioral response to a physical stimulus. Sex, because of the emotional intensity of the encounter, can act as a medium of exchange in the emotional system.

The sexual component of the affair, in the strict sense of sexual interaction between the involved spouse and the lover, can partly be understood as being related to the sexual chemistry between two people. At this level, the sexual chemistry could be seen as the physiological stratum of the individual, which would be a yet more limited level of the overall system. Although this physical attraction is a valid and real factor, it cannot begin to define the far-reaching repercussions of the sexual/emotional connection in an extramarital relationship.

Whereas the physical activity may be between the involved spouse and the lover, the emotional activity, and the emotional meaning of the physical activity, includes the noninvolved spouse and has the potential of including other people in the system as well. In other words, the supposedly isolated act between an involved spouse and lover is really a vehicle for addressing the emotional and dynamic balance in the entire emotional system of the two people having sex. Looked at from this vantage point, the emotional communication between the two people involved in the sexual act may actually be the least important level of emotional meaning to be derived from the act.

As a piece of a much larger jigsaw puzzle, the topic of sexual involvement must be understood to be a piece that helps to make the puzzle complete. Understanding feelings and reactions regarding the sexual involvement can help to illuminate some of the more critical dynamics at play. But to assume that it is the only cause of the involvement is naive and shortsighted. Even with isolated one-night stands that are never repeated, there are systems dynamics that set the emotional stage. And with longer and more involved relationships, sex rapidly diminishes in dynamic importance and must be seen as a medium of exchange in the emotional system.

A Definition of an Affair

What, exactly, is this book about?

Chances are good that the title of the book left little doubt about the subject matter. After all, everybody knows what an extramarital affair is. But after this brief exposition of the range of activities, it should be clear that it is not clear what is meant by an extramarital affair. More precisely, the range of idiosyncratic meanings and experiences leaves room for serious misunderstandings. Where one person may have an isolated incident in mind when using the term, another person may have a long-term relationship in mind. Where one person may assume sexual involvement, the other may be seeing the possibility of an emotional preoccupation that was not culminated with physical involvement. It remained "an affair of the heart."

Given these various permutations, it is quite impossible to arrive at a simple and concise definition of an extramarital affair. It would be easier to define extramarital sex, since that is behaviorally specific. But that very specificity has two drawbacks. First, it leaves unattended the problems created by nonsexual extramarital relationships, and second, it establishes a focus on the sexual dimension of the experience that further minimizes the emotional and dynamic elements.

An extramarital affair is not about sex.

It would be possible to define an extramarital affair as an infidelity. That leaves open the question of sexual involvement, since it is possible to be unfaithful in any number of ways. And it also opens up the question of the contractual understanding in the marriage, which is useful in discerning an affair. For example, if a husband and wife have an agreement that they will not go out for lunch with some other member of the opposite sex, breaking that contract could be defined as an infidelity. But does that mean that there was an extramarital affair? The answer to that question is, maybe yes, maybe no. Essentially, it is impossible to articulate a concise but flexible definition of an affair.

An affair can be defined more clearly in terms of its function than in terms of the behavior involved.

An affair carries out a range of functions that will be developed throughout the book. One specific function of an affair related to the marriage is to alter the emotional distance. In other words, an affair is an emotional involvement between one spouse and an outside person which, by its very existence, modifies the emotional distance in the marriage. This remains true even if the affair did not entail "love."

The notion that there can be physical involvement without emotional involvement is a popular one, but it misses the point. The emotional exchange between the spouse and the lover may not be the critical exchange. If a man engages in sex with another woman in response to an unsatisfactory relationship with his wife or in response to any of the other dynamics that will be developed later, that "purely physical" act with the other woman still has an impact on the distance in the marriage. It may create more distance if there is a need to keep a secret; it may create more closeness if the affair is revealed, and the couple confronts and resolves the meaning of the act.

Specific behaviors and events are ambiguous indicators of any meaning and importance in an affair.

This premise formulates the emotional foundation of extramarital affairs with a slightly different perspective. In an admittedly nonscientific survey, *People* magazine (8/18/86) asked its readers to indicate what constituted an affair. Twenty-one percent of the respondents indicated that infidelity was possible by simply thinking about an involvement. Another twenty-one percent defined an infidelity as being a dinner and drinks, twenty-four percent defined kissing and petting as an infidelity, and twenty-six percent defined an infidelity as being sexual intercourse.

The professional reader who is grounded in the rigor of academic and scientific research methods may want to dismiss this type of data as being irrelevant. In fact, it is quite representative of one particular part of the emotional system that may be more relevant to a client than the more limited world of academia. It certainly highlights the confusion about the definition of an affair in the general public. This confusion relates to the struggle to define an affair with a specific behavior, or thought, rather than by way of the emotional impact on the marriage and on the overall emotional system.

The disagreement about the definition can be reconciled by an understanding of an emotional definition of affairs rather than a behavioral one. Sometimes a person can be having an affair with another person by simply going out for dinner and drinks, whereas another person may experience the same type of evening as a simple, unencumbered, social evening. The people in the first example may be feeling a strong infatuation and attraction, and correspondingly, they feel an impact on their marriages. The feelings they have for each other detract from the marital relationship. The people in the second example may feel attracted to each other and enjoy each other's company but are confident of their marriages and feel comfortable with them having higher emotional priority.

In summary, an extramarital affair is a relationship between a person and someone other than his spouse that has an impact on the level of intimacy, emotional distance, and overall dynamic balance in the marriage.

The specific impact will be a function of the behaviors, events, and overall emotional context of the extramarital relationship relative to the primary relationship. The emotional repercussions may only be seen when the involved spouse is spending time with the lover rather than his spouse. Or they may be seen by way of the involved spouse being distant and disconnected when he is with his spouse. Or they could be seen in the form of the noninvolved spouse being hostile and aggravated about the situation. Regardless of how it is expressed, the affair, by definition, will have some impact on the emotional distance in the marriage.

The Professional Community

The community of mental health professionals is more reactive to extramarital affairs than to many other problems. In other words, it's possible to identify a level of anxiety around extramarital affairs that is higher than usual in the professional community. In professional seminars on this subject, dialogue can become heated and unresolved. Casual conversations among professionals tend to be tempered by uncomfortable humor, and up until recently, there has been a noticeable dearth of literature related to the problem. This paucity of literature stands in sharp contrast to the statistics that suggest that most marriages will, at some point, need to resolve the emotional trauma created by an affair.

Clearly, the minimal attention in the literature would suggest the possibility that there is an emotional basis for that coincidence. It would be easy to speculate that some of that anxiety is related to the question of affairs in the life of the therapist, a subject that will be developed in Chapter 4. There is also a lack of a coherent, broadly accepted model of the meaning of affairs. As a result, different authors will offer different interpretations that could be challenged as being thinly disguised attempts to justify a certain emotionally reactive point of view.

One somewhat predictable perspective that could be an emotionally reactive point of view would be to challenge the common assumption that affairs are "bad." For example, Weil (1975), in a "reappraisal" of extramarital affairs, suggests that they may not always disturb marital interaction. He suggests that an affair may be enjoyable and may help a marriage survive, because the individuals are finding other avenues to have their needs met. The author encourages consideration of the consequences of discovery, which may result in a threat to the stability of the marriage. Although there is the acknowledgment that the individuals involved may eventually want to leave their marriage, that danger is minimized and tempered with the belief that the extramarital relationship may actually strengthen the marriage.

In a similar vein, Meyers and Legitt (1975) argue that extramarital affairs can provide additional passion, tenderness, and stimulation for a person in a good marriage. They see the potential for a temporary respite from home problems, help with expanding sexual and relational repertoires, kindness toward spouses who are seriously ill or preoccupied, and opportunities to fulfill needs for variety. The need for variety is also emphasized by Block (1978). He argues that people are, by nature, interested in variety, and that extramarital affairs offer a chance to experience the needed variety. And in a well-publicized book targeted for the general public, the O'Neills (1972) developed the concept of an open marriage, which has since become, in a variety of forms, a basic alternative model for monogamous relationships.

Another perspective on the positive potential of extramarital relationships that seems to carry a high charge of emotionality is in the area of heterosexual/homosexual lifestyles. For example, Coleman (1981, 1985) and Brownfain (1985) use a research format to develop the problems and possibilities of men in heterosexual marriages having a homosexual lifestyle in addition to their marriage.

And J. K. Dixon (1985) explored the improvements in the lives of married, heterosexual women who became involved in a bisexual lifestyle.

There is, of course, literature that is founded on a perception of affairs as problems. This literature is characterized by a diversity that mirrors the diversity in affairs. It can be seen both in the development of the dynamic meaning of affairs and in the subsequent treatment planning. For example, Walster, Traupmann, and Walster (1978) used the model of equity theory to examine affairs. Sprenkle and Weiss (1978), from another vantage point, applied a script theory framework. And Strean (1980) examined affairs from a psychoanalytic point of view.

The most common approach to affairs in the professional literature is one that is descriptive. Beginning with Kinsey (1940, 1958), who collected data regarding the incidence of affairs, the professional community has based much of the analysis of affairs on interpreting statistics. The statistics frequently focus on what percentage of people do what with whom. The models emerging from these statistics tend to be phenomenological more than dynamic.

One of the most prolific writers in this style has been A. P. Thompson (1982a, 1982b, 1983, 1984a, 1984b, 1987). His writing has ranged from research, and research review, to the more descriptive. He identifies six points that he sees as being key to understanding affairs and achieving a satisfactory clinical outcome in treatment: cognitive and emotional turmoil, unresolved relationship issues, defensiveness, pressures related to the extramarital partner, a search for an interpretive framework, and decisions about the future.

Another frequent contributor to the study of affairs has been F. G. Humphrey (1976, 1984, 1985a, 1985b). His recommendations for treatment planning are based on attention to the time of involvement, the degree of emotional involvement, the presence or absence of sexual intercourse, the element of secrecy, the question of single or bilateral involvement, and the question of heterosexual or homosexual involvement (1987). His ideas regarding the etiology of affairs are founded in client self-reports and include such reasons as variety, curiosity, retaliation, and preserving the marriage.

The descriptive perspective can also be seen in the work of Pittman (1987, 1989). In a witty and provocative style, Pittman refers to the involved spouses as infidels, the noninvolved spouses as cuckolds, and he describes four types of affairs. The types are identified as unique, habitual, and structural infidelity, and falling in love. His views on etiology, or as he puts it, "why people screw around," bridge the gap between his description of styles and more traditional dynamic formulations including systems pressures and individual psychological makeup.

The professional literature, as an expression of the emotional system of the mental health community, reflects the uncertainty and latent anxiety related to affairs that can be seen casually. There is uncertainty about what actually takes place, because the statistics are chronically open to challenge related to validity and accuracy. And there is uncertainty regarding meaning, because each different model suggests a slightly different perspective that cannot be totally dismissed. As the complexities of the emotional system are developed through this book, it will become clear that neat and simple answers are rare. The approach here is to acknowledge the different levels of the system and to develop the interactional possibilities.

Values, Moral Judgments, and Affairs

The professional literature in some ways is a microcosm of the range of opinions and perspectives in the general population. There seem to be two burning questions related to affairs. Along with the age-old and complex "why?" is the equally formidable question "good or bad?" It is clear from the few opinions noted above that there is support for both answers. The definition of an affair as being an emotional solution rather than a sexual or behavioral response can, perhaps, add a new dimension to consider regarding the question of good or bad.

Before elaborating on these new possibilities, it must be acknowledged that any value judgment is culture bound, and this consideration of extramarital affairs is no exception. This dynamic portrait of an extramarital affair is making no attempt to describe or evaluate cultural practices that sanction various types of multiple relationship patterns. Concubines, for example, have been accepted in Chinese culture, and other cultures have accepted other forms of multiple relationships as well.

Returning to western culture, there are sharp trends that can be identified. Affairs have been judged to be immoral, therefore bad, throughout much of western history. This relates to the religious foundations previously mentioned, and it clearly weights the emotional and cognitive balance in the direction of retaining this principle. As mentioned above, there are, on the minority side, the voices extolling the positive potential in affairs. Perhaps that position needed to be articulated as a developmental step away from the rigid and largely unexamined position condemning affairs. But affairs don't need to be championed as being "good" any more than they need to be condemned for being "bad."

Affairs are emotional solutions to emotional problems.

Defined as emotional solutions, the question of values related to affairs takes on a slightly different perspective. The classic position that affairs are bad can be related to several factors. Extramarital affairs that include sexual involvement increase the possibility of spreading sexually transmitted diseases. This, especially in the time prior to the medical control of most of these diseases, was not to anyone's benefit. This same liability still exists, especially in view of the epidemic of AIDS, which at this time is still life-threatening.

A second factor that could be identified as being "bad" about affairs is the emotional trauma they often trigger. Assuming that most people would prefer to avoid that type of trauma, it could safely be proposed that affairs were seen as bad because of this type of impact.

An alternative view is found in the potential for the trauma to stimulate growth in the marriage. If the crisis leads to the development of a new level of awareness and understanding about the individual needs in the marriage, and if it stimulates the necessary motivation to redress the emotional balance, does this then mean that the affair was good?

Proposals in favor of affairs are just as complicated. The idea that they could infuse new life into a stale marriage is ambiguous and unclear. Is the new life a function of guilt over "bad" behavior, thus prompting a type of overcompensation? Or in the case of the emotional lift that can be seen in the initial stages of a brief affair, does the covert and unacknowledged preoccupation with the lover mean that the "attention" given to the spouse is really a type of displaced or transferred emotional attention grounded in feelings for the other person?

The idea that a long-term affair could help to maintain a marriage, because without it the marriage would fail, is even more vulnerable to questions. What type of emotional balance exists in a marriage that can tolerate the long-term intimacy deficit endemic to that situation? If, indeed, all three people functionally accept the balance that the affair creates, does that mean that they all fear intimacy and that both relationships, the marriage and the extramarital one, are shallow facades? If the marriage is being maintained for the children, what type of relationship do the children see as a model?

These types of questions challenge the simplicity of the good–bad evaluation of affairs. Are affairs good or bad? They inevitably signal some type of individual and relationship dysfunction. But the human condition is such that some type of emotional symptom is usually needed before there is motivation for change. If the affair is relatively short-lived, and it prompts a useful restructuring, it could be a painful but ultimately helpful crisis. And in that sense, an affair may be a less harmful symptom than, for example, a pattern of violent and physically destructive behavior. This is not in any way meant to condone or encourage involvements in extramarital affairs. It is only meant to emphasize the perspective that emotional trauma in people's lives does occasionally lead to dysfunctional patterns. Affairs are one of those patterns.

The Clinical Implications of Value Judgments

The complexities regarding values directly impact on clinical work. If a therapist begins with the bias that affairs are bad, and refuses treatment until the affair is terminated, he is trying to alter the emotional and dynamic balance in the marriage based on supposition and prejudice, rather than on a dynamic assessment. Or take, on the other hand, therapists who believe that some marriages must be balanced by discreet extramarital involvements. If they continue to see individual clients who are involved in this way without an ongoing therapeutic relationship with the spouses, they are making therapeutic decisions based on personal bias and contact with just one part of the system, rather than on a therapeutic relationship with both partners.

In contrast to either of these positions, an understanding of the emotional basis of affairs suggests the need for a clinical position that is based on neutrality. Specifically regarding affairs, the neutrality will be expressed in the suspension of "good versus bad" judgments, and villain versus victim formulations. Treatment will be more effective if begun with a willingness to postpone specific interventions until the emotional meaning of the affair can be fully developed. It is unhelpful, and at times not even possible, to demand one solution or another.

   Whereas there is evidence to suggest that some mental health practitioners have been willing to make value judgments about affairs, there is a reluctance to make public value judgments about healthy versus unhealthy. The mental health field has retreated into sterile, behaviorally specific descriptions of experience. The words healthy and unhealthy are somewhat eschewed in the field of mental health, at least in part because of the possibilities of inflammatory political debate. What is seen as healthy from one perspective is seen as unhealthy from another.

   I do not intend to become preoccupied here with the endless possibilities of discussion regarding the concept of health, but merely to reveal the opportunity affairs present to consider its operational meaning. It would, of course, be possible to retreat into the sterility of behavioral specificity, or the pragmatism of concepts that could be synonyms, such as "effective" or "workable" rather than healthy. This tack would likely be less provocative. In the case of the pragmatic ideas such as effective, however, the definition is no more specific than that of health. The intention is to offer an opportunity to consider the richness possible with the notion of health, while maintaining a primary focus on affairs.

   The premise that an affair is an emotional distance modifier in a relationship has implications for the ultimate resolution of the crisis as well as the concept of health. It is virtually impossible that a healthy relationship, with or without marriage, can be maintained over the long term with the emotional impact created by enduring involvement(s) outside of that relationship. By definition, an affair creates a deficit in the level of intimacy that is unhealthy and is bound to have profound negative effects on the individuals, the marriage, and any children in the family.

AN INTEGRATED MODEL

   The complexity of affairs calls for a complex and sensitive model for understanding them. The various levels of the emotional system mentioned at the beginning of this chapter, including the individual, the nuclear and extended family, and the broader social system, need to be expanded and enriched. Each of these elements constitutes a part of the emotional system that demands an elaborate map for itself, and one that will demonstrate its interface with the rest of the system.

To note, for example, that a study of the nuclear family may reveal something useful about affairs is similar to suggesting that a study of Texas may reveal something about problems with oil resources. The study of Texas may indeed be somewhat useful, but a map of Texas is needed for the study, and the problems must be linked to a much broader system as well. This broader system needs yet more maps. The maps of psychotherapy are the models, concepts, and other theoretical formulations that act as the basis for clinical intervention. Here they need to be brought to the task of understanding extramarital affairs.

The model that will act as the superstructure throughout this book is rooted in the premise that any one psychological model is necessarily limited in its scope. The most flexible model will be one that incorporates the strengths of several different models. It should be noted at the outset, however, that the integration of psychotherapeutic models is a continuous process (Moultrup, 1986), and any one statement is but a static representation of one point in an evolutionary progression. In other words, even the model presented in this book should be understood as being a step that will be followed by others.

The model has been integrated from theories in family and individual therapy. It was originally intended to organize the various dimensions of family therapy (Moultrup, 1981) and certainly was not designed as a model of extramarital affairs. The model has evolved since its first formulation to include a stronger emphasis on intrapsychic elements as well as social system dimensions beyond the family system. Extramarital affairs, as typical happenings in family life, fit perfectly with the overall model, and in fact offer a rich context for the development of a broadly systemic model of human life.

Extramarital affairs are so transparently systemic that even non-professionals are inclined to see the systemic nature of the crisis, without necessarily having a model to organize the ideas. It is such an intuitive fit, that extramarital affairs could be the type of common life experience that will help illuminate systems theories in the general population. Whereas the mental health field was introduced to systems thinking by way of the study of schizophrenia and major mental illness, the general population may be inducted into systems thinking with a systemic model of extramarital affairs.

The model is designed to highlight the dynamic dimensions of the emotional system. This would be in contrast, for example, to highlighting some integration of clinical intervention techniques. The emotional system is centered around the individual, and the primary relationships in his or her life, which include the family of origin, family of procreation, and the extended social network. Visualizing the model is hindered by two-dimensional representations that attempt to demonstrate experience that includes the dimensions of depth and time. A simple outline of the model can begin to suggest connections between the elements of the system noted at the beginning of the chapter and the theoretical models that address those elements:

I. Self and the family
   Differentiation
   Structure
   Power
   Communication
   Behavior
II. Time and the family
   Nuclear family life cycle
   Multigenerational patterns
III. Individual dynamics
IV. Social context

These concepts are most usefully understood as different dimensions of the same experience. A metaphor that may be useful is that of the polarizer. Photographers recognize the polarizer as a filter that enhances the color saturation of photographs. Each of these concepts can function as a polarizer that enhances the view of that particular dimension of life. All of these issues can be, and usually are, present at every moment. At any given moment, some of them will be more pertinent than others.

Just as the visualization of the model is hindered by two-dimensional representation, so too is the articulation of the model hindered in the usual way by the structure of language. Only one idea can be presented at a time, with complex formulations necessarily dependent on a sequential presentation of ideas that are not sequential. The sequence developed here begins with an overview of the ideas that will be developed throughout the book, with some of the primary applications to affairs.

Differentiation

Edward, the man described at the outset, illustrates one of the fundamental characteristics of the turmoil of affairs. It occupies the inner emotional world of the individual as well as the individual's connection to other people in the system. Edward didn't understand his own internal state and didn't understand his relationship with the people in his life. This is a turmoil that is related to self-image and to loyalties and obligations. Differentiation, as a concept, provides a conceptual tool for exploring that territory.

A concept taken from the work of Bowen (1978), differentiation addresses the complex and fundamental questions concerning the relationship of one individual with the family. An ambitious concept, it spans several different areas of emphasis. The primary intraperson-al dynamic it defines is the ability to "differentiate between thinking and feeling." It also addresses the vague, but very real notion of the definition of a self.

In the interpersonal realm, the concept of differentiation ad-dresses the ability both to be involved in an intimate relationship and to establish a healthy balance between connection and independence. It can be thought of as the freedom to be connected and the freedom to be separate. The concept of differentiation as a process within and between individuals in a family is pertinent both within one genera-tion, and across the generations in a family, as highlighted in Figure 1.1.

As the many different facets of differentiation are developed in Chapters 2 and 3, it will become obvious that the question of con-nectedness and separateness in families is at the very heart of the dynamic process of extramarital affairs. It is not simply at the center of the person who went outside the marriage, although it is critically

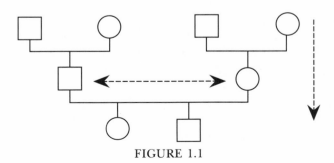

FIGURE 1.1

important there. Indeed, the questions are relevant to everyone, including the noninvolved spouse, children, and the lover, as well as the involved spouse.

Structure

When Lois, who was introduced earlier, began the evening class with Don, several important shifts occurred in her family. For one, since she had other time constraints, she could not fix the family dinner on class nights. That left her husband, Glenn, responsible, and it effectively altered the structure of the family. That type of altera- tion of the structure is not necessarily a trigger for an affair, but in this situation it did facilitate the extramarital involvement. In its simplicity, it illustrates the potential importance of that dimension of family life.

Families develop structures that reveal patterns of relatedness. The structures can relate to tasks, generations, gender, and so on. The structure manifests itself in the form of various subgroups and emotional alignments in the family. To the extent that the subgroups that form are operating in a way that promotes effective individual and family functioning, the structure of the family is a healthy one. Much of the focus on this element of a family in treatment can be traced to the work of Minuchin (1974), and since that time, the focus has evolved with the contributions of numerous others.

This has been a popular focus of treatment in the field of mar- riage and family therapy, because the structure of a family can be quite transparent. This structure also can be responsive to concrete, straightforward interventions. For example, if a husband and wife have been emotionally distant and follow a directive to spend more time together in the form of an evening out or a weekend away, it generally has some noticeable impact on the emotional balance be- tween them. Experienced therapists know that the exact impact will be impossible to anticipate, thereby establishing the need to monitor the effects of the interventions, and to evaluate the dynamic meaning of the outcome.

There are a number of key structural patterns in families bal- anced by an affair. These will be developed at length in Chapter 2. The most critical structural pattern is in the distance between the involved spouse and the rest of the family, as illustrated in Figure 1.2.

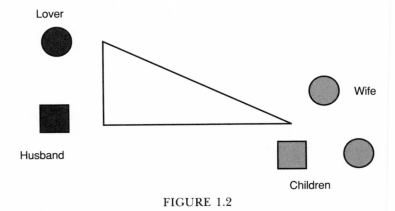

FIGURE 1.2

Although there may be claims that "there has been no effect on the children or on the spouse," it is impossible for this to be so. If a person has another life, one that is secret, one that must be kept from the awareness of other people who are supposedly close to him, it is quite impossible for the emotional consequences of that life not to have an effect on the family relationships. It, by definition, creates a gulf between them. If the affair is an overt one that has been accepted and incorporated into the structure of the family, the implications are that the distance is acknowledged and needed by everyone.

Power

Jake presents an interesting view of power that illustrates the complexity of the concept. The fact that he held a position at work that gave him a certain authority over others, and the potential to leave work at will to create his own lifestyle, might suggest that he held at least some power in his life. Since he flaunted his extramarital activities to his wife, it might suggest that he was powerful enough to maintain his marriage yet "enjoy" himself outside the home.

But Jake was not powerful enough to extract himself from the pain of his lifestyle. He was not powerful enough to enjoy the warmth and intimacy of his relationship with his wife. He was not powerful enough to create a marriage in which his wife did not need extramarital involvements. In many ways, Jake illustrates the pathos of a powerless person rather than the rewards of power.

Power as a concept is a new addition and was not included in previous presentations of the model (Moultrup, 1981, 1985). It is included now because it offers the potential to call attention to important areas of emotional functioning in a relationship. The problem with the concept of power, and the primary reason for its intentional absence from earlier works, is that it can be seen more accurately as a derivative of many of the other main topics in the model, such issues as definition of self.

Even the definition of power is problematic and can stir considerable controversy. Ultimately, the definition adopted is a reflection of the overall emotional process in the person and system. For example, if power is defined as the ability to wield influence in the relationship, then the question becomes, why does one person have the ability to influence more than the other? The answer usually points back to one of the other elements of the model, such as a weak definition of self. This suggests the ubiquitous nature of power, as a derivative dynamic rather than a primary one.

One of the power patterns that is important to monitor related to affairs is the passive and active use of power. Whereas the involved spouse may portray the noninvolved spouse as being domineering and impossible to control, the involved spouse may in turn exert power by physical and emotional presence or absence. So, although the noninvolved spouse may actively try to exert power in the relationship, the involved spouse frequently exerts even more power, in a passive style, simply by not being present. The provocative potential to be with the lover during physical absences increases the emotional power of that strategy. The other strategy of emotional absence while being physically present is equally powerful.

Despite the many problems with the concept, attention to the notion of power has proven itself to be clinically useful. Some couples will not see any problems in their relationship that they define as "power" problems, whereas others will appreciate the concept and find it a useful label for their experience. For this reason, it is included in the model. Power manifests itself throughout the emotional system, and it will be considered throughout the book in various forms.

Communication

The dimension of communication is included in the model because it is popularly recognized as being important to effective and

healthy family functioning. The premise of its importance in this
model is somewhat different than some may see as the standard
approach in the field. It is closer to the dynamic function described
above for power. Communication is seen as a reflection of the more
abstract dynamics of an emotional system, rather than as a "cause" of
those dynamics.

In other words, it is not enough to say that a couple is having
problems because they don't know how to talk with each other. The
miscommunication signals some type of problem that must be understood and addressed. Sometimes, there are minor misunderstandings that can easily be addressed by emphasizing the use of different
words or phrases or by emphasizing careful and active listening. But
in more important areas, or when seen in repetitive patterns, the
miscommunication is not the primary problem. There is some type of
emotional underpinning that is critical.

For example, if a husband expresses surprise at his wife's anger
when he neglects to do the simple chore of bringing home milk in the
evening, it may mean many things. He might contend that he didn't
happen to hear her when she called out to him on his way out the
door. It may mean, if it is a repetitive pattern, that he consistently and
selectively ignores her. Or it may mean that she is consistently demanding of him, or some combination of a problem on both sides.

The combination of those tendencies usually can be traced to
abstract dynamics such as differentiation, structure, or other dimensions of the integrated model. Understanding those dynamics is
far more crucial, and its impact on the couple will be much more
durable, than simply teaching them communication skills related to
bringing home milk in the evening. As the dynamic balance shifts, the
communication patterns will evolve to reflect the new balance.

This does not eliminate the need to attend to communication
patterns in treatment. Indeed, abstract dynamics that are far too
subtle to articulate concisely, can be addressed under the heading of
communication. It is difficult, however, to be precise about what
patterns to address. Communication patterns specifically related to
extramarital affairs will relate to a number of areas, including patterns of denial and patterns of the expression of affect.

Sally's story, described earlier, offers an interesting look at the
potential for denial. Despite the fact that her husband, Larry, had
sanctioned an unconventional sexual encounter in the past, she felt
compelled to deny the possibility of sex with Bill during their recent

encounter. Denial in this instance was not an example of poor communication but was a function of a much broader dynamic base. Any intervention focusing exclusively on honest, open communication in the marriage in this situation would be doomed to failure. As the various dimensions of the model are developed through the book, the element of communication will be developed as a continuous sub-theme.

Behavior

Behavior is yet another dimension that expresses the abstract dynamics of experience, but again is useful to address on its own merits. Along with the pertinent intrapsychic motivation, individual behavior can be understood in the context of the overall emotional system. The expansion of the behavioral perspective to the whole system implies correlating the behavior of all of the people in the system, rather than attending to the behavior of one individual.

This can be framed in the form of chains of behavior, with behavior A preceding behavior B preceding behavior C, and so forth. Or it can be framed in terms of reinforcement patterns and consequences. The purpose here is not to provide a review of behavioral theory, but more to emphasize the integration of behavior as a specific dimension into the model.

As every experienced clinician knows, attending to behavior clinically can lead to important and useful modifications for the individual and the system. Given this pragmatic approach, the question of the relationship of behavior change to dynamic change is a moot point. Sometimes people change their behavior after they understand the dynamic meaning, but sometimes they change their behavior before any cognitive understanding. Indeed, there are times when there is never any understanding of the dynamics, but the behavior changes anyway. Good psychotherapy cannot be encumbered by a rigid, ideological refusal to avoid interventions because change shouldn't happen in a certain manner.

Extramarital affairs present particularly difficult challenges when we consider the possibility of behavioral intervention. Although behavioral theory and technique will offer some ideas about why and how to intervene, the difficult questions of what behavior and when to intervene are made considerably more difficult with the anxiety and trauma surrounding an affair. There is a tendency to get caught up in the anxiety of the emotional system and to focus on reactive behavior that is less important to change than the more basic behavior expressive of the primary dynamics.

Lois again comes to mind as an example of this potential. The behavior that cries out as significant is the evening class with Don. If that behavior were altered, it would eliminate the opportunity for the two of them to cultivate a relationship, and it would realign the structural configuration between Lois and her family, presumably with more closeness as a result. Targeting that type of shift as a treatment goal would be naive and shortsighted. If there is a dynamic need for the emotional involvement, it will resurface in another way. If there is a dynamic need for the distance from husband and/or family, that too will resurface in another way. If there is a need for a behavioral intervention with Lois, it must be developed out of a broader view of the balance of the system.

Another common example of a trouble spot for behavioral intervention involves comparisons between the noninvolved spouse and the lover. These are often considered by the noninvolved spouse to establish some sense of who is "better than" and who is "worse than." If the therapist gets tricked into focusing on the "behavioral inadequacies" of the noninvolved spouse under the guise of eradicating problematic behavior, the therapist will be grossly missing the important behaviors and the important dynamics of the situation. Behavior, like power and communication, will be one of the ongoing subthemes throughout the book.

Nuclear Family Life Cycle

One of the key ingredients missing from each of the vignettes at the beginning of this book was a detailed development of the temporal element of the lives being described. This has the effect of drawing dramatic attention to the current crisis, and it fosters the illusion that the crisis is unrelated to the context of time. This illusion is grossly inaccurate. The timing of an affair is absolutely critical to the dynamic basis of the crisis.

The concept of time is organized here by way of life stages, specifically the stages of the family life cycle. Just as individuals evolve through a life cycle, so too does the family experience a similar process. There are several different models that outline a developmental life cycle for the nuclear family. Duvall (1977) developed an eight-stage model based on the age of the children. Haley (1973) proposed a model that is somewhat more general. In both models, the transition points in the family are crucial and key moments for the eruption of symptoms.

The two most common transition points associated with affairs are the advent of children and the death of a parent. It is with those two changes in the makeup of a family that an affair can be experienced as a welcome source of emotional support. The changes around the birth of the first child include the role demands of parenthood and the emotional closeness in the marriage. If the parenting demands are experienced as overwhelming, the need to distance from them can be acute. Or, if one spouse, the wife, for example, becomes so engrossed with her role as parent that the type of relationship in the marriage changes dramatically, there could be resentment regarding that change. The marriage begins to represent an unsatisfactory type of connection, one that needs to be avoided. The affair becomes the distancing mechanism.

The dynamics related to an extramarital involvement triggered by the death of a parent can include a need to distance from the intense grief in the family, a need to reaffirm one's own vitality by proving attractiveness, or far more complex and involved dynamics related to either positive or negative identification with the deceased parent. Frequently, there is no awareness of a connection between the death and the extramarital involvement. It generally is revealed during history taking, and it may even be unrecognized until the connection is noted by the therapist. Just noting the connection does not establish any dynamic connection. That becomes the work of the therapy in the sessions to come.

Multigenerational Patterns

Time offers fertile ground for philosophical consideration as well as the clinical conceptualization of life cycles. Where does the past break from the present and future? Does the distant past have any relevance to the crisis of an affair? The melding of the philosophical with the clinical comes with the possibility that the past lives in the present by way of multigenerational repetitions of patterns in the lives of individuals and families. This element of the model attends to those possibilities.

By now it is clear that none of these dimensions can be separated from any of the other dimensions. The model reflects the complexity of life in that way. This dimension is closely related to the concept of differentiation, and it can be seen as being related to life cycle concerns as well. The conceptual tools that have been developed to define multigenerational dynamics include Bowen's concept of the family projection process (Bowen, 1978) and Boszormenyi-Nagy and Spark's (1973) ideas related to obligations, indebtedness, and family loyalties.

The focal point of this dimension of the emotional system is the transmission of individual behavioral patterns and broad interactional patterns from one generation to the next in a family. Patterns can be repeated in a variety of forms. Two of the most common are the exact repetition of a particular pattern and a reversal from one generation to the next. In any case, contemporary life and the problems associated with it can be a result of rather invisible forces connecting the generations in a family.

In keeping with the pragmatic approach to theory established with the integrated model, there may be more than one specific formulation of the concept that is possible. Clinically, that is of less consequence than the attention to the dynamic in the course of treatment. The client, generally, will resonate to one set of ideas more than another. Where one client will light up at the idea that there are unresolved loyalties to a parent, and they have been influential in the extramarital involvement, another will dismiss that idea but in turn resonate to the idea that she is "identifying with" that parent.

The expectable area of attention regarding affairs is the extramarital patterns in the previous generations of the couple in treatment. In Figure 1.3, for example, both spouses came from families

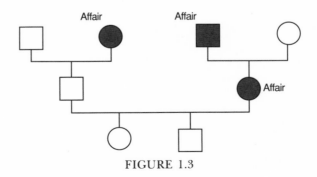

FIGURE 1.3

where there was a history of extramarital involvements. The pattern illustrated is one in which the wife was the involved spouse. Her father and her mother-in-law had both been involved in affairs. An understanding of the implications of that pattern is central to the treatment and will be explored throughout the book.

Although it will be quite useful to know about the patterns of affairs in previous generations, it would be a mistake to limit the exploration of multigenerational patterns to the patterns of extramarital involvement. That is one somewhat peripheral manifestation of the more profound and important patterns of differentiation and relatedness in the family. Knowing the established patterns of power, of role definition, of closeness and distance, of family structures, and so on, can suggest unconscious factors that have conspired to create the unhealthy situation that was the precursor to the affair.

Inside—Outside

The individual dynamics and the social context represent the inner and outer boundaries of the emotional system of the affair. Both are so complex that they could each command the attention of at least another whole book. The individual elements, which will be developed in more detail in Chapter 3, include the internal process of self-definition, cognitive and perceptual characteristics, and affective characteristics typical of the people involved in affairs. The social system, that part of the emotional system which is outside the family, will be developed at the end of the book in Chapter 9. Included there are the forces in the immediate social network of the couple as well as the broader social influences.

WHY AN AFFAIR?

This brief sketch of the integrated model demonstrates the complexity possible when addressing the "Why?" of an affair. Affairs defy simple explanations. As the model is developed throughout the rest of the book, many of these ideas will be seen from more different perspectives than might be imagined at this time. Affairs are not unique in this way. Any emotional symptom can be dissected to reveal the same range of dynamics. But the universality of the features involved in an affair give them a personal relevance that makes the idea of an emotional system come to life.

CHAPTER 2

Triangles and Emotional System Patterns

L ove triangle. As a synonym for an extramarital affair, as a description of the problem, and as a metaphor of the emotional shape, this phrase is timeless. This perspective of an affair conjures up impressions of a process among three people in which two are vying for the love and loyalty of the third. This image is one that must be faced early in the treatment of affairs. Frequently, the noninvolved spouse assumes that he is competing with the other person for the affection and love of his spouse.

This competition-based triangle suggests that the person who "wins" will remain in the relationship, whereas the "loser" will have to go off and find some other person. It can also suggest that the winner will win because of traits or characteristics that are superior to those of the loser. Ironically, it carries little in the way of insinuations about the person who will be making the choice, the person over whom the two others are supposedly competing.

In more recent times, mental health professionals have used the notion of triangles to describe a wider range of relationships in families. In contrast to the competition model of triangles, Bowen (1978) described the triangle as the fundamental unit of an emotional system. He defines the triangle as being the mechanism by which tension is dissipated in a system. When there is tension between any two people, they act to defuse it by "triangling-in" a third person or object.

The process of triangling-in is one in which emotional energy and attention is focused on a third person or object. By focusing on this third corner of the triangle, the tension that had existed between the original two people is avoided. This process of triangling-in a third person is effective as an avoidance strategy, but ineffective as a strategy for the resolution of the conflict, and as such carries long-term negative consequences.

This type of dynamic triangling is a natural process in all relationships. In other words, every relationship can be seen as being part of a triangle at various times. As people struggle with tension in relationships, and as triangles develop in response to that tension, the people can be seen as "being in a triangle." These triangles can be plotted, with the shape of the triangle reflecting the relative emotional distance between the people involved.

Bowen defined triangles as being permanent in a system. He posited that there is a fundamental basis of tension in any relationship related to the naturally occurring lack of differentiation in any two people. This naturally occurring tension sets the stage for the on-going existence of triangles. The shape of the triangles can change with different circumstances, and the desirability of the various positions changes with the level of tension. Bowen noted that in times of calm, the inside position in the triangle is the desired one, and in times of tension, the outside position is the desired one (Figure 2.1). The notion of a differentiation-based, baseline level of tension in any relationship removes the dynamic process of triangling-in from the more concrete focus on tension as a function of observable conflict.

Extramarital relationships are transparent examples of this dynamic model of emotional triangles. The tension that existed in the primary relationship is avoided by the focus on a third person. Attention can be focused on almost anything, including jobs, hobbies, children, or various objects. In this way, affairs are one variation on the natural process of triangling in a system.

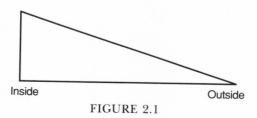

Inside   Outside

FIGURE 2.1

The Expanded Triangle

The anxiety-based model of triangles is a powerful one that can help to illuminate a wide range of phenomena in an emotional system. But it is restrictive and can be more confusing than necessary. For example, if we consider a triangle between a man involved in an affair, his wife, and her mother, it can be cumbersome to define the functioning of that triangle as being entirely related to the tension of differentiation. In a more expanded view, the triangle suggests the interconnection between the three people and could offer ideas about expectations, loyalties, and various other dynamics between them.

In this way, the anxiety-based model of triangles obscures the potential for using the geometry of triangles to shed light on other dimensions of system functioning. One element of the system that is undeveloped with the anxiety-based triangle is that of positive connections between people. Positive connections between people can be clarified when examined in the context of emotional triangles (Figure 2.2). The premise is to understand the impact of one relationship on the other and the impact on the individuals involved.

As the functioning of triangles is expanded, it is necessary to reemphasize their fluid nature. Assume that the shape of a triangle—the length of the lines and the degree of the angles—can be drawn to visually suggest something about the emotional experience of the people in the triangle. This shape is not static. The same three people can shift to form a triangle of a new shape depending on the issue that is active or even the time of involvement.

This expansion of the action of a triangle opens up possibilities of using the triangles to gain access to a wider range of emotional

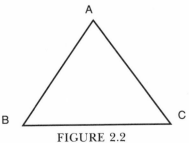

FIGURE 2.2

A triangle suggests the interconnectedness of the combinations within the triangle. A↔B is influenced by A↔C and B↔C. In like manner B↔C is influenced by A, and A↔C is influenced by B.

business in the system. Obligations, loyalties, and various emotional identifications can be tracked throughout the system by way of the permutations of triangles. Those triangles will be developed later in the chapter. Beginning with the critical triangle of the extramarital affair will provide a rich foundation for those later triangles.

THE CLASSIC TRIANGLE

The potential for tension, confusion, and chaos that is created when one spouse becomes emotionally involved with another person sets the stage for real life drama, and it sets the stage for an extramarital affair to be seen as the classic triangle. The expanded definition of a triangle, moreover, suggests potential for extracting a rich array of interpretations regarding the meaning and emotional function of this triangle. Each relationship in the triangle has meaning within itself, and relative to the other two relationships.

The basic triangular mechanism of the affair is the increase in distance between the two spouses as a result of one's involvement with another person. The beginning configuration is one in which the two spouses are closer to each other than either one is to an outsider. There are various people in their lives, whether they are co-workers, neighbors, friends, or strangers, who would be potential liaisons. Prior to the affair, however, none of these people is as close as the two spouses are to each other (Figure 2.3).

With the commencement of the affair, the configuration of the triangle changes. To the extent that the involved spouse is focusing emotional energy, attention, and time on the lover, there is an increase in distance between the two spouses and a corresponding increase in closeness between the involved spouse and the lover (Figure 2.4).

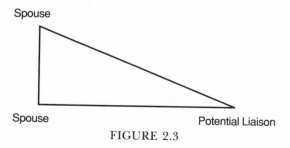

Spouse

Spouse   Potential Liaison

FIGURE 2.3

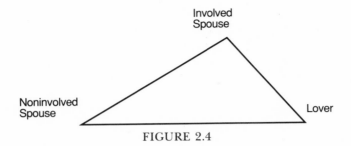

FIGURE 2.4

This triangle can be drawn with the lines and angles reflecting the perceived degree of involvement. Any changes, however, will be in degree and not in dynamic principle. The distance between the spouses has been increased as a function of the extramarital involvement.

Covert Themes

The obvious shift represented by these two triangles suggests significant shifts in the dynamic balance in the marriage. It raises questions concerning the need for the increase in distance and suggests a level of preexisting tension that prompted the distancing. In addition to the more transparent dynamics, however, there are interesting covert and at times paradoxical themes that emerge regarding the functioning of this triangle. If the triangle has evolved into a particular shape, there must be some emotional benefit to all of the parties involved. Although they may not all benefit equally, looking for the benefits develops an awareness of the unseen emotional needs in the system.

The Involved Spouse

This person is usually seen as the most obvious beneficiary of an affair. Beginning with the titillating prospect of sexual variety, and looking at the advantages of having an opportunity to form intimate rapport and understanding with another person, the common myth is that the involved spouse is the one with everything to gain and nothing to lose. Add to this the possibilities for distance from a spouse who is labeled, perhaps, as not understanding or seen as deficient in several dozen ways, and the involved spouse is often seen as the clear "winner" in the classic triangle.

The reality of this is not a given. The involved spouse, for example, may well be distraught and anxious about the confusion created by having attachments to two people. Although the lover may offer certain things that were not found in the spouse, they are often recognized for being deficient in themselves, and perhaps recognized as being poor candidates for a long-term, monogamous relationship. Simultaneously, the spouse is recognized for having certain strengths that are attractive. The likelihood in this case for guilt related to the disloyalty to the spouse, and ambivalence regarding the relationship with the lover, leave the involved spouse in a less enviable position than is commonly portrayed.

There are, of course, times when the involved spouse is benefiting from the triangle, but for different reasons than are commonly assumed. And there are unrecognized costs that accompany these benefits. In instances when the involved spouse is not bothered by guilt or ambivalence, they have created a lifestyle that is defined by a lack of integration. To the degree that one relationship is secret from the other, there is a need to divide one's inner emotional life. The intimacy in each relationship is compromised by the need to withhold certain information. Even when people say that they can talk about "anything" with their lover, there are occasional feelings, opinions, or other items that are conveniently avoided.

One of the more interesting expressions of this theme involves the definition of the marriage that the involved spouse offers to the lover. Often these men or women are unable to reveal the actual nature of their marriage to the lover. They frequently portray the marriage as an empty shell. If, later, the lover discovers that in fact there was an active sex life and emotional life in the marriage, the lovers can then feel as if they were the ones who were betrayed, rather than the noninvolved spouse.

The paradox of this situation has to do with intimacy. The lack of intimacy that is endemic to the involved spouse's corner of the triangle is so significant that it must be seen as a reflection of a certain level of ambivalence or even fear of intimacy. This fear can lead to the creation of a facade of intimacy with one while with the other. Although this "works" as a solution to the fear of intimacy, maintaining this facade inevitably leads to stress. This facade may be purported to be a "perfect set-up," but the ongoing stress cannot help but have various consequences, such as the increase in the potential for stress-related physical symptoms. Or at the very least, there is a loss in the richness of intimacy.

The Noninvolved Spouse

This person is usually seen as the loser, or perhaps victim, of the extramarital affair. Although it is true that she has not had the benefits of another person to relate to, she is part of the triangle. The very existence of the triangle creates the need to question the emotional function of the triangle for the person in this corner. This person represents half of the original relationship that has been altered by the distance generated by the triangle. To what degree did she contribute to establishing the added distance in the relationship? Given the complexities of the negotiations regarding emotional distance in a couple, it is totally impossible to see the product of those negotiations as being a unilateral initiative.

The notion of differentiation between the couple is one perspective on the establishment of this type of distance. Assuming the original relationship was characterized by a type of fusion that was uncomfortable to both the husband and the wife, they both stand to benefit from the emotional distance provided by the affair. This benefit is realized in the sense that the intensity and demands of the fusion in the marriage have been detoured and defused by another relationship.

This type of benefit is difficult to simplify and illustrate with one concrete example. One that comes close is the relief a noninvolved wife can feel when her husband doesn't come home at night. Her anxiety about his demands for such things as conversation and sex have been avoided, and she has been freed to be involved in her own separate life pursuits. The price is her fears over his involvement with someone else and the possible feelings of rejection. Seen from this perspective, the affair offers a paradoxical solution to her emotional problems.

A slightly different twist on this same principle has to do with the noninvolved spouse feeling inadequate. This sense of inadequacy leads to a desire for the needs of the other to be met by some other person. A flagrant and controversial example of this is in the case of one spouse crippled with some type of chronic disease, such as the example of Sally and Larry in Chapter 1. There are times when people in similar situations contemplate and even encourage their spouses to go elsewhere "to have their needs met." This same process occurs in many ways with real and perceived inadequacies. The result is that the noninvolved spouse can, in those instances, tacitly approve and encourage the extramarital involvement of her spouse. This again makes the affair a two-person process and not a one-person venture.

A third theme is a repeat of the avoidance of intimacy noted for the involved spouse. If the noninvolved spouse has some reason for ambivalence or fear regarding intimacy, the distance created with the spouse's involvement creates a context in which she can be seen as the helpless victim, while at the same time avoiding the intimate connection. Although she is not benefiting from a connection with another person directly, she is relieved from the responsibilities of the primary relationship and may actually be more satisfied as a "married single person."

The critical principle is to consider the possibility of unconscious emotional benefits gained by the noninvolved spouse. These benefits may come in the form of relief with the added distance in the marriage or in the unconscious need to relive some type of multigenerational pattern. Whatever the dynamic, they represent possibilities for the noninvolved spouse to "benefit" from the affair. Only rarely will the noninvolved spouse consciously see the affair in any beneficial terms.

The Lover

A complete model of the function of the classic triangle must include a perspective on the third corner, the lover. Again there are covert themes that require a careful shift in perspective. One of the interesting perspectives involves the possibility of terminating the marriage and establishing a permanent relationship, or marriage, with the lover. A common myth is that the lover is benefiting from the development of a relationship with a special person but is somewhat foiled by the presence of the stereotypically inept person, the noninvolved spouse. If it weren't for the marriage, the relationship with the involved spouse would be as close to idyllic as possible.

The necessary shift in perception here again involves exploring the need for the triangle to be the shape that it is. Rather than seeing the distance between the lover and the involved spouse as being something out of their control and generally an obstruction to the relationship, seeing it related to the needs of the people involved creates new hypotheses. The lover may need the distance from the involved spouse. The question is why?

One initial dynamic involves the same ambivalence over intimacy described for the two spouses. The person in the role of the lover can enjoy rather uncomplicated time with the involved spouse, without many of the burdens of day to day living. This very lack of complication has certain rewards. To the extent that a person tolerates a less-than-total relationship of this type for any length of time, there is a question about the need to retain this level of involvement, and in turn to avoid the demands of a total, integrated relationship.

A second hypothesis is a repeat of the theme of inadequacy. The lover may feel inadequate and basically unable to fulfill the needs of the involved spouse. Consequently she tolerates and actually needs the noninvolved spouse to provide in ways she is unable or unwilling to provide. This perspective suggests the existence of an almost invisible relationship between the noninvolved spouse and the lover, as demonstrated in Figure 2.5. The relationship between the lover and noninvolved spouse is then built on their respective perceptions of the place of the other person in the life of the involved spouse.

In summary, covert themes in the classic triangle can be developed that are founded on the assumption that the shape of a triangle implies a series of emotional needs and suggests a functional basis for the triangle. The people in the triangle need the emotional benefits derived from the triangle, but they may be suffering unwanted consequences. As the function of the triangle is developed, the possibilities for change are increased. There are many more covert themes that can influence this triangle, including ones derived from multigenerational triangles in the family. These will be developed later in the chapter.

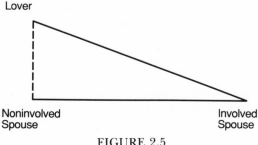

FIGURE 2.5

EMOTIONAL DISTANCE

The concept of emotional distance is one of the cornerstones of this model of triangular functioning in an emotional system. It is not, however, a known quantity. It is not simple or universal in its characteristics. A stereotype of emotional closeness and intimacy in a couple would be a warm feeling between them and textbook perfect communication that is accurately stated, then received and interpreted by the listener as the speaker had intended it. In addition to this perfect communication, there is major agreement on vast areas of opinion and a mutually fulfilling sex life. The reader is excused at this point if he finds himself muttering something about pie in the sky!

Emotional distance, on the other hand, is frequently defined as the opposite of this rosy picture. It is characterized by coldness, poor communication, lack of agreement, and a general sense of tension and dissatisfaction. The corollary to these stereotypic images is the value judgment that accompanies them. Based on these descriptions, the natural conclusion would be that emotional closeness is better than emotional distance. There are two major drawbacks to this conclusion. There are times when close can be too close, if it stifles individuality. And there are times when close is expressed negatively rather than positively.

Negative Emotional Closeness

Although there may be some connection between the characatures depicted above and the relationships they are meant to portray, by and large the descriptions are vague and misrepresentative. Even in the best of worlds, communication is not always perfect. There are times, moreover, when people are actually closer than either one of them may report. Two people can be close in a way that is based on negative interaction.

John and Linda offer a typical example of this type of closeness. John is an intense and insecure person who can be demanding of Linda's time and energy. He expects her to help him with projects, which monopolize Linda's time. If she balks at helping him, he becomes angry and confrontative. Linda does want to help John, but not to the exclusion of any other activities. She also is intimidated by his style, which borders on being abusive.

Linda married John because she saw in him many of the qualities she prized, including intellectual ability and career ambition. She also had concerns that she might not find anyone else to marry. Linda's attraction to John, in that way, was partially based on an attraction to John's qualities as a person and partially based on feelings of insecurity. These feelings contributed to Linda's willingness to tolerate John's behavior, her reluctance to confront John with her concerns, and her reluctance to consider getting out of the relationship.

Scott and Nancy provide another example. Scott stepped into a marriage with Nancy after years of their involvement as childhood sweethearts. The early years of their marriage recapitulated the emotional dynamics that had been established before they were married. The pattern included a high degree of passivity in Scott, with Nancy being more assertive and outspoken. With the birth of their first child, Nancy was clear in her expectations about Scott's role as a father and the level of his involvement. Scott began to feel suffocated. He had begun to realize that there had been no time in his life in which he had had the opportunity to develop his own ideas, aspirations, and lifestyle. He had come from a family with high expectations, and now he found himself in a very similar situation, albeit in a different role.

Linda, in the first example, and Scott in the second example both had affairs. Linda fantasized about being involved for quite some time before she became involved; Scott took action with relatively little delay. In both instances, they were distancing themselves from a type of closeness that was intense and in some ways negative.

Sue and Bob provide a similar example, from a slightly different perspective. Sue is an elementary school teacher and Bob a psychologist. Their five-year-old girl had been demanding and frequently misbehaving for most of her life. She had even been identified as a behavior problem at the day-care program she attended. Bob and Sue admitted that disagreements between them about child rearing were likely to be central to their daughter's problems.

Sue, meanwhile, felt constrained and burdened by Bob's expectations of her. Bob valued family time and activities and was forceful in expressing his expectations to Sue. He wanted her to be more active in her mothering, and active with him, both in activities as a couple and with all three of them. She frequently complained that she didn't have enough time for herself and that Bob didn't respect her values and priorities. She saw him as wanting everything his way. Sue, like Linda and Scott, found herself involved in an affair.

All three of these couples illustrate the potential for negative closeness. Strong expectations of connection, a deficit of individual autonomy, and an inability to change the balance within the relationship left Sue, Linda, and Scott vulnerable to the emotional benefits provided by an extramarital relationship. The closeness described in these examples is negative in many ways, despite the positive elements in the relationships. What becomes clear is the multidimensional nature of emotional closeness and intimacy in a relationship.

The Dimensions of Emotional Connection

There are four different levels of emotional connection in a relationship that will be developed here (Figure 2.6). They operate in different ways and can produce seemingly contradictory feelings and behavior. Although all four will be given full treatment momentarily, here is a brief introduction. At the base level, there is an abstract attachment that is relatively fixed. This is the degree of *fusion and differentiation.* This level of fusion is expressed in the second level of emotional connection by way of broad *operational styles,* which can be characterized as falling on a continuum between enmeshed and cut-off.

The third level of emotional connection is a more transient phenomenon, labeled here as *operational accessibility.* This level of emo-

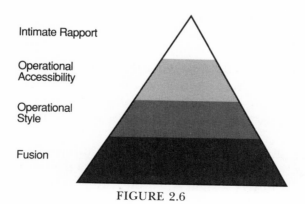

FIGURE 2.6

tional connection is frequently the one in which distance is increased during an affair. Operationally, people position themselves relative to each other by way of lifestyle choices that include time together, emotional attention, and the operational level of vulnerability to each other. To the degree that the functioning on this level is positive, the relationship is experienced as more satisfying.

The fourth level of emotional connection is a distilled experience of level three. Labeled *intimate rapport* for purposes of this discussion, it is sure to be called different things by different people. Expressed positively, this level of attachment can be experienced as the most satisfying, but transient feeling of connection and warmth possible between two people. In a negative valence, this level of connection can be seen in intense, consuming hatred that can almost create a cocoon around the people involved.

Fusion

The basic level of emotional connection between two people in a marriage can be described as the distance established by the interaction of their respective definitions of self. This dimension is a deeper, nontransient state that reflects their mutual ability to connect without losing a sense of self. The theoretical concepts that have addressed this level of connection include enmeshment (Minuchin, 1974), fusion (Bowen, 1978), and symbiosis (Mahler, 1967). Although it may be possible for the astute theoretician to discern subtle differences between these three concepts, it is beyond the scope of this discussion to articulate those differences. There is considerable experiential overlap that is the concern here.

The experiential core of these concepts is the process of defining a personal identity and knowing the limits of that identity. This definition of self allows for intimacy without a loss of self, closeness without a merging of the two people involved, and autonomy without a sense of isolation and rejection. It is at the crux of the fundamental struggle of separateness and connectedness in a family. More views of this process will be seen in the next chapter on the definition of self.

Bowen proposed that people operate at different levels of fusion/ differentiation, and that people usually chose others at basically similar levels of differentiation when they were looking for partners. This can be understood as a formal attempt to articulate the intuitively appealing suggestion that "birds of a feather flock together."

People with equally strong or weak definitions of self are attracted to each other, associate with each other, and eventually marry each other.

Operational Style

People develop broad operating styles that can be seen in the relative level of involvement with other people in their lives. On the close or enmeshed end of the continuum, people operate in such a way as to be highly, and sometimes overly, involved in the lives of people around them. Many times they expect the same type of involvement from others in their lives. This involvement comes in the form of such things as decision making on a daily basis, talking with and supporting each other, and general involvement in each other's lives.

On the distant or cut-off end of the continuum is the style of disengagement, which can go to the extreme of no contact for extended periods of time. Sometimes this lack of contact can be triggered by conflict, sometimes it is simply an expression of a personal lifestyle and has no direct or indirect connection to any type of obvious conflict. Neither the enmeshed nor the cut-off style are necessarily correlated to geographical location. People can stay in contact with family when they are scattered around the globe, and they can be cut off from family who live in the same town.

Although the premise is that people marry people of similar levels of fusion, the same is not true regarding operating styles. Indeed, people often seem to seek out others of the opposite style, almost in an attempt to counterbalance their own tendencies. For example, one person who has a distant, almost cut-off style that he has developed in his family of origin may seek out a person who has a strong style of engagement, also developed in her family of origin. The balance would be one in which the more distant person gained the warmth and connection and the more engaged person gained some of the independence represented by the more disengaged style.

The crucial dynamic to factor into the equation is the relative level of differentiation and fusion. The level of differentiation in the cut-off style is seen as basically the same as the level of differentiation in the more engaged style. The juxtaposition of the two operational styles, however, inevitably creates problems.

Operational Accessibility

As mentioned above, this is the level of emotional distance that is most affected by an affair. Within any relationship, people have varying degrees of accessibility to each other. This is seen in concrete ways such as amount of time spent together, the relative level of peace/conflict, and daily operational business. The obvious example in this book is, of course, an affair. To the extent that a person is physically absent, whether it be a late evening at "the office," a business trip that has a clandestine traveling companion, or "errands" that must be attended to on days off from work, these absences produce a diminished level of contact and a diminished level of accessibility between the two spouses.

Certainly, these same activities do happen in every relationship, without the malignant overtones of an affair. At times they are simply the normal fluctuations in emotional distance between any two people. Any relationship experiences these types of fluctuations. As they become more pronounced and severe, they begin to signal more substantial problems for the couple.

They become more than the normal fluctuations in distance when they are accompanied by the more intangible expressions of diminished accessibility in a relationship. These expressions include the distance that can be communicated by one person who is preoccupied and distant when the couple is together, who is mistrustful of the other, who is busy thinking about furtive contacts with someone else, or is contemplating the possibility of terminating the marriage. This more intangible distance can be communicated in the form of distant, formal, or superficial communication. It can also be communicated in the form of diminished sex drive, a lack of involvement in the more casual expressions of physical intimacy, or a lower threshold of irritability.

Intimate Rapport

This is a very complicated level of emotional connection. Generally, it is quite transient, and generally people consider it in its more positive form. This more positive form is one in which a strong feeling of closeness develops between two people. This feeling of closeness can include or lead to sexual involvement, but even more critically, it includes a sense of trust, acceptance, understanding, and intimacy that is invigorating and fulfilling.

The complications in this level of involvement are not so much phenomenological. It is not all that difficult to describe, and most people will have a number of personal experiences that instantly help to identify the involvement. The complications come with the dynamic motivation and meaning of the involvement. In a new relationship, for example, this feeling can be seen as being similar to what Tennov (1979) described as limerence. The new-found intimacy is given added appeal because of the barriers that are being broken in a new relationship.

Finding this same feeling is unlikely in more mature relationships, thus making the experience of emotional rapport in a more mature relationship much different. One of the most common perceptions of people in longer-term relationships is that they have lost the feeling of infatuation that existed early in the relationship. Usually, it is this level of intimacy they are tracking in that assessment. In older relationships, the capacity to establish this more intense level of intimacy is directly related to the more pervasive question of operational accessibility. Frequently it can be seen in a capacity to discuss feelings, aspirations, reactions, and the full range of personal experiences. This would be in contrast to an insidious process of editing those feelings, thus creating a relationship with restricted boundaries and a lack of intimacy.

When an intimate emotional connection develops between a spouse and a lover, it isn't encumbered by the link to operational accessibility in the same way as is the intimacy in the marriage. This makes the extramarital relationship look "easier" and thus more attractive. Additionally, the mere fact that the two people are less familiar with each other changes the nature of the rapport. There is a greater likelihood of idealizing someone who is more of a stranger and a greater chance of projecting qualities onto the other that may not actually exist.

Multidimensional Emotional Connection

These four concepts describe the different facets of emotional connection in a relationship. There is no value judgment intended. One level of the connection is not better than another level. They are simply different layers of the complex experience of emotional connection and distance in a relationship.

Intimate rapport is not the goal of a relationship, although every good relationship operates such that the people experience that level of connection regularly. The four dimensions can and often do exist simultaneously. They are not stepping stones to the ultimate relationship. But in more mature relationships especially, the daily operational accessibility will be far more critical than the intimate rapport. It will be a product of the level of fusion/differentiation and the operational style of the two people involved.

Distance Regulation

These four levels of emotional connection translate into subjective experiences of closeness between people. Understanding the fluctuations in this distance becomes a critical element in the model of emotional distance. For example, with the notion that an affair increases the distance between two people, two basic questions arise: what is an optimum amount of distance, and how is this distance established and maintained?

Distance Measurement

In a controlled research study, Crane and colleagues (1987) found that emotional distance in families can be correlated to physical distance. In uncontrolled clinical work, people consistently measure emotional distance in their relationships with no hesitation. When asked, for example, to measure the distance in a relationship in units of one to ten, with one being the closest and ten the most distant, people will easily choose a number that they see as appropriate. This can readily be expanded to accommodate a comparison between different points in the history of the relationship.

Obviously this measurement is entirely subjective and idiosyncratic. It would be most accurately seen as measuring some imprecise, experiential combination of all four levels of emotional distance. Sometimes the measurement can be consistent between both members of a couple, and sometimes quite different. If one person in a couple has been very dissatisfied, and has been suppressing or hiding this dissatisfaction, there will usually be more distance reflected in that assessment than in the spouse's. Conversely, if the conflict and tension are known to both partners, or they are both reporting on a time that was genuinely conflict-free and satisfying to both of them, it is quite possible for considerable agreement in their measurements.

The personal and subjective nature of measurement lays the

groundwork for problems in the definition of an optimum distance. Variables related to operational style and operational accessibility impact negotiations for optimum emotional distance. What is optimum for a person with an operationally enmeshed style may be too close for a person with a cut-off style. What is optimum for a person with a more distant style may trigger fears of rejection and abandonment in a person with a more involved style.

Distance Maintenance

There is no simple answer as to how emotional distance is established and maintained in a relationship. The relative definition of self of each person again acts as the foundation and establishes the abstract structure. The couple develops an operational style, or characteristic balance of enmeshment and disengagement, that reflects the two individual styles. Finally, the level of tension at any given time will have an impact on the level of operational accessibility in the relationship.

There is considerable potential for paradoxical movement on the various levels of emotional distance. Begin, for example, with two people who each have a strong need to fuse with another person, to augment weak and inadequate definitions of self. The abstract schematic of fusion in Figure 2.7 suggests the way in which the relationship is defined at that level by an unhealthy degree of fusion. It is characterized by a strong centripetal force, or energy pulling toward the center.

This pattern of emotional closeness can be tempered at the level of style by way of a person with a cut-off style pairing with a person

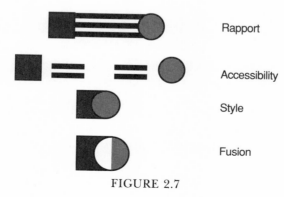

FIGURE 2.7

with an enmeshed style. If, on the other hand, the enmeshed style predominates, as demonstrated in Figure 2.7, it can create considerable tension in the relationship. The tension created by this difference increases the emotional distance in the relationship. It is almost like the type of reaction seen with identical poles of two magnets: they repel. This tension, and the resulting distance, is seen at the level of operational accessibility, and again demonstrated in Figure 2.7.

Although the tendency is to see the person opting for the cut-off style as being the distancer in the relationship, oftentimes the one bidding for a more enmeshed style is pursuing in a way that alienates the other, thus pushing her away. Not only does this make the distancing process a two-person dance of distance, but it influences the type of intimacy possible. They are set up for both intense conflict and the corresponding negatively expressed intimacy and rapport. In other words, conflict is the vehicle for closeness in the relationship.

A real-life example of this process can be developed from this same Figure 2.7. The classic example would be the man who operates with a cut-off style and the woman who operates with an enmeshed style. They both have equally strong needs to fuse together, in response to inadequate self definitions. The woman has imposed her more enmeshed style of operation at the stylistic level. The husband resents this, and is brooding and distant, creating distance on the level of accessibility and tension on the level of the intimate rapport between them.

MULTIPLE INTERLOCKING TRIANGLES

Although the classic triangle is the one that commands the initial attention, it actually is not the crucial triangle to explore for the dynamic meaning of the affair. There is a series of other triangles that operate in every family system and have particular relevance to the system dynamics in affairs. Defining these triangles is a complex process and represents the basic step toward a systemic understanding of affairs. Developing the triangles is not an idle intellectual exercise. The ability to perceive triangles and explore their significance to the situation at hand is an indispensable dimension of "thinking systems" and an important skill for the execution of systems-based psychotherapy.

The basic premise is that the emotional system breaks down into a series of interlocking triangles. These triangles all have their own internal dynamic balance and have varying degrees of influence on the functioning and balance in the total emotional system. Readers who are less familiar with triangles will probably be asking about the possibility of squares, rectangles, pentangles, hexagons, and other geometric patterns. If we can imagine triangles in emotional systems, why not other shapes as well? This might seem particularly appropriate, given possible examples of the classic triangle being expanded to include one other significant person, such as a parent.

The conceptual and dynamic problem with other geometric shapes is that they can always be broken down further, into a series of interlocking triangles. A square, for example, can be broken down into four interlocking triangles. For each point added to the shape, the number of triangles increases accordingly. Two-people units are defined as unstable and labile, therefore creating the potential for unresolved tension being diffused by the triangling-in of a third person. This then leaves the triangle the basic emotional unit.

Each different triangle operates in slightly different ways and creates different meanings in the lives of the people involved. Emotional business related to one relationship can be brought into another relationship and influence the course of events in covert and seemingly inexplicable ways. Tracking these triangles offers a systemic basis for explanation.

Although the notion of interlocking triangles is fairly straight forward once the pattern is established, simply keeping track of the people involved can become cumbersome and confusing. In the interest of keeping the project as uncluttered as possible, the husband in these examples will be the involved spouse and the wife the noninvolved spouse. In these days of militant anti-sexism, there are sure to be men who are offended by this somewhat stereotyped formulation. And there will be women who are quick to cling to the female prerogative to become involved in affairs, and they, too, will cry foul. This pattern is developed only in the interest of clarity and is not intended to carry the weight of unspoken gender stereotypes.

There are three final considerations before getting caught up in all of the triangles. First, not all of the triangles will be equally meaningful in each situation. Indeed, one of the primary clinical objectives is to identify the most relevant and reactive triangles. Second, triangles can be formed placing more than one person on any of the corners of the triangles. These are called complex triangles, and offer the advantage of presenting the triangular interaction of individuals and groups of people.

Finally, a brief comment on the basic neutrality of the triangles and on the need for a neutral approach to the understanding of the triangles. The process of identifying and exploring triangles can be value-laden and skewed to reflect certain narrow prejudices, such as seeing the involved spouse as the villain and the noninvolved spouse as the victim. The triangles are neutral, and they can best be used conceptually and theoretically with that in mind.

Multiple Triangles with the Involved Spouse

The involved spouse is often thought of as the more symptomatic member of the couple, to the extent that he is breaking the contract for an exclusive emotional bond in the marriage. The assumption relates to a perceived higher level of agitation, so high that he needs the solace and benefits to be gained from the extramarital relationship. The assumption that he is more symptomatic can frequently be incorrect. It is correct much of the time, and is *thought* to be correct even more often. As such, it needs to be considered in the therapy. These triangles begin to offer hypotheses as to why this level of discomfort exists.

Husband–Lover–Family

In this triangle, the husband's current family, his family of procreation, including wife and children, are taken as a unit, with the husband and his lover occupying the other two corners (Figure 2.8). By taking the family as a unit, we de-emphasize the relationship with any one person in the family, such as the wife in the classic triangle,

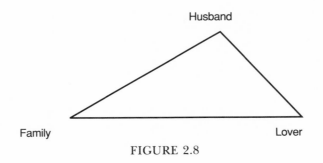

FIGURE 2.8

and emphasize the stresses and dynamics pertinent to the family as a unit. The triangle with the lover raises questions about the function of the relationship with the lover and the balance this establishes with the family at large.

Whether it be the time spent with the lover instead of the family, or the emotional preoccupation with the lover that distracts attention and emotional energy away from the family, the relationship with the lover must increase the distance as discussed previously. This triangle questions the possibility of preexisting tensions between the husband and the family. This can come in the form of lack of comfort with role expectations, such as the parent role, the provider role, or the husband role.

Edward, the man described at the beginning of the book, is an example of this type of triangle at work. Edward had purchased and moved into a large house in the months preceding his involvement with his co-worker. Along with specific troubles with his wife, Edward was also uncomfortable with the financial commitment to the house and the obligation to decorate and maintain the house. The house symbolized the shackles of family life to Edward, and his desire to escape from these obligations had peaked shortly before his extra-marital involvement.

This triangle also calls attention to the relationship between the lover and the family. If the lover is a single person, it raises questions about the possibility that she may need the family, perhaps to provide the husband with a family experience that she does not want. His family, in other words, provides him with the family she is unwilling to tolerate. She has the advantage of having a relationship with a "family man" without having the family obligations herself.

Husband—(Wife/Lover)—Mother
Husband—(Wife/Lover)—Father

Although these are two different triangles, they operate with the same basic mechanism. Coupling the wife and the lover on one corner (Figure 2.9) accents one of the most critical dynamics to track with the involved spouse. These two people are generally bringing two sets of traits, values, attitudes, and general styles into the emotional life of the involved spouse. The differences can include the romantic—practical split, or the creative—mechanical distinction, among others. The dilemma is the chaos and confusion created by the split between the spouse and the lover.

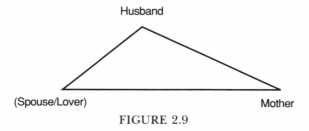

FIGURE 2.9

This split has profound implications. Very frequently the involved husband will have unrealistic perceptions of the two people,
and he will have strong convictions that one would be unwilling, or
unlikely, to express much if any of the qualities he sees in the other.
For example, if his perception is that his wife is romantic but im-
practical and that his lover is practical but not romantic, he may be
unable to imagine either one developing the other's traits.

The split can involve a negative–positive set of images. The lover
is kind, understanding, and nurturing, and the wife is hostile, distant,
and cold. Again he may have considerable difficulty in accepting a
more well-rounded perception of either one. The creation of the
triangle with both the spouse and the lover on one corner establishes
the precedent of pairing the traits in question and looking at the
family of origin as the likely source of that split. The treatment
questions that evolve from this triangle are: What does this split
between the lover and the spouse say about the husband's perceptions
of his mother? What does it say about his relationship with his
mother?

A common scenario involves a man "marrying a woman who is
solid, dependable, and domestic, like mom," and getting involved
with a woman who is "sexy, sensual, and romantic," but not being able
to marry that type of woman. Creating this triangle helps to focus on
the man's perceptions of his mother as a person and explores his ideas
about others' perceptions of her. As these are compared to the split he
sees between his wife and his lover, his unconscious expectations are
revealed. If, for example, he is distancing from his wife, whom he
views as similar to his mother, is he really distancing from his wife, or
in a subtle way distancing from his mother?

It is important to emphasize that this is more than fancy theoretical footwork. If the man is indeed distancing from his mother
as part of the dynamics of the affair, careful examination of the

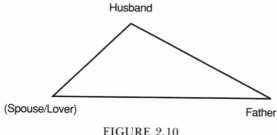

FIGURE 2.10

possibilities for reconciliation with the mother and establishment of a more comfortable closeness in that relationship present themselves as important and viable therapeutic goals.

The Husband–(Wife/Lover)–Father triangle (Figure 2.10) is interesting for its unexpected potential. The usual interpretation of affairs looks more toward the relationship with the mother as being dynamically significant, primarily relating it to gender identification of one sort or another. But if character traits are examined rather than gender, the triangle with father emerges as having the same dynamics as the one with the mother. It is possible, then, that the split between the wife and the lover is more reflective of, and pertinent to, the husband's relationship with his father than with his mother.

Steve provides a good example of this dynamic. He is a lawyer who married his childhood sweetheart shortly after college. Joan, his wife, was never totally accepted by Steve's parents. Steve's father was also a lawyer and spent much time away from the family. Frequently, when he was with the family, he was tired, irritable, and harshly authoritarian. He died unexpectedly when Steve was in high school. As Steve became involved in his own career as a lawyer, he was frequently compared favorably to his father and was told many glowing stories of his father's fine character and wonderful disposition.

Steve became involved with a woman around the time that his first child was born. His perceptions of his wife, as compared to the other woman, assumed an extreme negative–positive split. He saw his wife Joan as irritable and bossy and his lover as being kind, understanding, and sympathetic to his needs. Exploration revealed the split between his wife and his lover as paralleling the split that he experienced between his first-hand experience and perception of his father and the positive stories he heard about his father from professional associates.

Husband–Lover–Parents
Husband–Lover–Siblings

By now the pattern of the triangles should be emerging. Here again are two triangles with the same basic mechanism. The first triangle, with the deletion of the wife, focuses on the meaning of the husband's relationship with his lover as related to his relationship with his parents (Figure 2.11). Admittedly, deleting the wife from the equation is artificial. It is quite impossible to imagine a person involved in an affair where the relationship with the spouse is of no consequence in the evolving dynamics. But focusing on the meaning of the husband's affair in the context of his family of origin highlights the multigenerational dynamics at work, with the simultaneous de-emphasis of the marital dynamics.

The power this triangle, like every triangle, offers is in the questions that it presents. The basic question is, what does the husband's relationship with his lover say about his relationship with his parents? This can be developed into a series of more specific questions. Does his affair recreate a pattern of one or both parents? Does it violate a strong conviction of the parents, thus creating a cut-off between him and his parents? Was his relationship with his parents so conflicted and entwined that the affair is almost entirely an attempt to struggle emotionally with that entanglement? Is this triangle relatively unimportant in the etiology of this affair?

These questions need only slight modification for the triangle with the siblings. His relationship with his siblings could be one of the least relevant triangles in the evolution of his extramarital involvement, but focusing on the triangle in the sessions with the involved husband helps to verify this conclusion and avoids prematurely dismissing or ignoring the potential in these dynamics. With both trian-

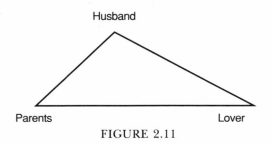

FIGURE 2.11

gles, the influences are likely to be either unconscious or covert. Careful questioning is imperative in eliciting accurate impressions about the relevance of these triangles.

Multiple Triangles with the Noninvolved Spouse

The pattern of creating triangles with the noninvolved spouse, here the wife, continues in the same vein as developed above. Each different permutation will offer a slightly different perspective on the emotional balance. The main theme to be tracked will be the relevance of extramarital affairs in the various triangles.

Wife—Parents—(Husband/Lover)
Wife—Mother—(Husband/Lover)
Wife—Father—(Husband/Lover)

These three triangles are all variations on the same theme, with varying degrees of specificity and slightly different points of focus. In the two triangles with each parent individually, the question the triangle highlights has to do with the nature of the relationships between the wife and each parent. In the triangle with both parents together on the third corner of the triangle (Figure 2.12), the question of their relationship with each other, as well as with the wife, is highlighted. The objective in detailing the different permutations is to create a structured opportunity to look at different facets of the same scene.

In each different case, the specific facts will, of course, be the basis for examining and interpreting the triangle. With that in mind, Audrey is a useful example of all three triangles. Audrey began therapy with her husband, Dan, after he announced that he was

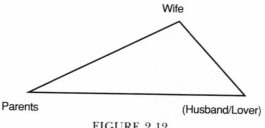

FIGURE 2.12

involved with another woman. They had been married three years earlier. Their first three years had been occasionally troubled for her, but she found out in this crisis that it had been much worse for Dan. He had experienced her as domineering and had been unable to discuss the problem with her. In the course of her discussions with him after beginning therapy, she realized that he had interpreted many of her comments as commands rather than statements of preference.

Audrey was quick to point out that her father had been involved in an affair when she was a child and that one of her strongest fears when she married was that Dan would become involved with another woman, just as her father had done. That Audrey ended up experiencing her worst fear is interesting and perhaps not very surprising. The basic hypothesis would address the possibility of some type of multigenerational recapitulation of family patterns. The triangles help to organize the thinking about this process.

The first triangle with both parents together sets the stage to explore the parents' relationship as some possible precedent for the Husband/Lover split. There are at least two sets of variations this triangle can suggest. The first variation is more interactive. What characteristics of the interaction between Audrey's parents have any relevance to an understanding of the relationship between Audrey and Dan? This question, of course, is fundamental to any marital therapy, but can specifically be focused on the theme of extramarital affairs.

The second set of variations this triangle can suggest is precedents in Audrey's parents' relationship to the relationship between Dan and his lover. For example, Audrey saw her parents' relationship as being tempestuous and labile, with stormy periods interspersed with periods of intense romance. Temperamentally and stylistically she is not suited to this type of relationship. Not only is she even-tempered to the point of suppression of emotional display, she also made a semiconscious decision early in her life to avoid the kind of emotional upheaval she saw in her parents' relationship, at any cost. Some of that cost came in the form of avoiding the periods of intense romance as well as the periods of intense conflict.

It was clear in this situation that Dan had captured some of that romance outside the marriage. Audrey was again in the position of viewing a relationship between the important man in her life and another woman, in which there was more romance in the other liaison than there was in her relationship with him. Did she prefer the isolated and lonely safety of the outside position to the intensity and vulnerability of the close position?

The triangle with her mother (Figure 2.13) raises questions about the process of identification. Did her identification with her mother set her up to choose a man with the potential to become involved with another woman? Did she conduct herself emotionally in the relationship in a manner similar to her mother, contributing to the emotional climate that would be fertile for extramarital involvements?

Although both of these questions probe the possibilities of old business between Audrey and her mother, there may be possibilities related to their current relationship as well. How does Dan's involvement influence Audrey's current relationship with her mother? Has she had a renewed closeness with her as a result of confiding her troubles, which ended years of distance and negativity between them? If so, what would Audrey anticipate about her continuing relationship with her mother if she works things out with Dan? Will she again become distant from her mother? The range of possibilities in this situation is so vast that it would take a full-length novel to develop it in detail.

The questions that are raised in the triangle with her father must, by now, be getting rather predictable. They again can be considered as reflecting both longstanding issues and current ones. Was Audrey attracted to a type of man who was similar to her father? Did this similarity have something to do with a certain style of intimacy, or lack of intimacy, which she saw in her father and to which she had grown accustomed? Did she, in some rather nebulous way, "learn" from her father that men are not satisfied with one woman? The word nebulous here is perhaps the most significant. Audrey was able to contemplate these questions and saw the significance to her relation-

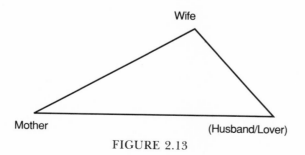

FIGURE 2.13

ship with Dan. She was unable to offer solid, concrete answers.
She was in keeping with the norm in both ways.

Multiple Triangles with the Lover

By this time, specific and detailed exploration of the various
permutations of these triangles can get redundant. But that does not
mean that the triangles should be ignored. The problem with including the set of triangles related to the lover has to do with the availability of information. Although there may be occasional instances in
which the therapist has the opportunity to interview the lover, far
more frequently that will not happen. At those times, the therapist is
left guessing, or making assumptions based on comments from the
involved spouse.

Lover–Father–Mother

This most fundamental of all triangles is mentioned precisely
because it is easily overlooked or forgotten. The "other man," or
"other woman," is a real person with parents. He or she is not some
mythical person who exists out of the context of any emotional system. Taking note of this triangle can rehumanize and recontextualize
the "other." It is considered with all of the usual questions relevant to
this triangle. Thematically, attention to the meaning of extramarital
affairs in their emotional system will begin to offer insight into the
emotional agenda the lover brings to the relationship with the involved spouse. This, in turn, fortifies the understanding of the
relationship that the involved spouse is using as a contrast to the
marriage.

Returning to the case of Steve, the lawyer, and his wife, Joan,
provides a good example of the power and importance of this triangle. The woman Steve was involved with was Cindy. Steve had talked
at great length with Cindy about her family background and, indeed,
was drawn to Cindy because of her neediness. Steve took time in one
of his individual meetings to talk at length about Cindy. Although it
was clear that the information was second-hand, and that the agenda
of the session was Steve's reaction to the situation, the facts are quite
consistent with other similar cases.

Cindy's father had left her mother for another woman. She
remained with her mother for the duration of her growing-up years,

but she had a tense, conflictual relationship with her. She was convinced that her father had left her mother for good cause and that he had little, if any, complicity in their poor marriage. She then made a conscious and effortless transition to her relationship with Steve, and his to Joan. She was fiercely determined to save Steve from a horrible relationship with Joan and offer him the warm, nurturing relationship that she felt he deserved.

Lover–Father–Husband

This triangle is a natural extension of the first triangle and, indeed, was insinuated in the previous example. By focusing specifically on this triangle rather than with the parents, the opportunity is created to look more carefully at the trend, in Cindy's case, to idealize her father and, in turn, idealize Steve. It is accessible by way of the full range of questions developed through the other triangles in this chapter.

Lover/Involved Spouse Triangles

The position of "lover" in the classic triangle frequently overlaps with the position of involved spouse. Obviously, if two married people are having an affair, each one is in turn an involved spouse in the marriage and the lover in the emotional system of his or her lover. Only an unmarried person can occupy the position of lover without the other complication.

This complication of the system adds the multiple triangles from each of the two emotional systems into the overall equation (Figure 2.14). This specific combination of triangles will be a consideration that can add objectivity to the view of the system that each couple has

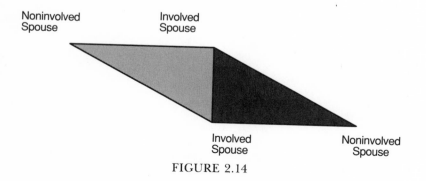

Noninvolved Spouse

Involved Spouse

Involved Spouse

Noninvolved Spouse

FIGURE 2.14

about themselves. Generally, the complications of the triangles extending into each family system are understood to be in existence, but they are rarely pertinent to treatment.

A FINAL WORD

The ideas about triangles and emotional distance in a system that have been developed in this chapter offer a series of lenses for viewing situations that are universal experience. The relevant levels of the system are primarily in the interpersonal realm, although it is impossible to ever stay cleanly in either the interpersonal realm or the intrapersonal realm. This level of the emotional system will continue to be relevant as the intrapersonal dimensions are highlighted in the next chapter.

CHAPTER 3

Inner Life

The interface between the individual and the broader elements of the system remains one of the more problematic points of conceptualization in mental health. This difficulty has often been circumvented by disregarding one level of the system in favor of a useful but incomplete emphasis on the other. Indeed, one of the catalyzing factors for the development of family systems-based therapy was the inadequate attention afforded to the broader system in the field of individual psychology and psychiatry. It is curious to note the frequency with which this tack led to the development of schools of therapy that neglected the individual dynamics in favor of attention to broader systems dynamics. This clearly can be seen as the same mistake from the other side of the fence.

The dynamic and experiential complexity of extramarital affairs is such that it is quite impossible to be allowed the luxury of ignoring either level of the system. Despite the usefulness of the triangles developed in the preceding chapter, the psychological makeup of the individuals must be reckoned with throughout the therapy. The question is not whether it is important but rather how it is important, how it can be conceptualized, and how it can integrated with the rest of the systems model.

The classic individual approach is one that emphasizes individual characteristics and traits, individual development, and individual diagnoses. Although this has some usefulness, there are a number of serious drawbacks to this approach. One primary drawback is in this very same interface of the individual with the outside world, and most significantly, with "significant others." In individually based theoretical models in which the relationship between one individual and the

world he lives in is acknowledged as important, the notion of systemic
interaction is underdeveloped. For example, the label of "object relations" conveys the sense of one individual interacting with "objects" in
his world. People aren't objects in the way that a table is an object.
Two people interacting in an emotional system are not two separate
individuals, each interacting with a separate object. The system includes two individuals and the resulting chemistry of the system.

The inescapable conclusion is that both the systems models and
the individual models are but parts of the whole. This may help to
balance the accounts, for those who need to keep score. And for those
who want to integrate the two levels, the task assumes a level of
difficulty that commands considerable respect. It undoubtedly implies a long gestation period prior to a desired level of clarity. But the
work will not wait for the conceptual clarity, so the inner life of the
individual must be brought in, as effectively as possible, as part of the
emotional system of the extramarital affair.

The complexities of internal psychological processes cannot ade-
quately be covered in one brief chapter. The volumes devoted to
internal psychological processes that already line the shelves of librar-
ies stand as a clear indication of that. The modest intention here is to
focus on three different internal dimensions that have special relevance to the phenomenon of affairs: the question of classic medical
diagnoses in the treatment of affairs, the broad question of the differentiation and definition of self, and elements of individual cognitive
styles that are pertinent to involvement in affairs. These elements,
which are very much related to the inner life of the individual,
inevitably relate to the broader emotional system as well. With that in
mind, we will also begin to develop the intersection of these internal
factors with that system.

Individual Diagnoses

The standard medical approach is to base treatment on diagnosis, which carries with it insinuations about etiology and treatment.
But the diagnostic scheme enjoys a rather mixed reputation in the
mental health field. There will be those who totally dismiss the diagnostic categories and refuse to base any part of the treatment on the
assumptions implicit in them. On the other hand there are those who
cling to the diagnoses and use them as the core of the treatment

approach. The premise here is that the diagnoses can have relevance in the treatment, but they should be used with a willingness to examine assumptions and consider ideas that may be at odds with the diagnostic model as well as at odds with the experience of the individuals in treatment.

Psychosis and Affairs

One of the major categories of diagnoses relevant to involvement in affairs is psychosis. There are times when people in the process of a psychotic decompensation can become involved in an affair. In cases such as these, the dynamics of the affair are more appropriately seen as secondary to the more severe individual deterioration of the psychosis. Although the triangles developed earlier may have some relevance, the primary initial treatment goal will be to gain control over the psychosis. Indeed, the affairs can only loosely be seen as affairs. They are more accurately seen as expressions of grossly disorganized thinking.

The primary psychotic disorder that can present as "affairs" is a manic–depressive syndrome. In that situation, people in the process of a serious deterioration can fall into sexual, and psuedoemotional relationships with other people. If the psychotic process is severe, the involvement can be with people who are strangers or almost strangers. The relationships are psuedoemotional because the emotions can be vibrant, and described with the vocabulary usually applied to new-found infatuations, but there is a psychotic lack of reality to the connection.

Meg offers a poignant example of that potential. She was a thirty-seven-year-old woman who had been married to her husband, George, for twelve years. Over the years of their marriage, she had experienced mood swings and had been encouraged by George to seek out treatment. She usually managed to swing back to a midpoint in such a way that she chose not to seek treatment, and George did not demand a follow-through on the plan. Treatment was finally initiated when their nine-year-old son, Ted, developed behavioral problems in school and was referred for treatment.

Meg and George joined Ted in the initial session. In that interview, it was obvious that Meg was anxious, but the full extent of her anxiety and agitation was not apparent. The treatment continued on with the primary symptom being seen as Ted's behavioral problems in school. There were several diagnostic clues provided early in the treatment that suggested a level of disturbance in Ted, and also in Meg, that was greater than a simple school behavior problem. Meg identified with Ted, and she reported a history of school problems herself. She said that she, too, had a history of "losing it," which to her referred to times when she became so "hyper" that she knew that her judgment became poor.

About two months after beginning family treatment, Meg called and asked for an individual appointment. She indicated that she had told George that she wanted to come in and discuss some things without him. Since this was quite consistent with his earlier wish that Meg would get some help for herself, he readily agreed to the plan. In that session, she said that she was in serious trouble and needed help. She reported that she had gone out to a well-known singles bar recently, and she had intentionally gone back to a hotel with a man whom she had found at the bar. She didn't even know his name, because she wasn't sure he had given her his real name.

She was very confused about the experience. On the one hand, she knew that it was dangerous for her physically. She also knew that she was in "one of those states," meaning she was very agitated, and her judgment was poor. On the other hand, she knew that she had a very exciting time and hoped that the man would call her for another date. Even though she was hoping for him to call her, she was aware of the fact that this represented involvement in an affair and realized that it would be bad for her marriage.

Although Meg's reports of her "states" were suspicious, during the session she continued to control herself in a way that made arriving at a conclusive diagnosis extremely difficult. The probability of a type of manic process seemed quite high, but it was difficult to establish with certainty. Within a week after that session, however, George called to say that Meg was very depressed, and they needed help. When Meg came in for the session, it was clear at that point that she was indeed so depressed that hospitalization was indicated. While in the hospital, Meg leveled out in a way that made diagnosis just as difficult as it had been previously. On the strength of her history of mood swings and her more recent concern over her own states, she was diagnosed as manic–depressive and started on a program of lithium carbonate treatment.

Meg chose not to tell George about her whirlwind affair. She was embarrassed about it, saw it as a byproduct of one of her states, and was very hopeful that with the help of the lithium these states would not be recurring. She knew that she did not need other relationships like that, and she was anxious to build a new, more even life at home. She reported feeling a significant and much appreciated improvement in her level of control, which she attributed to the medication. She continued to follow through on her intentions to develop a new life and reported continued prosperity for George, Ted, and herself two years after the conclusion of therapy. Ted, by the way, showed a significant improvement in his behavior at school and made a remark about being pleased that his mother's mood was better.

Although Meg's story has a much better ending than many extramarital involvements that involve a psychotic decompensation, it is typical in the way the extramarital involvement fits into the overall experience. The affair is an unbridled episode of someone who is out of control. The use of the medication was essential to help Meg regain control, and it provided her with the distance and objectivity to personally understand her previous mood swings.

Character Diagnoses

Another dimension of diagnosis is the identification of character types. Each of the protagonists in the classic triangle could be diagnosed as some particular character type. For example, one of the most likely diagnoses of this type to be seen as relevant to extramarital affairs is the label of the narcissistic personality. There could be an inclination to label the involved spouse as a narcissistic personality, with the stereotypical suggestions of a lack of self-confidence masquerading as conceit, and a desire to have two different people express love and admiration. Other diagnoses that might be seen to be appropriate to the involved spouse would be any of the psychosexual dysfunctions that might fit, or the broadly used category of borderline personality.

The potential for character diagnoses is present for the other two people in the triangle as well. If the noninvolved spouse, in her emotional pursuing, is seen as dependent, she could be diagnosed as a dependent personality, or some variation on that theme. Or she may be given some type of diagnosis that would reflect a dominating personality. If the lover is a person who has been unable to establish any type of meaningful emotional life other than the affair, she might be diagnosed as an inadequate personality.

If these constructs are used in a way that is sensitive to the overall emotional system, and avoids the trap of viewing the people in the affair as three different, disconnected black boxes, they can be a useful element in the conceptualization of the problem. Indeed, there is a need for careful assessment of individual genetic and developmental predispositions that can be enriched by these models. If, on the other hand, they are used in a way that focuses attention on one individual, and labels that person as being the sick one, the diagnoses can foster a narrow, and less helpful, treatment approach.

Affect

People involved in extramarital affairs are acutely concerned with two different levels of affect, levels that become significant in the treatment. The first, and in some ways the easier one to handle in the course of the treatment, is the anxiety and depression that may benefit from judicious use of medication. Any of the players in the drama of an affair can be likely candidates for acute distress which needs, and will respond to, medication. The clinical treatment of such situations is standard therapeutic practice.

There should be an emphasis on careful attention to the distinction between anxiety and depression. Accurate assessment should lead to careful consideration of the appropriate medication regime, if any medication is used. Although it is important to assess possible indications for medication, the therapeutic attention to those symptoms does not end there. There are trends that are significant to the outcome of the therapy.

Anxiety and Depression

The balance between the level of anxiety in the involved spouse and the level of anxiety in the noninvolved spouse is a crucial indicator of the viability of the marriage. This balance is particularly significant at the outset of the therapy. A clinical pattern that has emerged may need empirical validation, but it is useful as a beginning hypothesis:

> *The greater the level of anxiety about the affair in the involved spouse at the outset of therapy, the more likely the marriage will remain intact and the affair will terminate. Conversely, the lower the level of anxiety in the involved spouse, and the greater the level of anxiety in the noninvolved spouse at the outset of the therapy, the greater the chances of the termination of the marriage.*

This trend is partially related to the pattern of emotional pursuing and distancing in the relationship. If the noninvolved spouse is very anxious at the outset of therapy, she usually is concerned about her adequacy as a spouse and the viability of the marriage. This concern frequently evolves into a highly charged and generally unhelpful level of emotional pursuit that creates *more* rather than *less* distance in the marriage. In the attempts to "prove" her worth, she conveys anxiety and a severe lack of self-confidence. She is likely to look for a level of commitment from her husband that he is not emotionally capable of giving, at least at that time. The involved husband sees his wife acting as the inadequate person he has come to believe that she is, and he gains resolve to terminate the marriage.

On the side of the involved spouse, the level of affect fits into the flow of the dynamics by way of the element of the differentiation of self. If the involved spouse has decided that the new relationship has emancipated him from the shackles of a relationship that was suppressing his true identity, he is likely to be calm and ready to move toward a divorce. If, on the other hand, the extramarital relationship has generated a high level of confusion and ambivalence related to appropriate loyalties, it is more likely that there is enough of an attachment and enough of a foundation in the marriage that he may want to return to rehabilitate that relationship. His level of anxiety then relates to a fear. He has discovered that he had needs that were *not* being met in the marriage that *were* met by the lover. There is a fear that if he recommits himself to the marriage those needs will again be ignored.

Once past the beginning stages of the therapy, the level of anxiety and agitation in the individuals will continue to play a role in both daily life and the progress of the therapy. The level of anxiety usually needs to be high enough to motivate the person to examine the emotional structure of his or her life, but low enough to allow that examination to proceed with solid cognitive functioning. This necessitates an ongoing therapeutic agenda that moves to provoke a helpful amount of anxiety at times when motivation is waning or helps to defuse an unhelpful level of anxiety when it is so high that objectivity and rationality are not to be found.

Love

The other feeling that is central to the therapy will be love. At the outset of therapy, the meaning of love becomes even more ambiguous than usual and is approached by way of questions. The obvious question centers on who loves whom. Does the involvement in the affair mean that there is no more love for each other? Frequently, the involved spouse is totally unable to make sense of his feelings of love at the outset of therapy.

While the noninvolved spouse may be agitating for an answer to her question, "Do you love me?," in fact, the involved spouse may not be able to answer that question. The noninvolved spouse may come to the conclusion that her husband really doesn't love her anymore and is simply trying to "break it to her gently." But more frequently, the involved spouse is torn between feelings, which he recognizes as some type of love, for his spouse and feelings for the lover as well.

The feelings of the noninvolved spouse also can be confused, but for slightly different reasons. She may desperately *want* to rehabilitate the relationship, and she may be aware of strong feelings of love mixed with disappointment, anger, and feelings of inadequacy. This leads to a certain cautiousness and ambivalence in her emotional accessibility. As the communication of those feelings is interpreted by the involved spouse, he may fear that she has ceased loving him because of his transgression, because he is "no longer worth it."

This leads to a symmetrical experience of a lack of love. Whether each person is most acutely aware of the lack of love for the other in themselves, or a lack of love for themselves in the other, it can have a profound effect on the course of the healing. Generally, the feelings that people are searching for in that situation are most accurately described as the feelings of intimate rapport and accessibility that were developed in the preceding chapter. Those types of feelings, however, are rarely found at that time. Certainly it is unrealistic to expect that delicate feelings of rapport, and even the more mundane operational accessibility, would be able to surface in the midst of the crisis of an affair. Whether the pair love each other, however, is a much different question, and usually an unanswerable one in the initial stages of treatment. Love is a far more complex type of attachment that relates to all four levels of emotional connection.

Similar to the level of anxiety discussed above, the question of love will take on different forms at different points in the therapy. At the beginning of therapy, this confusion can be taken to mean that if the involved spouse can't feel, and in turn express feelings of love, it truly means that the love between the couple is gone, or perhaps was never there. Either one or both of them can then reach the conclusion that the marriage should be terminated. Generally, it must be expected that whatever feelings of love *did* exist between them would be substantially altered at the outset of the therapy, and no decisions should be made based on the form those feelings assume at that point in the process.

The question of love takes on a different form later in the therapy. As the couple explores the history of their relationship and the history of their attraction to each other, they are likely to come to the realization that at least some part of their initial attraction to each other was based on needs they now see as immature and unhealthy. They then can begin to question the nature of their love for each other from the beginnings of the relationship and doubt its validity.

Suspicious Beginnings

Jack and Bea provide a good example of that type of concern. They entered therapy after Bea admitted to Jack that she had been involved with a man she met at work. Jack was very distraught about Bea's involvement and desperately wanted to make the marriage work. Bea, on the other hand, was somewhat interested in continuing the marriage, but she was concerned that the marriage had begun at a time when she had needed a different type of relationship than she needed currently.

Specifically, Bea had met Jack nine years earlier, when both of them were in their early twenties. Both had graduated from college, but Bea had returned home to live with her parents after graduating. Jack, in contrast, was living on his own in an apartment. Bea had begun to realize over the months preceding her affair just how intensely she had needed to be free of her parents at the time that she had met Jack. She had felt suffocated living with her parents, and at that time she had made the assumption that the only way out was to get married. She now believed that she should have moved out of her parents' house and lived in a place of her own prior to getting married.

As the therapy progressed, Bea came to see how she had unconsciously felt just as trapped by the marriage as she had felt in her parents' home following college. She saw Jack as the type of responsible person who would have met her parents approval when she began dating him. He was successful in his business, but the temperament that yielded that success also gave him the inclination to be the dominating one in their marriage. Bea came to see, even before the affair and before the therapy, that she had traded one oppressive living situation for another.

Jack was somewhat unaware of this process until the therapy began. But as he explored these dynamics in the therapy, he came to realize that he had been vaguely aware of the problem from another point of view. He recollected that the two of them had talked in some depth when they first began dating about their mutual need to be in a relationship founded on independence, respect, and equality. He then tracked the development of the relationship into the dynamic balance that existed in the year prior to Bea's affair. He remembered having thoughts during that time that he did not share with Bea. It seemed to him that Bea was waiting for him to make most of the decisions and deferring to him on decisions that should have been joint efforts.

The multigenerational patterns in their respective families shed light on their own emotional evolution. Both of them came from families that were dominated by their fathers. Both of them consciously desired to reject that style of a relationship, but as they worked their way through the therapy, both came to see that they had colluded in recreating the very pattern they had intended to reject. They came to question the love they had for each other at the outset of the relationship. It seemed as if they had a symmetrical predisposition to look consciously for an egalitarian relationship and, unconsciously, to establish a relationship based on male dominance.

Bea's affair signaled a desire to escape that type of relationship. She had known that she was oppressed in her marriage to Jack, but it was not clear that she was truly looking for a different type of relationship. She now could see, with hindsight, that the person whom she became involved with could easily fall into the pattern of male dominance as well. She became suspicious of the split between her conscious desires for a relationship and the apparent unconscious motivating forces. Who was she going to love, and what type of relationship would evolve?

Jack, meanwhile, was questioning the type of relationship he wanted to have. He came to realize that he had indeed become the dominant one in the relationship with Bea, and he now could see how that dominance was unhealthy for both of them. He was intent on establishing the type of relationship they had both consciously desired when they were first dating. As the therapy progressed, Bea came to believe his intentions; she also came to understand that her own predisposition to recreate her family pattern was as much a part of the evolution in their marriage as were any tendencies toward dominance in Jack.

Fortified with that insight, they were able to understand the type of immature love that had characterized the beginnings of their relationship. They also were able to see the potential in themselves, in each other, and in the relationship for which they had hoped at the outset. Establishing a new balance of power did not come quickly, but they both consciously attended to it. The feelings of love they had for each other became very different. They both described it as a sense of a more mature and understanding love.

DIFFERENTIATION AND THE DEFINITION OF SELF

The process of differentiating and defining a self is at the very core of the internal factors associated with extramarital affairs. Considerable confusion arises, however, in the way that the concept addresses the interface between intrapsychic functioning and interpersonal emotional connections. That confusion is further compounded by two other factors. First, the common understanding of the concept has become blurred, thus leading to the same type of linguistic imprecision that was reviewed regarding affairs. And second, the classic definition of differentiation truly needs to be expanded, in the same spirit as the expansions on the notion of triangles.

The linguistic problems can be illustrated with a series of different examples.

"Is Joe more differentiated than his brother Matt?" This sentence illustrates a usage that implies an assessment of the two brothers and a value judgment that one "level" of differentiation is better than another. Differentiated, in this sense, suggests a state of being beyond any conscious awareness or control.

"I felt more differentiated from the family after my discussion with my father." Although this sentence suggests an understanding that differentiation is a rather broad concept that has to do with one's relationship with family, the belief that one conversation could have an impact on the level of differentiation suggests a more contained experience. No doubt the speaker felt something different, but it was probably a sense of greater distance, which may or may not have been

comfortable. It was not differentiation in the more abstract sense of the concept. Differentiation cannot be felt in that way.

"*I was trying to differentiate myself from the emotionality of the disagreement.*" This usage makes differentiate into a verb that connotes an attempt to avoid tension. It implies a conscious level of activity that can be initiated at will, rather than the more enduring features of level of functioning and definition of self.

"*She couldn't differentiate her thoughts from her feelings.*" This sentence implies a cognitive activity that is examining both thoughts and feelings and using an awareness of that distinction for some purpose. This usage again suggests a more conscious activity that is subject to at least some measure of personal control.

The confusion emanating from these different usages can be minimized somewhat by more clarity in the definition and a stricter protocol for use of the word. When Bowen brought the word into the vocabulary of family systems from the physical sciences, he intended it to refer to a level of human functioning that was more pervasive than behavior that was under any type of conscious control. But, by way of the folk process, the original, specific intention has been blurred over time. For example, the person who wished to "differentiate" herself from the emotionality of a disagreement is not using the word with the original family systems meaning. A simpler word such as "avoid" would actually be clearer in that situation.

The concept of differentiation only becomes slightly easier to understand once the linguistic problems are eliminated. By way of bringing some order to the relevant ideas, we will begin with a development of the classic components of the concept that need elaboration and then move on to expand on certain areas that need new development.

Thought or Feeling?

This distinction can be an extremely elusive one. The haphazard use of language has numbed our sensibilities and obscured the difference between thinking and feeling. The confusion can go in either direction. Sometimes thoughts are reported as feelings, and sometimes feelings are reported as thoughts. In most instances, language provides the necessary clues.

It is all too common to hear someone say something such as "I felt he was wrong when he bought the smaller car." Now it may be that the speaker did have a feeling about the purchase, but the activity she was reporting sounds more like a cognitive one. In other words, she is suggesting that she had evaluated the features of the smaller car versus whatever option was available and had made a decision that the smaller car was less useful than the other option. That decision is a thought more than a feeling, and it would have been more accurately reported by saying, "I thought that he was wrong when he bought the smaller car."

Statements that begin with the first person and switch to the third person can suggest the confusion of a thought for a feeling. "I felt *he was wrong*" does just that. "I felt" establishes the expectation that a feeling is going to be reported, but the second phrase does not fulfill that expectation. "He was wrong" is a judgmental phrase, which is a cognitive activity and clearly does not report on an internal feeling.

The woman who provided that example had been involved in an affair when she and her husband entered treatment. She had mentioned that "feeling" in the middle of a discussion about the differences between them. The therapeutic challenge is to clarify the distinction between thinking and feeling, and identify the feeling that *is* involved. That entails focusing on different vocabulary, words that identify internal feelings such as angry, sad, upset, and so forth. This different vocabulary is the access to a different dimension of experience in the individual, the affective dimension.

After making the initial distinction between thinking and feeling, even more subtle confusion is possible. It can be continued with a variation on the classic defense mechanism of intellectualization. Again, vocabulary provides clues about this confusion. For example, when I asked the woman how she *felt* about her husband buying the smaller car, she responded by saying, "I think I felt angry." Beginning the sentence with "I think" neutralizes the attempt to report on the feeling. She was not recognizing her feeling and reporting on it. She was cognitively assessing what she thought she was "supposed" to feel, and perhaps what she thought I expected her to feel, and proceeding to "think" about the correct answer to the question.

The reverse confusion, expressing a feeling rather than a thought, tends to be a bit more transparent. Take, for example, the husband's response when I asked him why he had decided to buy the smaller car. That question asks for *thinking*, looking for facts, figures, and so on. His response was, "I felt confident that the smaller car would meet our needs better than the larger car." He reported on a feeling rather than on the thinking process that went into the decision.

Although the most useful cues regarding the confusion between thinking and feeling can come from language, it is not a simple linguistic distinction. The two different dimensions of internal life operate on very different premises. Feeling is a nonrational or irrational experience, and thinking is a more cognitive and rational experience. The interaction between thoughts and feelings is such that it is quite impossible to have a thought that is totally divorced from feelings, or a feeling that is totally divorced from thoughts. As the distinction is understood, the interaction becomes more clear.

Thoughts, Feelings, and Separate Individuals

The distinction between thoughts and feelings takes on greater complexity when considered in the context of the emotional system. The capacity to sense another person's feelings and anticipate her thoughts raises the probability that one person could "feel the same" as another person, as a result of the process of identification with the other, or definition of self. This creates a false sense of connection, an inadequate sense of individuality, and generally blurry emotional boundaries between the people involved.

From another vantage point, a person could "feel what she was supposed to feel," meaning that she could feel and ultimately act out feelings that had begun as expectations of those feelings from another person. Here again is an instance in which feelings that appear to be "inside one person" are more accurately understood within the broader context of the interpersonal relationships involved. The conceptual structure can be augmented with established concepts such as projective identification, or a more thorough development of the nuances of fusion. The clinical treatment is founded on greater definition of the separate individuals involved.

DEFINITION OF SELF

The second intrapersonal dimension of differentiation speaks to the definition of self. Originally this referred to a vague combination of the ability to differentiate between thinking and feeling and the ability to know and express a personal opinion. The assumption regarding the expression of opinions was, if a person were able to know her own opinion, she then "knew herself," and she could differentiate her opinion from the opinions of others. The differentiation of opinions was tantamount to the differentiation of self.

The definition of self in colloquial usage, however, generally refers to a person's self-image. A person will have an image of herself as being a combination of different traits. These traits may be somewhat related to opinions, but in fact they offer a much richer image of the definition of self. A person may, for example, see herself as gregarious, or quiet, or strong, or weak, and so forth. The traits can actually be interpreted in different ways. Whereas she may use positive labels to describe those traits, someone else with a different perspective may label the traits with words that are less complimentary. This self-image eventually develops into a central ingredient to the emotional system of the affair.

TRAIT LABELS

Positive	*Negative*
Quiet	Uncommunicative
Strong	Dominating
Flexible	Wishy-washy
Interested in others	Intrusive
Caring	Suffocating
Independent	Isolated
Expressive	Gabby
Nurturing	Controlling

This pairing of opposites could be continued with the entire range of trait labels usually used to describe a personality. Although some part of the distinction between a "positive" trait and a "negative" trait is in the eyes of the beholder, some part of it is a function of the expression of the trait and the extreme to which it is taken. For example, independence, when taken to an extreme, can become isolation. It is, in fact, in the ultimate expression of these traits that the definition of self within a marriage becomes operational.

Fusion and the Definition of Self

The definition of self, in the context of a marriage, rests at the balance point of intrapersonal elements of the system and inter-

personal elements. Again referring to Bowen's original model, he
suggested that every relationship is defined by a certain level of
fusion. There simply is no relationship that is perfect. The level of
fusion is related to the relative definition of self of each individual,
which was primarily established in their respective families of origin.
And as was discussed in Chapter 1, the model suggests that people
marry people of equal levels of differentiation.

Within this structure, however, there are two other dimensions
that must be highlighted, *patterns of apparent dominance* in the relationship, and *patterns of similarity and difference*. Looking first at patterns of
apparent dominance, people experience dominance in a relationship
in a way that can be illustrated as retaining the integrity of the
boundaries of self. As the process of fusion evolves between two
people, one can experience oneself as either forfeiting self, or maintaining self. The beginning position (Figure 3.1) is one with a man
and woman, illustrated as usual with a square and circle, respectively.

As the two people connect in an intimate relationship, one or the
other of them can be experienced as being the dominant one in the
relationship. The other one in turn forfeits self and loses the integrity
of the boundaries of self (Figure 3.2). The figure on the left suggests
the loss of self in the woman, with the man being dominant, the figure
on the right suggests the reverse.

Sometimes one couple will evolve into a permanent, rigid expression of one of these solutions in every aspect of their relationship. In
some cases, a couple will adopt one pattern at one time, the other at
other times. For example, a couple may be seen as operating consistent with the male-dominated pattern during times that were seen
as conflict free and a pattern consistent with the female-dominated
pattern during times of conflict. Or a couple will be able to identify
one solution as typifying one period in their history, with the other
typifying another period.

Either one of these emotional solutions to the process of connec-

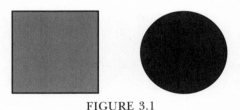

FIGURE 3.1

 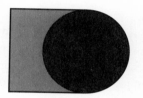

Male Dominance   Female Dominance

FIGURE 3.2

tion in the relationship is undesirable. Although it would appear that the person who manages to retain self-boundaries is gaining, what is gained is a false sense of augmentation to self. And the one who forfeits self clearly is losing the overall integrity of self-boundaries. A more balanced connection, one that is ultimately healthier, is one in which both retain clear boundaries and are able to experience a comfortable connection (Figure 3.3).

It should be emphasized that the emotional process of connection illustrated by these simple figures has vast implications for the daily life of the couple as well as broad-based operational and emotional trends. They can give meaning to such simple questions as daily decision making as well as the more enduring questions such as who is getting more of his or her needs met in the relationship.

The second dimension, that of the relative degree of similarity and difference, is somewhat related to the level of operational style developed in the previous chapter, with more emphasis on the respective definitions of self. The balance again rests on the degree of similarity and the overall level of connection. If there is process which establishes "connection through similarity," both may define themselves as being flexible, or being strong-willed, or some other established trait with which they identify.

If, on the other hand, there is a need to establish "separateness through dissimilarity," there will be a process that highlights the

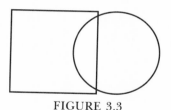

FIGURE 3.3

opposite nature of the two people in the relationship. In this instance, one may be seen as the strong one in control, the other may be seen as the dependent and incompetent one. Or one may be seen as the saavy, street-wise one, and the other would be the naive, prudish one. Or one may be seen as the sensitive, insightful one, and the other may be seen as the stoic, cold, and insensitive one.

Whether the process is one that accents connection through similarity, or separateness through dissimilarity, there is a rigidity to the definitions of the people involved that establishes a false definition of self, diminishes the healthy process of self-definition, and compromises the functioning of the individuals. Although each has a definition of himself that is known, it is not a healthy definition based on individual abilities. It is a function of the fusion in the relationship.

In extreme cases of separateness through dissimilarity, people can develop patterns that put them at polar opposite ends of various continuums. For example, one will be rigidly independent to a point of isolation, and the other will be excessively dependent to a point of physical and emotional dysfunction. In extreme cases of connection through similarity, people can collude in unhealthy extremes of behavior, such as alcohol abuse. In those cases, like relationships built on opposites, the potential for the healthy, flexible, definition of the two people involved has been sorely compromised.

Multigenerational Fusion and the Definition of Self

This process of self-definition occurs across generations in a family system. Both patterns of dominance and patterns of similarity travel from one generation to the next. The process is dependent on both the relationship a person has with her parents and the relationship the parents have with each other. The process of connection through similarity has been given other labels, such as identification. And the process of separateness through dissimilarity has been given such labels as rebellion. Obviously, either tack taken to an extreme is an unsuccessful attempt to define a self. The notion of the definition of self in one's family of origin is a slightly different facet of the same process developed in Chapter 2 related to the multigenerational triangles in the family.

If a person defines herself as being "similar" to a particular parent, she may adopt life style patterns that mimic the parent with whom she has identified. If a woman, for example, had a father whom she knew to be involved in affairs, and she, because of the usual array of reasons, defined herself as being similar to her mother, then there is some reason to consider the possibility that she may tolerate and even need a marriage that mimics her parents marriage. Her marriage, also, may be characterized by her husband's extramarital involvement.

Does this mean that she needed her husband to have an affair? Only in the broadest and least specific meaning of the word need. Does this mean that her self-image in some way contributed to the overall process? Possibly, is the only accurate answer that can ever be given for that question. This same model can be applied to both the involved spouse and the lover. Generalizations are not particularly helpful. The specifics will depend on the definition of self, how it relates to the multigenerational process in the individual's family, and the implications of that definition for her particular involvement in the affair.

Affairs and Fusion

An extramarital involvement usually signals some attempt to reckon with the emotional complexities of the fusion. When the primary emotional motivation for the affair begins with the fusion in the marriage, the affair can offer a false sense of escaping from it. The involved spouse is usually more aware of this feeling of escape than is the noninvolved spouse. Frequently, the affair will be with a person who will accept and even encourage a different definition of self than the one rigidly defined in the marriage.

Take, for example, a person who is locked into a definition of being functional, responsible, and in control in the marriage. She may find herself in an extramarital relationship with a person who will accept and encourage a frivolity and irresponsibility that is not seen in the marriage. In a marriage characterized by the pairing of two strong-willed personalities, the affair may offer respite by way of establishing a relationship with a person who, for reasons of her own, is content not being in control.

The extramarital relationship offers an opportunity to establish what appears to be a different definition of self. Initially, there is a sense of liberation from the old constraints and a sense that the new relationship is "better" than the original relationship, because there is the ability to be someone new. There is a feeling that this new person and new relationship finally offer the opportunity to express and/or develop an element of self that was buried in the marriage.

Frequently, however, as the new relationship continues to develop, it becomes clear that the process of defining a self in the new relationship will be just as difficult as in the original relationship, but with a different set of parameters. For example, for the person who found a new sense of carefree frivolity in the affair, it can become clear as that relationship deepens that it is difficult to establish the sense of ongoing responsibility characteristic of the marriage. Or if the affair happens to be with someone who is originally seen as less strong-willed than the spouse, she may eventually be seen as too dependent and not sufficiently self-motivated.

The Involved Spouse and a Split Sense of Self

The involved spouse, more than either of the other two people in the classic triangle, is faced with the realization of the differences between the two relationships. The standard interpretation is that someone has been found who is a "better match" in some ways than is the spouse. The feeling is that he has unlocked a part of himself that was lost in the marriage.

Although this is often interpreted as being inherent in the personal differences between the lover and the noninvolved spouse, it is also a function of the different definitions of self brought to each relationship by the one in the middle, the involved spouse. For example, whereas the lover may be seen as more sensitive than the spouse, the spouse involved in the affair may present an image that is more conducive to eliciting sensitivity when with the lover. In a sense, the lover and the noninvolved spouse are more neutral than Figure 3.4 suggests. The split is more intrinsic to the definition of self of the one who is involved in the two different relationships, as suggested in Figure 3.5.

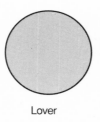

Lover

Involved
Spouse

Noninvolved
Spouse

FIGURE 3.4

Lover   Involved
         Spouse   Noninvolved
                   Spouse

FIGURE 3.5

The Noninvolved Spouse and the Rigid Definition of Self

In contrast to the split and rather confused sense of self seen in the involved spouse, the noninvolved spouse tends to have a self-image that may be defined so strongly as to be somewhat rigid. As seen through the eyes of the involved spouse, the noninvolved spouse is someone who is "just a certain way." Frequently, almost by way of fulfilling the image, that person may conduct himself in ways consistent with that image. And he may overtly agree that the image is basically accurate.

There are two examples of this process of self-definition in the noninvolved spouse that are seen frequently. When the woman is the one who has become involved in the affair, the husband is often seen as overly controlling, and sometimes insensitive as well. When the husband has become involved, the wife is often seen as insensitive, and unresponsive. The definition of self by the noninvolved spouse in both of these situations is eventually seen and understood as being just as constricted and unhealthy for him or her as the split is for the involved spouse.

The Lover and the Weak Sense of Self

A brief consideration of the third corner of the classic triangle is useful both for times when that is the individual in treatment and for when there is some consideration of the emotional system that extends beyond the couple in treatment. The involvement of one married person with another married person is likely to involve the types of dynamics reviewed in the two preceding sections. But the single person who becomes involved with a married person frequently exhibits a rather weak sense of self.

Sometimes this weakness is expressed paradoxically, in the form of a strong external facade that conveys the impression of refusing to be duped into the folly of marriage. Such individuals allow a type of involvement that is, by definition, limited and steadfastly maintain that any serious encroachment on their independent territory will be grounds for termination of the relationship. This type of image is founded on a fear of the loss of self in an intimate, total relationship. It is founded on a fundamental sense of personal weakness.

A second presentation of weakness of self-definition in the lover is the person who agrees to "string along" in a relationship with a married person for an extended time, under the pretenses that the marriage is dead and will be terminated imminently. The assumption is that the lovers will marry after the divorce. As time passes, and it becomes more clear that any plans of divorce and remarriage are specious, the weakness of self-definition of the lover is one of the cornerstones of the continued affair. She is not strong enough to leave the relationship, nor does she feel capable of establishing a healthier relationship.

INTEGRATION OF SELF

All three of these styles of definition of self are obviously problematic. The underlying theme in all three styles is a lack of integration of the different elements of self-definition into one healthy image. All three people involved in the triangle bring incomplete and disintegrated self-images into the emotional system of the affair, which in turn contributes to the evolution of both the overall balance in the system and the affair itself.

In contrast, there is the potential in a healthy, well-functioning individual, to be able to express and experience a wide range of feelings, traits, and facets of "self." Sometimes these various traits have a superficial contrast that makes them seem mutually exclusive, but more accurately, they are seen as integral parts of a broader whole. Whereas a capacity to be responsible, for example, would be an indispensable element of healthy functioning, the excessive drive to be over-responsible, and the inability occasionally and appropriately to "loosen-up" is not in the best interest of the individual or the system at large.

Whatever specific features of self-definition characterize the people involved in the emotional system of the affair, the focus is on the task of greater integration of the healthy elements of self that have been lacking. It is at this point that the self-definition of the individuals must again be examined and understood in the context of the overall emotional system and in the self-definition of the other people as well. As noted above, the definition of self in the marriage is a function of both multigenerational and marital fusion, as well as individual traits.

The somewhat simplified trends in self-definition developed above can offer a model for the development of thinking about the definition of self, and its interaction with the emotional system. The split in the involved spouse speaks to a need to be able to integrate the different images of self and to express them appropriately in one relationship. The repercussions, both for that individual and the other person in the relationship, need to be understood if that range is developed. Frequently there was a fear, prior to the affair, that expression of that wider range *in the marriage* would have been ill-received, or even impossible.

The rigid definition of self in the noninvolved spouse operates dynamically in much the same way. There was a fear prior to the affair that an expression of a wider range of self in the marriage would be ill-received, or perhaps would leave the overall functioning of the marriage and family compromised. If the noninvolved spouse evolved into a self-definition that was skewed in the direction of being, for example, the overly domestic one, there are implications for the therapy.

The therapist, and eventually the client, must have some understanding of the individual and systems factors that conspired to produce that type of functioning, and the corresponding image of self must be challenged. An emotional balance in the marriage, which would help to unburden them of that role, must be contemplated and eventually implemented. The negative implications that balance would have for the two people must be anticipated and defused.

Integration of Self and Interpersonal Boundaries

In marriages that were characterized by separateness through dissimilarity, the development of self is likely to develop in such a way that both spouses become "more like the other." In other words, the initial, unhealthy balance in the relationship was such that each of the partners had adopted a specific range of expression that was different from the other. This helped to create a sense of separation between them, but, in fact, each became parts of the whole. If each of them redevelops elements of self that have been lost in that process, they will develop elements that might have been primarily expressed by the other. The task, individually and collectively, is to maintain healthy and appropriate boundaries between them in this process.

In marriages that were characterized by connection through similarity, the process of integration of self will likely involve the integration, or perhaps recapturing, of a wider range of self not previously seen in the marriage. One may become free to recapture, for example, a trait such as a capacity for leadership, which may have been an integral part of a self-definition prior to marriage, that had been unexpressed in the marriage. This same process can evolve in the reinvolvement in activities integral to the definition of self prior to marriage but that had withered away during the marriage.

Examples of this include personal involvement in some avocation such as the arts or music that had been particularly meaningful but neglected through the marriage. The dynamic balance regarding boundaries needs to then take into account the need to retain an optimum level of connection, while at the same time facilitating the needed level of autonomy. This notion is at once complex and difficult to define in a manner that is generalizable, yet at the same time possible to evaluate in specific relationships with specific people.

COGNITION

Cognition is yet another aspect of individual functioning that has commanded considerable attention. Again, the intention here is to focus on elements that are particularly relevant to the emotional system of the affair, and not to provide a comprehensive treatment of cognitive theory and/or therapy. The point of departure is the simple observation that individuals' perceptions of themselves, others, and the world are critical to their involvement in affairs. This certainly will come as no surprise. But again, certain trends and central themes are noteworthy.

The Involved Spouse

Rarely can a person become involved in an affair and be unaware of the unflattering overtones of the involvement. The sanctions against affairs are simply too embedded in the social fabric, the sprinkling of apologists notwithstanding, to be able to ignore that viewpoint. The ability to proceed with an affair in the face of this is founded not only on the dynamic, emotional, and systemic factors that have been developed but also on a cognitive perspective that serves to explain and justify the involvement.

There are four common cognitive structures that counterbalance the negative image of extramarital involvements and in some way emphasize the premise that extramarital affairs can be "good." These mechanisms can be employed individually or in combinations.

Cultural Norm

"Affairs are just a way of life. Everybody that I know has had an affair."

At one time, this model may have been more common for men than for women, although by the late 1980s, statistics (Hite, 1987) may offer women the same rationale. The basis is the perception that everyone is involved in affairs, and it is acceptable behavior given whatever conditions are defined. Sometimes "everyone" is meant to be everyone in the neighborhood, or gang, or ethnic group. The group identification defuses the negativity of the individual behavior and offers a perceptual lens that justifies the affair.

The Defective Self

"I am a defective person who is incapable of a healthy marriage. The best way for me to take care of myself, and make my marriage endure, is to create a parallel relationship that will take the pressure off me and my marriage."

This contrived quote could be the oath of a person whose cognitive structure is based on the premise of a defective self. The intersection of this model and the question of definition of self is of course rather blatant. The premise of a defective definition of self must be understood with the array of concepts previously developed. The cognitive structure adds even more weight. It helps to minimize the cognitive dissonance that could be encountered in the juxtaposition of a good self-image with involvement in a bad activity.

The Defective Other

"You drove me into the affair because of your problems."

A logical corollary to the previous cognitive stance, the perception that the other is defective or inadequate not only justifies the affair, but it takes the focus off of self. Here again, there is a seamless connection between this stance and the question of definition of self in the emotional system, with particular reference to the fusion in the relationship. Despite the necessity to consider the vast implications of the definition of self, the cognitive element is powerful in and of itself. It is possible for an involved spouse operating in this vein to construct a distorted perception of the other that is unrealistically negative. She is seen as being unable to do anything acceptable and as ill-equipped to fulfill her role in the relationship.

Affairs Are Harmless

"I know that I probably shouldn't be doing this, but it really is fairly harmless."

Some may justifiably call this stance a form of denial. Although it has some relation to denial, it is extremely pervasive and can be seen as a lack of ability to perceive the impact of the extramarital involvement on self, spouse, or family. The construction of reality is such that emotions, and the usual signals that communicate those emotions, are interpreted to reinforce the belief that the affair has only a minimal impact on everyone concerned.

The Noninvolved Spouse

The cognitive patterns of the noninvolved spouse partially mirror the trends developed for the involved spouse, though there are other important areas of emphasis.

Evidence of the Affair

"Do I see anything that suggests involvement in an affair?"

This is perhaps the most significant cognitive/perceptual lens to track with the noninvolved spouse. The answer to the question can range from a denial that any evidence of an affair exists to the other extreme of seeing evidence of an involvement in literally everything. Like the cognitive patterns noted above, the style of the individual will be linked to the dynamic and affective components of the situation. In other words, emotional dynamics, such as the couple's collusion in the distance provided by the affair, and their affective response to the affair, such as a fear of the affair, will profoundly influence their cognitive pattern.

Defective Self, Defective Other

"I am an inadequate person. I understand (accept) that he is involved with someone else because I cannot fulfill his needs."

"She is involved with someone else because she has a problem."

These two patterns are reciprocal to the same patterns in the involved spouse, complete with the intersection of the dynamic and affective components. Either perception can reinforce a belief that the pattern of extramarital involvements will continue in some form, based on the perception of inadequacy in one or the other, or both.

Trust

"Can I trust her to be faithful?"

This, of course, overlaps with every other cognitive pattern, as well as being linked to the overall dynamics. Experientially, the noninvolved spouse will process a vast range of information, including minute behaviors in the spouse, to support any opinions concerning trustworthiness. Where a disinterested observer may see a person routinely going about daily activities, a suspicious spouse will see opportunities for secret rendezvous, unexplained contradictions in accounts of activities, and evidence of gift exchanges with lovers. In some situations, the totality of this world view cannot be overstated. Even in situations where the suspiciousness is less pervasive, the cognitive pattern inevitably emerges on an intermittent basis.

The Lover

The person in the third corner of the classic triangle, the lover, needs to have some type of cognitive structure to assist in the processing of somewhat discrepant data and feelings throughout the affair. In keeping with the trends developed earlier, the lover's style will be largely dependent on whether or not he is married. If he is married, his cognitive style will be very much in keeping with the style noted above for the involved spouse. If, on the other hand, he is single, there are two different cognitive styles that are common and offer a structure for understanding their predicament.

Patience and the Burden of a Bad Marriage

"I am patiently waiting for her to get out of her marriage. She has told me that it is a bad marriage, and she needs to find the right way and the right time to get out."

People adopting this type of cognitive structure frequently are competitive with the noninvolved spouse. He wants to believe that there are no feelings of love between his lover, the involved spouse, and the noninvolved spouse. He assumes that he needs to wait until some particular set of circumstances evolve to finally liberate the one person from the marriage and make it possible for the new match. These circumstances could have to do with children reaching a certain age, financial situations developing to a certain point, or perhaps the death of a key person in the family.

Savvy Self, Weak Other

"This person thinks that he will marry me as soon as he gets divorced. That's a joke. First of all, he doesn't have the guts to get divorced. And secondly, I don't want a thing to do with a marriage. I'm quite content with the relationship the way it is. I don't want any more money, time, or responsibilities."

The person operating with this type of cognitive structure clearly is in a much stronger position than the person described in the first example. She sees herself as the one in control in the relationship and believes that she has the situation just the way she wants it. That definition of the relationship is one of circumscribed boundaries, which protect the lover from the totality of a fully functioning relationship. This viewpoint is one that is quite transparent in its rejection of intimacy and commitment and, in that way, suggests a fragile vulnerability at the core.

INSIDE—OUTSIDE: A FINAL WORD

Many of the themes developed over the preceding two chapters have seemed somewhat redundant. It would be more accurate to understand the repetitiveness as the complex interconnections of core dynamics of the emotional system. It is quite impossible to dissect the various factors of the system and proclaim dogmatically that one element is totally intrapsychic in nature and another totally interpersonal. Inevitably, most of the elements bridge the gap in ways that are impossible to articulate perfectly. This results in the same phenomenon being explored both from the "inside" perspective and from the "outside" perspective. Each view of the same situation offers a slightly different perspective and a slightly different meaning. Neither viewpoint can be identified as being the only correct interpretation.

This fact is reflected clinically in the way that different people have different reactions to the various inter- and intrapersonal interpretations that can be developed to explain their lives. Some people will resonate to one interpretation, whereas others, in situations that would appear to be quite similar, will resonate to another interpretation and reject the one found useful by the first person. This type of difference creates the necessity for the therapist to be willing to forego the luxury of an attachment to theory as if it were religious dogma. Theory is merely the current map that is useful in the journey. The previous two chapters have developed the highlights of a theory that can be useful in the treatment of affairs, but even this model should not be seen as a static statement. Any useful theory is continually evolving.

Along with being evolutionary, theory also must be implemented. Certainly there have been many ideas thus far about treatment strategies, but with little specificity. The next six chapters explore the implementation of theory. After a broad look at therapeutic technique, the application of the theory and technique to the treatment of affairs will be developed, first by way of treatment planning concerns, then by way of case illustration.

CHAPTER 4

Improvisation and Therapeutic Technique

An effective exploration of the therapeutic technique involved in the treatment of affairs can only be accomplished by digressing from the subject of affairs and turning to the subject of technique. This chapter will be that digression. In an important way, the digression will mirror the type of "digression" that must happen in the therapy itself. If the therapy single-mindedly and myopically focuses on the subject of the affair, critical dynamics will be missed, therapeutic opportunities will be squandered, and generally, the therapy will be less effective than it could or should be. Likewise for this book.

The basis of effective psychotherapeutic technique is disciplined improvisation. Effective psychotherapy cannot be conducted without the ability to improvise. Improvisation is the type of activity that elicits more emotional reactions than cognitive ones. Some people are convinced that they are unable to improvise, before having any idea of exactly what is entailed. And others, with basically the same imprecise knowledge base, are equally convinced that they can improvise. This chapter is intended to take some of the mystery out of therapeutic improvisation and to look specifically at the improvisational potential in the treatment of affairs.

The techniques in this chapter will be seen by experienced clinicians to be very basic to the practice of psychotherapy. They are intended to be so. The premise of this model of systems-oriented psychotherapy is that there are basic concepts and techniques that combine to yield basic, effective, psychotherapy. The intention is to avoid defining a "new school" of psychotherapy for the treatment of affairs, or anything else. A second goal is to use ordinary language and to avoid the coining of words or phrases that establish new jargon. Words, ideas, and techniques are intended to be understood with the standard and most common usage. The intention is to integrate the knowledge available and put it into an effective structure.

IMPROVISATION

The cornerstone of artistic improvisation in painting, drama, music, sculpting, or psychotherapy is the disciplined application of theory to practice. Although an artist may paint different scenes and images, she superimposes a certain fundamental understanding of shape, color, and perspective onto each new painting. A musician may play different songs, with different harmonic and rhythmic characteristics, but there, too, certain basic principles are acknowledged in the musical statement. And a psychotherapist may conduct psychotherapy with a variety of different clients having a variety of different complaints, but there will be a thread of familiarity that runs through the work.

In this way, the treatment of extramarital affairs must be seen as being more similar to basic psychotherapeutic practice than it is dissimilar. In fact, it is only different in the way that each psychotherapeutic experience, each treatment hour, is different from any other treatment hour. The differences lie in the areas of emphasis created by the therapist and client, and in the stamp of personal style that gives the work a personal definition. The areas of emphasis begin with the conceptual model and begin to take shape with the broad treatment goals. Ultimately the specific comment, intervention, interpretation, or response, is an improvisational act.

The art of improvisation is endlessly complex, even when it appears to be basic or simple. The processes of growth and maturation create an ever-increasing appreciation for details missed in earlier times and an appreciation for the poignancy in simplicity. There are several elements pertinent to improvisation in psychotherapy, and in the treatment of affairs, that can be highlighted here.

In the Groove

Jazz musicians talk about a phenomenon called "being in the groove." This can refer to the level of compatibility and responsiveness between any one musician and the rest of the musicians in the band. Or it can refer to the band as a whole, as in "the band was in the groove." Whether the statement refers to one individual or the whole band, usually it is obvious to everyone involved. Not being in the groove can manifest itself as a lackluster performance, or worse, a performance that was characterized by tension and a lack of relaxation, fit, and "swing" to the music.

In contrast, being in the groove is experienced as a high level of responsiveness, vitality, and controlled intensity. The level of concentration is such that the musicians are absorbed in a unanimous flow and swing to the music, and are thoroughly engaged in playing. The added precision in execution, and the added emotional depth, create the difference between an inspired and an uninspired performance.

Exactly the same phenomenon exists in psychotherapy. There are times when the therapist is in the groove, and times when he is not. And even though there usually are not other band members to know about it, except in the case of cotherapy, the client/couple will know it in the same way an audience knows when a band is in the groove and when it isn't. The family, like the audience, may not realize it on a conscious level. They may not even know what they are experiencing, but they will be left with an unsettled feeling of being unsatisfied and perhaps being "out of sync" with the therapist. If the therapist is not in the groove with the clients, any misfit is a function of the therapist's state as well as being a reflection of resistance by the clients.

The therapist must depend on the same type of focused concentration, absorption, and engagement as an improvising musician. If the therapist is actively thinking about ideas from a book or a supervisory hour, he could try to fit the client's experience into those ideas. This can lead to a tension and struggle between the client's personal experience and the therapist's experience of the client's experience. This produces a misfit, and the therapist is not in the groove with the client. In a peculiar way, this suggests that the most effective use of the ideas found in this book will happen when there is no direct thought about the ideas, and the concentration is on the content of the session. In other words, forget about this book during therapy.

A more extreme example of this same type of dissonance is the therapist who has a very narrow world view and proceeds to shoehorn all of the client's experiences into this narrow model. An example might be the therapist who experiences the human condition as being organized around one specific idea, such as instincts, gender issues, or internal psychological constructs. If the therapist is so firmly entrenched in one narrow belief system that he is unable to relate to other experiences of the world, he is likely to be "in the groove" with the clients who happen to share his belief system and quite out of the groove with the rest. Given the controversial and provocative nature of extramarital affairs, the model adopted by the therapist is particularly relevant to this point.

A more mundane question related to being in the groove is the level of concentration brought by the therapist to any given session. If the therapist is preoccupied with basically ordinary and innocuous matters from other parts of his life, such as unexpected mechanical problems, upcoming vacations, or other normal life events, he may be unable to "get in the groove" in the therapy hour. Or if the therapist is overextended, with an overloaded caseload, there may be insufficient energy and concentration left for clients at the end of the day or end of the week.

The cues in all of these situations are going to be very subtle. They usually will revolve around a lack of intensity and a lack of cogent involvement by the therapist. Intensity doesn't mean histrionics or passion. It means engagement, absorption, and intense concentration on the process. If the level of concentration is focused, if the therapist is in the groove, the capacity for a spontaneous, wide-ranging synthesis of ideas will improve, and the ability to use those ideas creatively will improve as well.

"I Hear Ya"

One of Murray Bowen's favorite and most frequently used comments during a therapy hour was "I hear ya." These three words, with an array of different inflections, suggested a variety of different meanings. The one meaning common to all of the inflections was an indication of a deep understanding of what the client was saying, and perhaps was not saying. Although there is frequent talk of the client being able to "hear" the therapist, or other family members, the importance of the therapist's ability to hear the clients simply cannot be overstated.

Actually, "hear" is a misstatement, because the activity that is called for is a full-scale processing of every available cue provided by the couple. This includes all of the standard cues so well known to the general population, as well as the professional community, including body posture, facial expressions, seating arrangements, and so on. The actual words spoken in a session are but a fraction of the information a therapist needs to be able to "hear."

The importance of hearing most assuredly comes as no surprise even to neophyte therapists. There are, however, two points to emphasize regarding hearing in this context. First, and quite obviously, is the integral connection between hearing and successful therapeutic improvising. Second, it is essential to call attention to the distinction between various degrees, or levels of hearing. A brief comparison, again to music, may help clarify the notion of various levels and degrees of hearing.

A person totally unfamiliar with classical music may have the opportunity to be exposed to one famous work, perhaps Beethoven's Fifth Symphony, and feel satisfied that she is able to identify the famous "victory motif" when she hears it at a later time. A person with slightly more sophistication may be so familiar with classical music that she is able to hear, distinguish, and accurately identify different composers. Yet another person may be able to differentiate among different composers, but she also may hear differences between different renditions of the same work by different orchestras or performers. And lastly, there are people who are able to hear the differences between different performances of the same work and understand why those differences exist and how they were created. That person can then go on to use that knowledge either to create her own music or for any other creative purpose.

The process of hearing in psychotherapy is remarkably similar. Even though every trained psychotherapist is familiar with the learning process in the early stages of professional development, the process of improved hearing hopefully continues very long after training has been completed. In this way, details that were noted as significant in the early stages of learning are eventually taken in and recorded in an off-hand, almost instinctual manner. The concentration is instead focused on ever more subtle and hopefully more telling cues.

As the range of hearing gains breadth and depth, so too does the range of interventions available. Where the beginning therapist sees the seating arrangement in the room as reflective of family dynamics, and chooses to comment on that arrangement because that is the primary cue she is able to "hear," the seasoned therapist may also see the seating arrangement, yet choose to ignore it in favor of attending to a subtle comment buried in the middle of a seemingly unrelated point made by one of the clients. That comment, it turns out, offers rich opportunity to expose dynamics related to the seating arrangement and deeper, more poignant dynamics in the couple's relationship.

Consistent with the themes developed throughout this book, it must be clear that the conceptual model and world view of the therapist will shape what is heard. The therapist who sees affairs as examples of unilateral sexual acting out of internal conflicts will be able to "hear" comments that support that view. The therapist who is listening for comments revealing the broad-based systemic model developed here will be able to hear references which support that model. Although both models can be helpful in their own ways, there will be a different slant to both pieces of work.

Attention to Detail

This may be implicit in the discussion of being "in the groove" and hearing, but it is sufficiently important to warrant specific attention. Improvisation becomes more effective with more attention to detail. It is necessary, of course, to hear the detail, but it is also necessary to respond to it effectively. When an audience listens to a preeminent musician such as Louis Armstrong improvise, its members become caught up in the beautiful music and let their minds playfully wander into a variety of images.

The listener may imagine that the musician is doing the same, but the truth is that generally, he is not. He is carefully attending to thousands of details that are quite out of the awareness of the average listener. These details range from the performance of the accompanying musicians to the sound of any one note that he is playing. More often than not, the musician is not having the same emotional reaction to the music that the listener is having. As the therapist compares the experience of listening to a musician improvise, to improvising during psychotherapy, it is crucial to remember the difference between the active and the passive role. For a listener of musical improvisation, the role is passive. For a therapist conducting treatment, the role is active.

The comparison between musical improvisation and therapeutic

improvisation can be made even more graphic if the field of vision is
expanded to compare the improvising of a highly polished professional jazz musician, to a pleasant, well-meaning, but undisciplined
street musician. The professional musician *sounds* better: he is more
effectively responding to and solving the problems presented by the
music. One of the most critical distinctions between these two extremes is the attention to detail. Every minute aspect of the music will
be important to the polished professional, whereas the street musician
may only be able to perform certain parts of the music effectively,
glossing over other, "more difficult" parts. Both groups of people
may play a standard piece, such as " 'Round Midnight," or "Autumn
Leaves," but there is a different level of performance.

In the realm of psychotherapy, and especially the treatment of
affairs, the comparison is striking. Everybody has opinions about
affairs, and everybody seems to think he or she knows exactly what to
do about the situation. This includes neighbors, relatives, co-workers,
and so on. Many times, as will be discussed in Chapter 9, they are
quick to offer their ideas. Hopefully, the difference between professional input and the input of the "man in the street" is one that is
based on attention to detail and having a thought-out approach on
what to do with the information presented.

Notes on Style

Setting aside the distinction between the polished and the un-
polished musician and therapist, the differences in style are critical in
the overall musical or psychotherapeutic experience. For example,
even a totally untrained and unprepared listener could hear the
stylistic differences between the controlled improvisation of Coleman
Hawkins on the jazz classic "Body and Soul" and the raucous and
frantic improvisation characteristic of the experimental Ornette Coleman, or the late work of John Coltrane. The differences are simply
not subtle.

So too with psychotherapy, stylistic differences are going to be
evident. On one level, they are manifested in the amount of input
provided by the therapist. A far more critical distinction is the type of
input rather than the amount. Returning to affairs, the style of
intervention and the style of improvisation will grossly effect the
clients' experience. There have been attempts to develop ideas about

the stylistic possibilities of psychotherapy. Stanton (1981), for example, developed a model that integrated the structural and strategic models. Although this was a useful attempt at integration, it can only be seen as one small piece in a much larger jigsaw puzzle. At the other extreme is the work done by Bugental (1987), which is much more vast in philosophical focus but, again, has an idiosyncratic approach. Inevitably, the most effective style will be idiosyncratic.

The element of style complicates the question as to what theory, and what intervention, at what point in the treatment. Frequently the choice of theory and technique can be made from a set of appropriate choices. Rarely is there a situation that is explainable with only one concept and treatable with only one intervention. The choices made over the course of the treatment will have a cumulative effect on the course of the treatment and will define the prevailing style. Any one choice will have a relatively minimal impact on either the definition of the style, or the likely outcome.

INTERVENTION TECHNIQUES

The final ingredient in improvisation is the repertoire of techniques available. This is a difficult and perhaps even dangerous topic to explore. In psychotherapy, as in music, the capacity to improvise will be modulated by the technical skills available to the therapist and musician. This creates the need to acquire technical skills, which can take the form of techniques.

Certainly this is an important component of improvisation, but one which can be misused in both music and therapy. The musician who inappropriately inserts a technically difficult phrase in a solo is seen as using a "hot lick" in an amateurish fashion. The therapist who uses techniques with insufficient understanding of the underlying theoretical base, or the moment in treatment, will be misusing therapeutic technique. The efficacy of any given technique simply cannot be determined separate from the technician, target, and the context of the treatment.

With that caution noted, a few key techniques pertinent to psychotherapy, and the treatment of affairs, will be reviewed here. The purpose of such a review is not to provide a new and unusual model of intervention, nor is it intended to add to or comment on, the considerable body of professional literature already devoted to the techniques of psychotherapy. Indeed, there will be many common intervention strategies, such as the use of video and audio tape, the use of cotherapy, and the use of consultation teams, that are not explored here. The emphasis here will be one of establishing a pattern for the creative and disciplined use of technique in the treatment of affairs, and in psychotherapy in general. As that pattern becomes established, and is firmly rooted in the conceptual model, the potential for an ever-increasing range of interventions becomes almost limitless.

Questions

Questions are to psychotherapists what blue jeans are to cowboys—a basic tool of the trade. And just as blue jeans have been raised to the status of fashionable clothing with designer labels, so too have there been attempts to create designer labels for questions. Labels such as "circular" or "reflexive" questions beg for definitions of the term and seem to have more status than a generic question. Although there may be an occasional advantage to differentiating between different types of questions, the most critical ingredient to any question is the conceptual model that structures the implicit world view, and in turn leads to a series of hypotheses that can/need to be tested. In psychotherapy, the questions that need to be asked, in most instances, are vehicles that can provide information for the testing of those hypotheses.

Questions are more important, in some ways, than are the answers to the questions. Creative questioning can open up new vistas, by suggesting new and different ways of perceiving aspects of life that are so familiar as to have become almost invisible, or by framing new experiences in ways that make them more understandable. Questions are central to the process Duhl (1983) refers to as "making the strange familiar, and the familiar strange."

The emphasis on questioning in couples therapy, which must be made clear to the couple, is on the assessment of individual feelings, perceptions, and opinions. It is not on the collection of data, or the establishment of historical fact as in a court of law. For example, when a husband reports that his wife is inadequate because she totally ignores him when he comes home from work, the focus is on the husband's perceptions and his behavior rather than on the "in-

adequacies" of his wife. Thus, the information the husband is presenting is seen as more revelatory of him, as the speaker, than it
reveals about the wife. The distinction is critical, and it leads to
considerable reduction in defensiveness and editing in the answering
of questions. It also allows the silent, listening partner, to hear the
words without becoming defensive.

The individual feelings, perceptions, and opinions elicited by
questioning can be related to the entire spectrum of life in the family.
Indeed, a narrow focus on the presenting problem, such as the affair,
will inevitably be counterproductive. Frequently the questions are
unanswerable. For example, the question "Why did you become involved in an affair?" could be met with a blank stare by the client,
especially during an initial interview. If it isn't met with a blank stare,
the answer forthcoming may be superficial and unproductive. The
response could be, "It was just stupidity and irresponsibility on my
part." That type of self-deprecation, although appearing honorable
and contrite, rarely indicates any type of helpful understanding and
resolution of the pertinent dynamics.

With either the blank stare or the humble self-blame, the creativity of the therapist is challenged. Perhaps more questions, which are
narrower in focus, could prompt the client to reexperience and re-
frame the situation. For example, the question "What did you find in
your relationship with the other person that you had not found in
your marriage?" is both a statement and a question. Imbedded in the
question of "What did you find?" is the statement that you did find
something. This type of question also takes a step toward focusing the
client's attention on a more discreet and manageable understanding
of the complexities of the affair.

Instigations

This second category of interventions is one of the most important, and one of the most difficult to describe. Instigations, or offering directions to clients, are one of the most potent ingredients of any
psychotherapeutic experience, since the therapist is offering instructions that will have a noticeable impact on the lives of the clients. They
are difficult to describe because they beg the question of the pro-
verbial "bag of tricks," which at worst can be a series of mechanical
exercises, and at best can be what Guerin and colleagues (1987) refer

to as an experimental opportunity to disrupt established patterns in the individuals and families.

There is no list of directions that are perfect for the couple struggling with an extramarital affair. Nor is there a list of directions for the therapist treating (struggling with?) a couple involved in an affair. The most effective directions are improvised in the same way that questions are improvised, designed to test hypotheses about the functioning of the individuals and the system and firmly rooted in the underlying conceptual base.

One obvious target for directions is observable behavior (Figure 4.1). The question of what behavior, when in treatment, and why, cannot be answered simply or succinctly, because the possibilities are truly limitless. The "why?" can be explained by any concept, including a shift in the emotional distance in the couple, disruption in the pattern of distancer–pursuer, attention to some triangle in the family, alteration of communication patterns, a shift in decision-making patterns, and so on. The range of behavioral possibilities are even more diverse, beginning with powerful and major alterations in the lives of the couple, such as a temporary separation, or a weekend away with each other, and extending to the unending opportunities for shifting seemingly inconsequential daily interactions, such as dinner table conversation, checkbook balancing, and doing the laundry.

A somewhat less obvious and more intangible target for directions from the therapist is in the realm of cognitions and perceptions. The client can be encouraged to think about and perceive elements of life in new and provocative ways. Directions can, for example, take the form of "think about the assumptions you are making about your wife when you avoid talking with her during this coming week." The general thrust of any instigation of this type is to establish ex-

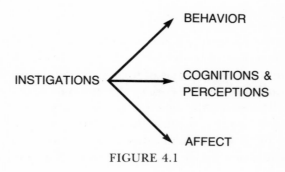

FIGURE 4.1

pectations that the client will think about his thinking and in turn think about the perceptions that influence that thinking.

A more ambiguous, yet vital, target for instigations is affect. Obviously, affect cannot directly be controlled, as in "Don't feel angry at your husband when he comes home late." Obvious also is the need to respect the distinction between thinking and feeling. This distinction is evident when clients are instructed to think about what they are feeling, which activates a conscious and cognitive assessment of affective states. The instruction to think about feelings helps to establish control and objectivity in the early stages of therapy, when emotions are peaked, and provides clues about double messages in the later stages of therapy.

An example may help illustrate this potential. Dick and Anita entered therapy after Dick revealed his extramarital affair to Anita. Initially, Anita was extremely angry and was prone to attacking Dick verbally at regular intervals throughout the day. Although she recognized the feelings of anger, she did not recognize any other feelings contributing to her dismay. She was instructed to continue her outbursts for a period of two days following the session but to think about other feelings that were intensifying them. She discovered feelings of rejection, abandonment, and betrayal that she associated with her discovery of her father's affair. This discovery, and the implications of unfinished business, offered fertile ground for exploration of her relationship with her father. This helped to diminish and defuse the intensity of the emotion directed at Dick.

Later in therapy, despite an absence of angry outbursts, Anita and Dick were reporting a lack of good communication between them. The subjects that were discussed seemed to be relevant, but both acknowledged that something was missing. They were instructed to think about what they were feeling during those conversations. They both reported feeling cautious and mistrustful of the other. As the discrepancy between their conscious intentions and their basic feelings was highlighted, the meaning and function of the mistrust was understood and eventually shifted.

They came to realize that the "right words" and the "right actions" may still be compromised by feelings that can sabotage the conscious goal. In both of these instances, and the initial example pertinent to the early stages of therapy, the clients were encouraged to experiment with different affective states. In other words, Dick and Anita were encouraged consciously to evaluate their emotional state during a conversation and to make an effort to drop the feelings of coldness, aloofness, and mistrust. These were to be replaced experimentally with warmer and more vulnerable feelings during the conversation.

Education

Interventions designed to educate the clients about the functioning of emotional systems are a constant throughout the therapy, and frequently they come in the form of observing the patterns and functioning of the clients themselves. Coming, as usual, from the conceptual model, the style of presentation varies from situation to situation. Generally, long and complicated speeches are counterproductive. Brief, cogent explanations about ideas pertinent to the topic are far more effective.

Sometimes these brief explanations can be augmented by offering reading material to clients. Sometimes they can be enhanced by using role plays, or by developing with the clients an understanding of the principle as it evolves into a pattern in their lives. For example, in an individual session with Anita, the wife described above, we role-played a conversation with her husband. During the role play, she became cold, cautious, and withdrawn in a way that mimicked perfectly her emotional posture with her husband. The contrast between that posture and her usual posture of trust and connection with me taught her the meaning of emotional distance in a way she had not understood previously.

Visualizing patterns and systemic functioning is an educationally oriented intervention that can be developed in various ways, again limited only by the creativity brought to bear on the situation. A chalkboard can be used by both the client and the therapist as a tool for visualizing the patterns, which frequently evolve dynamically such that they happened repeatedly, with the emotional dynamics operating with a circular effect. Figure 4.2 illustrates a generic model that can be individualized to fit the thousands of daily exchanges that transpire. This pattern can be used to highlight behaviors, perceptions, feelings, or a combination of all three.

Shifting of triangles offers another visual interactional pattern in the system. Triangles can be drawn to illustrate the relative emotional distance between the chosen members of the triangle at various significant points in the evolution of the system. Enough triangles were drawn in Chapter 2 to emphasize this point and make yet another

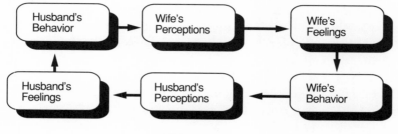

FIGURE 4.2

triangle here unnecessary. This type of intervention is generally more powerful if the client, rather than the therapist, draws the triangle. During a couple session, emphasizing the likelihood that each person will perceive the triangle differently intervenes simultaneously on several levels, in the encouragement of differentiation, and the cognitive awareness of systems functioning.

Patterns in the family can be traced and visualized in the form of developmental chains that can be sketched similar to Figure 4.2, with the emphasis on historical development rather than on circular interaction. The chains that are the most accessible relate to the same three areas of system functioning that were developed in the section on instigations: behavior, cognitions, and affect. Behavior can be tracked with a focus on broad patterns, such as the level of hostility and conflict between spouses from one year to the next in the relationship, or on a more detailed level that would track the nuances of behavior in the evolution of a critical incident. Each level of focus can be compared to a different lens in a microscope, and each offers different information about the system.

Cognitive and affective patterns can be traced in the same manner. For example, the destruction of trust in a relationship following an affair usually is a powerful theme and a significant focus of treatment. If trust is dissected into several component parts, it can be understood as being partly affective and partly cognitive in nature. Tracing the evolution of trust through the entire relationship can be very revealing about the eventual extramarital involvement. Frequently the couple will discover that the level of trust in the relationship prior to the affair was at best marginal, particularly on the part of the involved spouse. This lack of trust can come in the form of a fear that her needs will not be understood or met, or a lack of trust in the communication process in the relationship. One other common mistrust seen in the involved spouse is a fear that she will not be accepted for who she is, or who she thinks she wants to be.

"Love" ranks high on the agenda of couples in the initial stages of working through an affair. "What does the affair mean about our love for each other?" is the usual thrust of the question from the clients. Establishing the idiosyncratic meaning of love for each of them, and tracing the feelings over their relationship, will help to detoxify the issue until a more substantial appreciation for the complexity of the subject can be developed. Once some type of definition is developed, tracing the manifestations of it through their history amounts to a development of the pattern of their feelings. Creating some type of visual illustration on the chalkboard helps to crystallize the image.

Storytelling is educational in nature. As therapy proceeds, clients frequently want to know whether their woes are comparable to other situations. Discreet comparisons, with the appropriate attention to confidentiality and facts chosen for their relevance to the clients at hand, can have a beneficial impact on clients' understanding of their own situations. "Is it usual for a spouse to become reinvolved after one whole month of therapy?" "Am I the only one who feels this way?" These questions, and countless other situations, can be addressed with creative storytelling in the therapy.

Creative educational interventions will be interspersed throughout the therapy in the same manner as questions, instigations, and other interventions. The foundation of the treatment is on a broad-based process of healing rather than on the specific application of one intervention or type of intervention.

Paradoxical Interventions

These interventions can be as powerful in the treatment of affairs as they are with other symptoms. They are at a different level of abstraction than the interventions discussed previously, in that any of those interventions can be articulated paradoxically. The power in a paradoxical intervention is in the potential for disrupting the expected. The paradox is most effective when it is a paradox in the mind of the client and not in the mind of the therapist. For example, if a therapist instructs a couple to plan on having an argument at a certain time during the upcoming week, the couple will experience it as contrary to their goals for the therapy. This makes it paradoxical in their mind. If the therapist sees and understands the need to legitimize disagreements between them, prescribing the argument will be consistent with the broader therapeutic goals, and not paradoxical to the therapist.

One of the most common interventions in the initial stages of the treatment of affairs is to coach the noninvolved spouse in the subleties of emotional distance, and to encourage him not to react to the extramarital involvement by intense pursuing and "proving" he is the more deserving person. This intervention is perfectly reasonable and understandable, given the model developed throughout the book. But to the grieving spouse, it sounds as if he is being told to back away and let go of someone who is already trying to run away. Seen in this way, it is a paradoxical instruction, doing the opposite of what is expected.

Most paradoxical interventions in the treatment of affairs will probably relate to the dynamic of emotional distance, given the critical importance of that theme in the evolution of the symptom. The paradox could involve behavior, such as the example cited above, or it could involve cognitions or affect. An example of a paradoxical intervention targeted at affect would be the situation presented by Frank. When Frank entered therapy, he reported being involved with another woman, but he was extremely cold and denied being affected by his involvement. This denial, of course, was suspect, given his decision to come to therapy and try to do something about the situation. Along with questioning him in such a way as to provoke a realization of the chaos and pain intrinsic in the situation, which was buried and unacknowledged, he was encouraged to discuss these feelings with his wife.

Frank experienced this entire therapeutic strategy as being paradoxical. He expected to be helped to "feel better" when he came into therapy, and instead he was made to "feel worse." The questioning that revealed the uncomfortable feelings did not "create" those feelings, but merely made them overt. The paradox was in the misfit between Frank's initial naive expectations and the most effective treatment strategy. He expected to have help with explaining to his wife why her faults caused him to have an affair, and instead he found himself expressing his own feelings of confusion and anxiety to her as never before. Again, this is not creating something that isn't there. The assumption, which was substantiated by the success of the intervention, is that Frank did want to discuss this situation with his wife because he did want to resolve it and end the secret. This created a level of rapport and intimacy between them, with him being the one to open up and reach out.

There have been occasional challenges to paradoxical interventions based on questions of ethical treatment. Is it ethical to manipulate clients? Is it ethical to be dishonest with clients? These types of questions illustrate a fundamental misunderstanding of the premise of paradoxical interventions. Paradoxical interventions rest on the knife-edge of ambivalence and contradiction inherent in people and in systems. People may wish to be close to their spouse, but at the same time, they fear that closeness. Although they come to treatment to "fix" the situation and satisfy their wishes, to pretend that the fears do not exist is to ignore a powerful dynamic in the system. Paradoxical interventions provoke the ambivalence and are designed to defuse, eventually, the potential negative impact from those sources. Used properly, they are honest, effective, and quite ethical.

Paradoxical interventions have been seen in various forms in many, if not most, schools of psychotherapy. They have been described as reverse psychology, reversals, satiation therapy, prescribing the symptom, and paradoxical instructions. Used exclusively they would be sure to lead to treatment failures. Used responsibly in a more well-rounded therapy, they offer therapeutic power and leverage that is invaluable. They are, in fact so powerful that a word of caution is in order. Paradoxical interventions are extremely provocative, and are deceptively difficult to execute in a way that usefully provokes the client and maintains the therapeutic relationship. They will be useless as an initial intervention. The timing and context of paradoxical interventions are just as important as the interventions themselves.

Humor

Yes, humor is one of the ingredients that is critical to success. Yes, it is too complicated to describe neatly. Yes, there are some readers who will immediately and totally dismiss humor as "not professional" and skip on to the next section. But yes, there are also those who will be encouraged to tap into their own humor and rely on it to loosen up the clients, and perhaps even themselves, during the course of therapy. It is hard to imagine successful therapeutic improvisation that totally dismisses humor.

Humor frequently goes hand in hand with paradoxical interventions and can provide the emotional distance necessary for the success of the intervention. Aside from paradoxical interventions, laughing together helps to create an atmosphere of trust and rapport that is difficult to develop in other ways.

Therapist Self-Disclosure

A difficult to describe but noteworthy class of interventions can be described somewhat loosely as therapist self-disclosure. This type of intervention has been more common in family therapy than in many other approaches. Within the ranks of family therapists, self-disclosure has taken different forms. There are, for example, apocryphal stories of therapists telling stories to clients that are seemingly about the therapist's spouse and children in circumstances similar to that of the client. These stories were supposedly fabricated for purposes of therapeutic effect and emphasis. Although the intentions were noble and understandable in those instances, that is not the type of self-disclosure being advocated here. Fabricating stories about one's personal life, even for a beneficial effect, can be dangerous as a glib and perhaps disingenuous factor in what should be a solid person-to-person relationship between the therapist and client.

The type of self-disclosure that can be useful and provocative has to do with the therapist's feelings about the course of the therapy, the presentation of the clients, and the events as they are unfolding. The discussion with the noninvolved spouse who enters therapy shortly after learning about her spouse's affair could be an example of this type of intervention. Assume that she is so depressed that she is not sleeping well and has lost her appetite. She can be acknowledged with genuine feelings from the therapist, in the form of "I'm concerned about your depression." This can help strengthen the therapeutic relationship and make the client more consciously aware of herself as well. This intervention is distinctly different from the less personal and more aloof flavor of "Would you say that you are depressed?" or the even more sterile "How is your mood?" The power of the therapist will be in knowing when it would be most useful to use the various possibilities.

One of the complications regarding therapist self-disclosure has to do with his feelings about the affair. What if the therapist is outraged that the person is involved, or thinks he, the involved spouse, is a fool for "letting go" of a great spouse, or feels jealous that he has found such a wonderful lover? Are these reactions reported? The safe answer to that question would be "no, of course not!" The more difficult answer is that there are times, when the therapist is fully aware of and in control of feelings that have classically been referred to as countertransference feelings, that some type of creative use of those feelings may be possible. Effective and helpful use of those feelings undoubtedly relies on firm and healthy clinical judgment and sound intuition, and simultaneously defies a simple list of dos and don'ts.

The Art of Therapeutic Improvisation

Combining all of these elements and actually improvising in the therapy is not easy. Frequently people feel safer acting in a way that has been prescribed by some "higher authority." It is important to understand that improvisation does not mean creating something totally new at every moment. Creative implementation of standard techniques, and even classical use of standard techniques, weave through the process of therapy, just as they weave through the musical improvisation of the masters. There will be times when the now worn out cliche "I hear ya" will be the perfect intervention. There will be other times when a more explicit comment about the dynamics will be more helpful.

Different phrases, interventions, and even conceptual models enjoy periods of popularity and usefulness. An effective improvisor will have the courage to use what is useful and powerful at the time and have the courage to move on to new ideas and techniques when they are needed. Rollo May (1975) has suggested that the type of courage that is needed relates to the development of new symbols. The overall effect will be the presence in the therapy of a therapist who has defined a self, and has brought it to the therapy. This is in contrast to the therapist who has latched onto one static model and clings to it past any usefulness.

The need for improvisation in the therapist is similar to the task of therapy for the client. If the client is going to effectively eliminate the unhealthy and destructive life choices that brought her to therapy, she obviously is going to have to change. If the therapist is clinging to old patterns of behavior, old ways of thinking, and old ways of doing therapy, he is going to be modeling the opposite of what he expects from the patient, and he probably will have less empathy for his patient's dilemma.

TECHNIQUE AND TREATMENT PROTOCOL

Beyond the minute-to-minute demands of improvising an intervention based on questions, instigations, humor, and so on, an overarching approach to therapeutic practice and technique must be defined. In other words, there is a need for a structure that creates boundaries for the therapy. Again, the musical analogy is pertinent. The musical structure of a song, based on elements such as the harmonic and rhythmic characteristics, defines the basic structure of the improvisation. Without that structure, the improvisation would be aimless.

Psychotherapy has broad structures that are comparable. These broad-based structures traditionally have been defined by the number of people in the treatment room during the session, and have been labeled "individual therapy," "couple therapy," and "family therapy," depending on the situation. The structure developed here makes the classical definition of those terms obsolete. Although there are times when there are different numbers of people at any given session, that session is one part of a much broader structure, a structure of treatment that integrates the various permutations and uses them as different sections of a broader piece. The most obvious musical analogy would be the contrasting improvisational potential to be found in the different sections of the same jazz song.

Simultaneous Marital and Individual Treatment

This title is descriptive in the sense that it creates a reasonable image of the broad structure of the therapy. It is not descriptive in the sense that it belies the profound differences to be found. One of the key technical features to be stressed here is the incorporation of simultaneous marital and individual therapy done by the same therapist. This model is in contrast to the more traditional model of engaging the couple in marital therapy with one therapist and having each member of the couple in individual therapy with two other therapists. There is no perfect treatment model, and this approach is no exception. But the potential in this model is considerable.

Simultaneous treatment by the same therapist is an outgrowth of the movement toward integration in psychotherapy. As marital therapists integrated individual concepts and techniques, and individual therapists integrated marital concepts and techniques, the potential for combining the two streams became more apparent. The integration has moved beyond the idea of patching together two different systems of change. It is now clear that a broadly based approach to change, and health, is one which understands, acknowledges, and attends to the multiple layers of experience pertinent to emotional dysfunction, and the corresponding components necessary for healing. Rather than a crude patchwork of techniques, there is now the potential for a richly woven tapestry given vivid life by different threads.

The early developmental roots of this strategy have been in practice for quite some time, and they reflect a well-intentioned but rather elementary approach to the model. Individual therapists have, as an adjunct to ongoing individual therapy, scheduled sessions with a client and spouse. Frequently, the rationale for this approach has been to give the couple an opportunity to discuss a critical or volatile issue or to collect from the spouse a different perspective on various problems.

Marital therapists, on the other hand, frequently included individual sessions in the early stages of marital therapy for purposes of information gathering. There was a desire to collect information about secrets, such as affairs, which might affect the outcome of the marital therapy, yet was unlikely to be revealed in the joint sessions. From both the perspective of the individual therapist and the marital therapist, there was a focus on the *content* possibilities available with the other treatment modality and less emphasis and attention given to the *treatment process* implications of the expanded approach.

Integration of the Treatment

Combining individual and marital sessions ceases being a patchwork quilt and becomes a richly woven tapestry when there is the understanding that the sessions do not represent the combining of two different modalities, but in truth represent one comprehensive treatment approach. Each type of session offers an opportunity to access certain bands of information and emotional business in a way that would be less available in one of the other groupings. Whether the session is with an individual spouse, the couple, the nuclear family, the extended family, or some certain subgroups, the composition of the meeting lends itself to different approaches on the emotional dynamics of the system. The challenge for the therapist is to make use of the opportunities in any one session and to have a respect for and understanding of the intricacies created by the overall process.

The boundaries of this integrated form of treatment are much broader than either modality independently. Individual psychological concerns are approached in ways not usually as available in exclusive marital or family sessions. And certainly the broader system dynamics are more available than in strict individual treatment. It will be referred to here as *integrated treatment*. This is not an attempt to coin any new brand of therapy. Quite to the contrary. The use of a relatively generic term such as integrated is meant to convey the generic nature of the concept, to de-emphasize any exclusivity, de-emphasize any idiosyncratic vocabulary, and offer a shorthand for identifying the treatment process.

The Therapeutic Relationship

Typically, a therapist who is seeing one person exclusively in individual treatment is going to develop a more intimate relationship with that one person than a therapist who sees people only in combination with a spouse or other family members. Conversely, the relationship a therapist has with people seen in the context of a couple or family is going to have a type of leverage based on the first-hand experience of seeing the marital relationship that is untypical of individual treatment. Integrated treatment poses the opportunities for both forms of the therapeutic relationship, with a different set of challenges.

The basic challenge is to balance the intimacy characteristic of individual treatment with the neutrality that is critical to successful marital therapy. The result will be an intimate, but neutral relationship with each person. The one-to-one sessions will undoubtedly provide an opportunity to experience a more intimate, more vulnerable dimension from each spouse than they make available to each other, especially during the initial crisis of the revelation of the affair. Knowing "this side" of each person first hand usually provides clues about the potential assets and liabilities in the relationship.

Eric and Dale provide an interesting example of the interaction of the therapeutic relationships that develop in integrated treatment and the effect on the treatment. They were prompted to begin treatment by the revelation of yet another of what was a series of affairs Eric had been in. He was a successful businessman, and Dale had dropped her career to concentrate on their three children. Although Eric was very successful in his career, he was remarkably unable to exert any power at home. Dale, on the other hand, was at the very least a strong, take-charge person. Eric usually saw her as overbearing and intimidating.

Dale's defenses were such that early in treatment, she would put up a strong front during the couple sessions, successfully intimidating Eric. During the individual sessions, she was able to drop the strong front, and she began to understand the pain and fear that fueled her overbearing manner. Her understanding of the change in her relationship with me between the individual session and the couple sessions helped to free her up and allowed her to be more vulnerable to Eric both during the couple sessions, and at home.

The same set of circumstances provided the context for the development of a higher level of neutrality in me as the therapist. Eric was very convincing in his portrayal of Dale as an overly strong person. Dale was very accommodating in living out that image in the context of the couple sessions. It was only in the structure and safety of an individual session that Dale initially was able to let down her guard and exhibit the potential for warmth and vulnerability which she did have. If there had been no individual sessions, these qualities would have taken much longer to surface, if they would have surfaced at all.

There are two sides to this process. In one direction, the therapeutic relationship developed during the individual sessions offers a richness and depth to the relationships that can offer leverage during the marital sessions. And in the other direction, the first-hand experience of each individual in the context of the marriage offers a position of neutrality that can make many standard defenses of people in individual treatment much less effective.

Treatment Sequence

One of the interesting complications arising in this form of integrated treatment involves the seemingly inconsequential element of scheduling sessions. It can have a surprisingly powerful impact on the overall treatment process. It takes basic card shuffling to see the possible permutations when scheduling sessions with a couple, the involved spouse, and the noninvolved spouse. Sometimes couples will schedule more couple sessions than individual sessions. Sometimes travel problems and daily scheduling problems result in more individual sessions than couple sessions.

One initial problem for the therapist is to be alert to the scheduling sequence and to decide if the particular sequence represents some form of resistance. For example, "innocent" scheduling difficulties by one member of the couple may signal an unwillingness to come in for an individual session. Similar scheduling problems in which the couple cannot coordinate their schedule to have a joint session can represent resistance to the couple sessions. These types of difficulties must be addressed if they arise. People are consistently receptive to fairly gentle interpretations of resistance at this level, and they are willing to redress the sequencing problems.

This treatment sequence frequently leads to questions of content and process. There will be times when one spouse reports, in an individual session, an episode that transpired between the couple. This spouse may proceed to develop her perspective on the situation, seeing it as symptomatic of what is wrong in the marriage and frequently expressing belief that the other is the one to blame. There are two separate levels of therapeutic process that impact the approach to this problem. First, the individual who is present will offer the usual, immediate demands regarding interventions. Second, is the longer-term therapeutic process, which involves the spouse not present, and the couple together.

If the other spouse is already scheduled for an individual session before the next joint session is scheduled, there is the question of whether to address the incident, and how. At times, especially early in treatment, the other spouse may come in for his individual session and not even mention the incident the other saw as so critical. This is usually a function of their different perceptions and sensitivities to the problems, and it tends to diminish as treatment progresses. As their sensitivities to each other's perceptions increases, the spouses are more likely to know what the other sees as important and are more likely to raise the concerns in the sessions. But what if that doesn't happen?

Decisions about interventions in these instances are made with *attention to the overall process first* and the *process in the session second*. For example, if a wife doesn't discuss an episode that was discussed in great detail in an earlier session by the husband, the incident is *not* raised by the therapist, with the intention of challenging the resistance. Instead, discussion of the incident is deferred until a future couple session, at which time the husband and not the therapist could bring up the incident for examination.

Confronting the wife in the individual session might provoke the process in that one session, but it will undermine both partners' trust in the therapist and, as such, compromise the long-term process of the therapy. The content provided by the husband usually can be accessed more effectively during a later couple session when he, not the therapist, can raise the episode. In the meantime, the session with the wife can be used as an opportunity to learn about her priorities and to contemplate the defenses that are active in preventing her exploration of the episode previously discussed by her husband.

A second problem created by the integrated treatment protocol is that of *competition between the spouses.* There is the possibility that one spouse will feel competitive with the other spouse and have a strong desire to either please, entertain, or dominate the therapist in the individual sessions. They particularly want to do it "better" than the other spouse. These feelings signal a type of transference that is unusual for more traditional marital or individual therapy. They can usually be diffused rather easily, by acknowledging them, and possibly testing them humorously. If they prove to be persistent, and remain a theme in the therapy, exploring their genetic and developmental etiology, both in the marriage and in the family of origin, will undoubtedly offer dynamic clues about their meaning and usually diminish their impact on the treatment.

The "Nay-Sayers"

There undoubtedly will be those who express objections to this integrated model of treatment. It does, after all, represent a radical shift away from the more traditional school of treatment that advocates different therapists for all of the different "modalities" and people in treatment. That shift in and of itself will prompt a reaction. The response is the classic one to any change in a system. There is resistance and a push to return to the original *status quo.* As with any systemic resistance, some of it is understandable, and should be acknowledged as such, and some of it is purely resistance to change.

Certainly there are legitimate concerns that can be expressed regarding the limitations of the model. Much of the concern will relate to the therapeutic relationship. For those therapists who believe that the primary healing component of the therapy is in the therapeutic relationship of individual therapy, the complications in the therapeutic relationship developed above can be seen as an unhelpful distraction. And family therapists who have taken the extreme position of refusing to see people individually will cast a suspicious eye at the potential for losing neutrality, or being "triangled-in" to the system.

Another understandable reservation will relate to the burden of diagnosis and treatment being entirely on one therapist. The medical world is steeped in the ethic of consultations and team meetings to augment diagnosis and treatment planning. The mental health community is likewise familiar with the structure of supervision, consultations, and multiple providers involved with one family. The family therapy community, specifically, has refined that tradition in the form of unseen consultation teams, or "Greek choruses," observing and contributing to the therapy from behind one-way screens. The premise underlying all of these structures is that one person cannot and should not be responsible for the entire treatment.

The controversy over these points is far more complex than can be covered comprehensively here. Hopefully, this presentation will prompt an extensive reevaluation of these points, as well as other reservations to an integrated treatment model. Briefly, the concerns about the therapeutic relationship must be put into the context of the expanded relationship, one in which the therapist's role is far more complex than either limited model. Healing is somewhat related to the therapeutic relationship, in the mode of traditional individual therapy. It is also related to the actions people take themselves within their own family emotional system, in the mode of that type of therapy. Healing, rather than being an "either–or" proposition, is expanding by "and."

As to the concerns about the limits of any one therapist, those limits are undeniably present. This mode of therapy, however, does not eliminate the possibilities for consultations; these simply happen outside the strict boundaries of the sessions, rather than with an on-site consultation team. The consultation then includes a discussion of the entire treatment process, including the individual sessions and the couple sessions. This presumes the therapist will know when he needs to ask for a consultation, since there will be no one else with "hands-on" familiarity with the treatment process. In that way, it may be less suitable for students than for experienced practitioners.

Just as the therapeutic relationship concerns of "either–or" can be augmented by "and," so too can the concerns about the burden on one therapist be tempered somewhat by the benefits gained. The single-therapist model is cost-effective. Dynamics emerge quickly and with more clarity, given the characteristics of the different settings. The cost of on-site consultation teams is eliminated, and the potential for multidimensional healing is enriched.

Neutrality

Extramarital affairs severely test the notion of neutrality throughout the treatment. Again referring to a basic sense of the idea of neutrality, and not any idiosyncratic meaning, the premise is that both people must be seen to be equal partners in the process of change. They both are in emotional pain. They both want things to be different. Perhaps one has a more concrete focal point for disappointment. For example, the noninvolved spouse can be quite specific when viewing the relationship between the other two people, and say "that is the problem." But a neutral position would include an understanding of the potential for understanding that the other spouse may have problems with the *status quo* aside from the extramarital relationship.

A neutral position transcends the more myopic idea that there can be goals that will be good for one person but not for the other person. The treatment is founded on the premise that effective functioning of the system will mean effective functioning at all levels, including the individual and the couple. If a wife desperately is determined to get out of the relationship, it can't be good for her husband to keep her there against her will just because he would prefer to keep the relationship alive. Seeing the interaction of the multiple levels of the system provides a structure for decision making that is embedded in neutrality.

From one perspective, neutrality can be seen as more abstract and philosophical than it is technical. But it does have observable referents in the treatment. It gets reflected in concrete interventions and overall treatment protocol and is emphasized here with that in mind. It is conveyed in the relative relationships that are established with the various members of the family or couple. An overly sympathetic relationship with a noninvolved husband and a punitive, confrontational relationship with an involved wife is obviously not neutral. Reversing the polarity on the relationships doesn't "fix it." Neutral means neutral.

The sense of neutrality is most obviously, most often, and most powerfully communicated nonverbally. While clinical skills such as interventions and interpretations are frequently the focus of attention, neutrality is communicated by eye contact, body language, and attitudes conveyed. Nonverbal communication, in this way, will be yet another form of improvisational intervention, and another element of therapeutic technique.

A sense of respect, compassion, and acceptance is a necessity. Attitudes about affairs also influence the sense of neutrality that permeates the treatment. If the therapist believes that "all men" need to have an affair, and encourages or sanctions an involvement by the client for that reason, that is a decidedly unneutral position. On the other hand, if the therapist believes that affairs are immoral, and again imposes this belief on the client, it too would influence the sense of neutrality.

Affairs in the Life of the Therapist

These attitudes betray feelings the therapist may have about affairs. Whether these reactions and feelings are diagnosed as countertransference, understood as intuition that will guide the therapy, or are undetected factors that have a silent impact on the therapist's interventions, they are potentially a significant factor in the treatment. The personal experience a therapist has with affairs will undoubtedly be a major determining factor regarding these attitudes. The importance of the therapist's awareness of this impact cannot be overstated.

If a therapist has never been involved in any way with an affair but has experienced either ongoing or acute ambivalence about the potential of such involvement, it could increase the potential of acting on one side of the ambivalence or the other. For example, a therapist who acts on the negative side of his own ambivalence, the side against being involved, may demand an immediate termination of the affair or refuse treatment. Conversely, a therapist who acts on the positive side of the ambivalence, the side in favor of being involved, may unwittingly encourage a continuation of the involvement and derive a type of secondary satisfaction from it.

Personal Experience with Affairs

The therapist also has the potential of actual experience with affairs in his own life. Specifically, the therapist could have occupied any of the three corners of the classic triangle. The experiences of involved spouse, noninvolved spouse, or lover will each have specific impact on the reactions of the therapist in the therapy. There is, in addition to the three basic positions, one which could be called that of observer. If the therapist has observed extramarital affairs in other members of his family, especially parents, feelings and reactions to that situation can influence the conduct of the therapy as well.

The therapist as the involved spouse creates considerable potential for any number of feelings, depending on the status of his involvement. For example, if the extramarital affair is current, and is experienced as beneficial, the personal satisfaction can influence the thinking about the beneficial potential of the affair. On the other hand, if the involvement is in the past, or is in a stage of lower satisfaction or even guilt, those feelings, also, can be projected in subtle ways.

The therapist as the noninvolved spouse offers several interesting permutations of the themes developed throughout the book. Along with the potential to identify with the noninvolved spouse in treatment, the possibility of a lack of trust between the therapist and the involved spouse can mimic the lack of trust in the client's marriage and in the therapist's marriage. That trust is likely to be a function of the evolution of the therapist's knowledge of his spouse's affair. Different reactions could be expected if the affair were suspected and denied than if the affair were unsuspected and long-lasting.

If a married therapist is occupying the position of the lover in a triangle in his personal life while treating a couple struggling with an extramarital affair, the possibility of an intermingling of the emotional agendas would be limited only by the specifics of the case. The double triangle of two marriages connected by one affair developed in Chapter 2 is the basic structure. The full range of dynamics of both emotional systems intersects in ways that are far too complicated to encapsulate but are logical extrapolations of the entire model.

Therapists who have observed affairs of significant others in their lives, such as parents, can bring feelings such as pain and heartache, mistrust, or self-righteous morality. The experience of observing a parent in an affair has enduring implications. The potential for the therapist to recreate the parental triangle with the client couple is great. This also creates the dynamic potential to align with the person in the couple who is in the same position as the parent with whom they were aligned.

Therapist–Client Affairs

It is well known that some therapists occasionally get emotionally and sexually involved with clients. Although there are times that the involvement comes "after termination," there are those times when the involvement comes during treatment. It almost seems inadequate to call that type of involvement an affair. Certainly it is an affair to the extent that if either the therapist or the client is married, the basic structure is the classic triangle. And certainly it is an affair in that this model, complete with triangles, will help to explain some of the dynamics of the involvement. But an emotional and/or sexual involvement between a therapist and a client transcends an ordinary affair by virtue of the added dynamic of the therapeutic relationship and the disparity in power inherent in that relationship.

There is a high level of official disapproval for this type of involvement in professional societies, licensing boards, and the general public. A clear understanding of this model of affairs can only serve to augment that disapproval with the corresponding dynamic basis. They are unhealthy relationships and are such transparent examples of inadequacies at enough different points in the system that even mediocre judgment is lacking on both the part of the therapist and client.

The possibility of an affair between a therapist and a client who has terminated is modified slightly. In the best light, it can be assumed to be more a reflection of a "regular" affair, whatever that may be. Beyond that, there are legitimate questions about the continuing therapeutic relationship. As will be developed in Chapter 7 on long-term treatment, the concept of termination can be modified somewhat. It is quite possible to retain the usefulness of the therapeutic relationship for crisis points after the main thrust of the therapy has concluded.

Given this possibility, is it ever possible to assert that the therapeutic relationship has terminated and the relationship between two people who had a therapist–client relationship is now an "ordinary" one? If this is not possible, any romantic and/or sexual contact between a therapist and a client either during or after treatment can be seen in basically the same light. The emotional foundation is flawed.

THE JOURNEY THROUGH THE EMOTIONAL SYSTEM: A PROGRESS REPORT

With the conclusion of this review of therapeutic technique, this journey through the emotional system of the extramarital affair has developed interpersonal and intrapersonal dimensions of the system, as well as the basic tools of psychotherapeutic intervention. Chapters 1–3, although not exhaustive reviews of the particular subject matter, have established a pattern that can be developed. The application of these patterns will be explored in the next four chapters.

CHAPTER 5

The Opening Fanfare: Treatment Strategies at the Crisis Point

The early stages of treatment are like a rollercoaster ride. This is particularly true if the affair has recently been revealed, but simply initiating treatment changes the equilibrium in the system, even if the affair has been overt for some time. Either one or both of the people in the couple could become severely symptomatic, with anxiety and depression being the most prominent symptoms. There is also the expectable level of symptoms in the marriage, with the conflict potential heightened and the question of the viability of the marriage brought to center stage. The challenge for the therapist is to establish treatment priorities and choose effective interventions.

Most of the early decisions about treatment planning will be shaped by the circumstances presented to the therapist. If the therapist is suddenly presented with the affair by someone already in treatment, the conceptualization, goals, and strategies will be developed from the context of the preceding treatment. In that case, the therapist is likely to know much of the background and history already, and the affair takes on meaning as part of the ongoing therapy. The treatment goals will then follow from the treatment already in progress, although some of the goals developed later in this chapter may be relevant.

People who initially enter treatment at the time of the first, traumatic revelation of the affair present a somewhat different set of challenges. The therapist will be confronted with the emotionality of the crisis and the demands from two people who have strikingly different ideas about what they need. The treatment plans come, nonetheless, out of the conceptual model and basic treatment protocol. This is not to say that it is a formula. Quite to the contrary, the most effective approach will be individualized to the situation.

Although formulas and "cookbooks" for psychotherapy are destined for eventual failure, there are general strategies that are indispensable to a successful therapeutic course. The challenge is to know the potential in a basic structure without being limited by that very structure. Whereas the previous chapter developed the principles of going beyond structure by way of improvisational psychotherapy, this chapter will focus more specifically on the structural elements of the beginning stages of treatment.

To Stop or Not to Stop

One of the first major questions to be answered will address the continuation of the affair. If the affair is not a secret, and if it is acknowledged to be continuing, should the therapist demand that the involved spouse discontinue the affair as a condition for therapy? The answer is clear, firm, and unequivocal *NO!*

Any demand for a discontinuation of an affair is plagued by several major problems. First, the potential for deceit clearly puts the client in the position of having more power than the therapist, since that client can simply lie and maintain a facade throughout many hours of treatment. If the reader has not personally had the experience of discovering that a client, after months of treatment with absolutely no clues, was having an affair, it is certain to be rather easy to find a colleague who has had the experience.

This potential for deceit is exacerbated by the fact that it is impossible to monitor any contract or agreement to discontinue the affair. Despite visions of intrigue and private detectives, it is, in most cases, practically impossible to track and enforce a discontinuation of a relationship between an involved spouse and a lover. This leads to the second major problem created by a demand to stop the affair. If the therapist demands a discontinuation of the affair, he has immediately and effectively put himself in a less powerful position than the involved spouse.

A third problem is related to situations in which an involved spouse initiates treatment individually and requests that the extra-marital involvement remain a secret. If the therapist demands that the affair be revealed to the spouse and discontinued prior to treatment, it is unlikely that the client will agree to begin therapy. If the demand comes shortly after treatment has commenced, the probability that the client will bolt from treatment is great. Obviously, if the person balks at commencing therapy, or bolts from treatment already begun, the therapist's sphere of influence is a bit diminished.

A fourth consideration is feelings in the therapist, or what is commonly referred to as countertransference. A demand to discontinue the affair can suggest an emotional agenda on the therapist's part, as was discussed in Chapter 4. This agenda may relate to being in control, sexuality, or extramarital relationships themselves. If the agenda is such that a demand for certain action precedes the treatment, it clearly signals the need to reevaluate the motivation for that action.

There is one final consideration that may be the most critical of all. The affair has acted as an integral part of the evolution of the emotional balance in the couple. Particularly if the affair has been of long duration, the emotional distance in the marriage has been influenced and maintained by the affair for much of the time of involvement. At the outset of the therapy, it is quite impossible to know what dynamics prompted the affair. Specifically, it is difficult to know the possible need for distance by the noninvolved spouse as well as the involved spouse.

Demanding that the affair be terminated can cause as much concern in the noninvolved spouse as it does in the involved spouse. If the affair provided an emotional buffer zone between the spouses, the prospect of losing that buffer zone is sure to provoke concern in both people. Any demand to discontinue an affair should not be founded on a perceived need to "protect" the noninvolved spouse.

There will be times when the noninvolved spouse is highly agitated by the affair and is adamant that the affair should stop. In many ways, she is as powerless to enforce the termination of the affair as the therapist. Her desire to demand a termination of the affair is plagued with the same basic problems developed above. Usually, a spouse who gets quite agitated is responding to a relatively short-term affair. Focusing on the emotional function of the affair in the marriage and the dynamic meaning of his agitation can help defuse this agitation.

Therapeutic Pressure

Psychotherapy being the inexact pursuit that it is, there will inevitably be situations that are exceptions to the rule developed above. Those exceptions are more likely to appear in the context of long-term therapy. There will be times when the therapist will need to exert pressure in the direction of discontinuing the extramarital involvement. The premise would be that ongoing therapy devoted to the transformation of that person and his marriage cannot continue with the continuation of the other relationship(s). At those times, the therapist can use the leverage of the established relationship with the involved spouse to exert therapeutic pressure and encourage the termination of the affair.

This therapeutic pressure will be most effective if it is brought later in the treatment. Later in the therapy the therapist should have more power. By that time, there is a realistic possibility that the therapist could question the viability of continued treatment if the affair were to continue. Pressure later in the therapy puts the two people in opposite positions from the outset of the therapy, when the client had more to gain by the strategy of terminating than did the therapist. Later in the therapy, the involved spouse is more likely to recognize that a termination by the therapist could signal to his spouse that the goals of the therapy are in question. And more importantly, the contract of the marriage is in question.

Even though the balance of power between therapist and client is altered later in therapy, relying on that disparity is unlikely to be the most effective clinical strategy. The therapist will need to emphasize the desirability of the termination for the client. Highlighting the personal advantages in the termination, and the costs in continuation is one angle on this idea. Exacerbating the anxiety about those costs reinforces the point. Essentially, the approach is a variation on the age-old therapeutic strategy of setting the decision up to be the client's decision and not the therapist's decision.

Secrets

Secrets are simply part of the territory of extramarital affairs. The potential for secrets regarding affairs is so high, in fact, that affairs are one of the most frequently mentioned problems when the subject of secrets in therapy is discussed. The secret, of course, relates to the relationship between the involved spouse and the lover. Sometimes, the secret is at the level of the existence of the relationship. Does it exist, or does it not exist? Does the spouse know, or not? Other times the secret is at the level of the degree of involvement. Was there sexual involvement or not? Did they go out for an evening? Did they go away for a weekend? Yet other times the secret is at the level of the emotional involvement. Do they truly love each other? Is there a desire to divorce the spouse and make a new life with the lover?

The dynamic implications of the secrets will be decided based on the particular situation and will demand careful judgment by the therapist. These judgments can range from the very first clinical decision the therapist is called on to make and can continue all the way through the therapy. For example, if a prospective client reveals over the phone that she is having an affair that she wants to discuss, but does not want to reveal to her spouse, the question is raised even before the client and therapist meet face to face. Another typical pattern is to have the client refer obliquely in the initial phone call to "private difficulties," which she needs to discuss individually, and then reveal in the first session that she is involved in an affair that she wants to keep secret from her spouse.

Questions that arise later in treatment include whether to reveal the involvement to extended family members such as parents and siblings, whether to reveal renewed contact between the involved spouse and lover to the noninvolved spouse, and whether to reveal the affair to children. In the later stages of the therapy, the noninvolved spouse may be the one considering the possibility of revealing the affair to extended family and children. The involved spouse will also be considering what type of secrets to live with later in the therapy. At times of the highly usual reinvolvement of the person with the lover, she will be considering whether to admit the "slip" to the spouse, and to the therapist as well.

The potential for secrets permeates every relationship in the emotional system, and because of that it has considerable impact. The need to create and maintain an alliance with both members in a couple, and all the members of a family, makes these questions more complex and difficult for marriage and family therapists than for therapists who limit their practice to individual therapy. The ethic of privileged, confidential communication between a person and her therapist in individual psychotherapy is so strong that the question of conflicting loyalties is of less concern. The expectations of loyalty between a therapist and a client's spouse are radically different than for the therapist working with both members of the couple.

Secrets as Treatment Problems

The integrated model of treatment developed in the last chapter adds extra complications to the "secret problem." As time with both people together combines with time spent with each of them individually, it can become extremely difficult to remember whether a particular bit of information was revealed in the joint meetings or in an individual meeting. This, obviously, can put the therapist at risk for revealing information that was classified and not intended for general use.

The problems encountered with this treatment protocol are both dynamic and ethical. Will the alliance with the noninvolved spouse be harmed by withholding information regarding the spouse's affair? Will the involved spouse expect some type of deferential treatment from the therapist? Will the therapist lose the position of neutrality? Is it ethical to withhold information? Is the therapist in the position of coconspirator if he agrees to withhold information from the noninvolved spouse?

One of the popular strategies for neutralizing most of these problems and maintaining a clear and obvious position of neutrality, has been to avoid being included in any secret. This was usually done by stating to the couple that any and all information was expected to be shared equally, and that the therapist would not/could not take responsibility for sharing in and maintaining any secrets. A strategy somewhat related to this position is to avoid, or refuse to see anyone in the couple individually.

Although the open disclosure policy may have some shock value, it carries considerable risk as well. The first risk is an echo of the position taken in the earlier section, "to stop or not to stop." The clients, especially early in treatment, may terminate prematurely. If they do terminate prematurely, they may not seek out any further treatment. Or they may search out a counseling approach that won't demand raw, open disclosure. These options can include strictly individual psychotherapy, "alternative counseling" provided by non-mainstream therapists, and semicommercialized sensitivity seminars.

Although any one of these options may have some value to the clients, the need for healing in the emotional system as a whole is crucial. If systems therapy is to be an important factor in the recovery from the trauma of an extramarital affair, there is simply no room for dogmatic, self-righteous stances by the therapist. If a client is unwilling, unable, or not ready to divulge the secret, she is more likely to drop out of treatment than to suddenly be inspired to comply with the therapist's demand for open disclosure. If the client does comply, there is another potential risk, that being the timing of the disclosure.

If the disclosure is made prematurely, both of the spouses may be inadequately prepared both cognitively and emotionally for the disclosure. The key symptoms of premature disclosure include an excessively high degree of affect, including anger, guilt, confusion, and anxiety. This high level of affect can lead to a premature termination of the treatment and perhaps a premature termination of the marriage.

There is yet a third position that can be adopted regarding secrets, and it has proven itself clinically to be the most effective and pragmatic in the treatment of affairs. It is similar to what Karpel and Strauss (1983) have referred to as "accountability with discretion." They point out that there is a need to balance a therapist's need to know (about affairs) with the obligation to maintain trustworthiness in a way that works for the best interests of all the family members.

This translates into a therapeutic strategy that will consider each secret for the dynamic implications it presents, and clearly expects the probability that the therapist will be involved in "sharing a secret" with some members of couples. This is obviously not an easy position to take. It relies heavily on judgment, demands clear-headed thinking, and challenges the fundamentally neutral position of the therapist. The solid therapeutic relationship with each member of the couple is the basis for effective execution of this position.

Some examples may help sketch out the limits of the decisions that can be made about secrets. The typical problem usually involves the revelation by one spouse that she is, or has been, involved in an affair. This revelation comes either by phone, or in an individual session without the spouse present. The secret is created when the information is accompanied by a request to "not tell" the other spouse.

The key factors to consider when making the decision to reveal (Figure 5.1) are the timing of the affair (whether present or past), the dynamic meaning of the affair, the current status of the dynamics of the couple as reflected by the affair, and the dynamic implications of the decision to reveal. For example, if the affair was a one-time-only

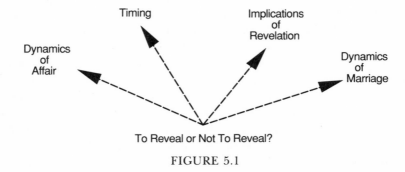

FIGURE 5.1

fling that happened in the distant past, at a time following a death of a parent, and the relationship of the couple was and is currently not affected by the emotional implications of the affair, then it should only be revealed if there is a strong desire on the client's part to do so. If she desires to "let sleeping dogs lie," then the therapist has an obligation to respect that decision.

In the event that there is a strong desire on the part of the involved spouse to reveal the type of affair described above, that desire must be explored and understood prior to the revelation. It is not enough to assume that the desire for open communication and disclosure is an indication of a healthy relationship. There is the possibility that the lingering secret is experienced as a block in the relationship and that removing that block would offer new potential for intimacy. A revelation in those circumstances may well accomplish exactly what it was designed to accomplish.

Concluded Affairs

On the other hand, it may be that the desire to reveal an old, concluded involvement is more accurately understood as a desire to shock the spouse and call attention to problems that are more current. In these cases, the initial dynamics that prompted the affair usually are unresolved and quite active in the relationship. The revelation of the affair in these situations, even if the affair is over, is usually helpful and necessary, but is more effective when both the involved spouse and the noninvolved spouse have been prepared to make use of the information and process the emotional meaning of the affair in a way that will be helpful and "healthful."

A typical example of this situation was Paul and Lisa. Paul was a successful professor, whereas Lisa had not developed a career outside the home. She had felt isolated, lonely, and left behind over the years as Paul had devoted much time and energy to his career. Approximately ten years prior to entering therapy, Lisa had a brief affair with a neighbor. She was able to recognize that the feelings of alienation from Paul prompted that involvement, and although the affair was long since over, the feelings of alienation were still plaguing her.

Lisa was reluctant initially to reveal that involvement, since she saw it as being over. As she became more aware of the similarities between the emotional state of the marriage at that time and in the present, she was able to see the affair as yet one of the repercussions of a longstanding situation. She also became more aware of her own contribution to the situation and was less prone to blame Paul for the entire problem. At that point she was ready to reveal the affair and make use of the revelation in a way that helped the current therapeutic work.

Paul, in the meantime, had been developing a clearer understanding of the problem of the alienation between them. He had prided himself on his attention to Lisa over the years, believing that his career had not interfered with his marriage. His attention to Lisa, however, had come at his convenience and largely on his own terms. He wanted Lisa available to him without regard to her schedule of activities or her needs. As he became more aware of the long-term coupling of alienation between the two of them with rigid demands on his part, he was ready to hear the revelation of the affair as yet one of the repercussions of the broader pattern that he and Lisa had developed together.

Secrets and Current Affairs

Current affairs, not referring to news but referring to extramarital relationships that are currently active, are difficult to keep as secrets. If it is a secret in a specific situation, the involved spouse will usually ask if she should reveal it. In most cases, the revelation of the affair will be a necessary step in the resolution of the conflict in the marriage. The revelation has the effect of placing an exclamation mark on the pronouncement that there are troubles in the marriage. If the involved spouse has initiated treatment individually, one of the first questions she will pose will be the question of revelation.

Generally people in that case have already made up their mind that they want to tell their spouse, and they are looking for the approval of the therapist. Especially if the therapist has not met the other spouse, he can have no idea about the reception the news will get from the other person. At those times, looking to the client for her ideas about how the news will be received can provide clues about the dynamic balance in the marriage. People frequently will anticipate that their spouse will be surprised, hurt, and upset, but that he will want to "work it out." In those cases, the revelation is not only inevitable, but it will be a necessary condition for the therapy to be successful.

The Secret Kept

There are exceptions to this policy. Mike and Charlene provide an example of the possibilities of not revealing an affair, and it being the best strategy for the couple. Mike initiated therapy after an out-of-town business trip created the opportunity to cultivate a relationship with another woman. He had been aware of a deterioration in the relationship with Charlene since the children were born, but he had been unable to do anything to change it. He knew that he did not want anything to do with multiple relationships. He had watched both parents destroy their marriage with mutual outside involvements.

He also knew that the out-of-town woman represented many of the opposite traits that he treasured in his wife. His wife stayed at home to raise the children. The other woman was a career person. Charlene was calm and reserved. The other woman was flamboyant and outspoken. His list continued with a number of opposites.

Mike entered therapy with the firm resolution to discontinue the relationship with the other woman and rehabilitate the marriage. He believed that Charlene would not be helped by knowledge of the affair and that dispensing of it was his problem. Charlene was reluctant to enter therapy, but Mike's agitation and mild depression convinced her that something was needed, so she agreed to come. The therapy was short-term, focusing on communication and the balance of parenting responsibilities with the needs of the marriage. Both Mike and Charlene reported significant improvement between them, and follow-up a year and a half later indicated that they remained very pleased with the current status of the marriage, and very pleased with the outcome of the therapy.

Concluding Thoughts on Secrets

Mike and Charlene's situation is the exception. More typically, a current affair will need to be revealed as part of a successful therapy.

Frequently the revelation comes before the couple calls the therapist and is, in fact, the stimulus for the call. Other times the involved spouse initiates the therapy to create an opportunity to reveal the affair, in a context that will be safe and structured. In these situations, the question of secrets is less significant, and more significance is found in the handling of the information and general treatment strategies. Although secrets are a complication, they are not an impossibility. Staying neutral, assessing the dynamics, and assessing the needs of the individuals will provide the basis for decisions.

DISTANCING AND PURSUING

The oscillation of distancing and pursuing in the relationship will be the premier concern initially, and it will need to be continuously monitored. The distancing–pursuing dynamic is conceptualized in terms of the triangles and levels of emotional connection that were developed in Chapter 2. People regulate distance in their relationships by way of behavior, attitude, and nonverbal communication. Much of the time this distance regulation is unconscious and at that level uncontrolled.

The common pattern regarding the operational styles of the couple is that the involved spouse is the distancer in the relationship, and the noninvolved spouse is the pursuer. In this way, the affair can often be an exaggerated crystallization of the basic pattern. At the level of operational styles, the pursuing is seen in an "ordinary" lifestyle presentation in which the noninvolved spouse is "just trying to keep the family together," perhaps in the face of someone who is aloof and unemotional and who perhaps spends too much time involved in individual pursuits such as work and other activities.

Seen from the other direction, the pursuing is seen as invasive, controlling, and insensitive to the needs of individuals. The counter-strategy of distancing is not seen negatively but is defined as simple attempts to establish reasonable individual territory. Frequently, both people are capable of balancing their assertions by offering examples in which they have reversed roles and truly understand the need for the other's position.

On an abstract level, the continual ebb and flow of the emotional distance in the couple is clearly related to the abstract concepts of fusion and differentiation developed earlier. This abstract level can also be understood in terms of boundaries between the two people and what is comfortable to each. For example, the pursuer in the relationship can be seen as a person who is more comfortable with closer boundaries in the relationship. This dynamic will manifest itself in the daily life exchanges, and it will be a continual focus of discussion.

A common expression of the distancing–pursuing pattern is one in which the involved spouse "behaves" better when the couple is together. The scenario goes like this:

The involved husband points out the demands imposed by his wife, and points to his own attempts at cooperation. The noninvolved wife, on the other hand, will contend that they hardly have any time together, and that she (the noninvolved spouse) is trying hard to make the most of the time. Each person, in this example is following true to form. The involved spouse, as the distancer, stays away and creates problems with this type of passive, indirect distancing. The noninvolved spouse is invasive, and possibly annoying while they are together, and creates problems with that style.

In the beginning stages of treatment the crisis has made the patterns more transparent. The activity is more unconscious—and therefore less camouflaged. As a result, identifying behavior as either distancing or pursuing is easier than in the later stages of treatment. As the couple gets more sophisticated about distancing in the relationship, there will be times when the intent and effect of a certain behavior will be unclear. At those times, having the couple define the nature of the behavior in question becomes the work of the therapy.

TREATMENT PLANNING

The flexibility that is the strength of this model of treatment could, from some corners, be seen as its undoing. Should there be more prescriptions for treatment? How are decisions made about where to intervene, at what time, with what intervention? It would indeed be reassuring to have at least some basic structure to use as a foundation.

The structure is founded on the full-scale integration of joint and individual meetings in the same treatment. Full-scale can translate into different ratios for different couples, but in principle, everyone involved knows that there will be a regular mix of individual and joint meetings. Neither forum will be neglected. Exactly how it is begun will depend on who makes the initial call, how the initial meeting is structured, and what the immediate needs are. But very soon after the outset of the therapy, this structure will be implemented.

As this structure falls into place, it will be possible to identify the different types of emotional agendas that are more accessible in the two different formats. The couple sessions will offer the opportunity to see the couple "in action," with their respective emotional presentations to the other being critical to the development of the therapy. These sessions will also offer the most helpful forum for each of them to learn about the other's perceptions, attitudes, and feelings. As each listens to the other talk to the therapist, each individual inevitably hears things never heard before. This is partly because things are said that are withheld at other times and partly because both are listening more carefully than they are likely to elsewhere.

The individual sessions are an opportunity to have each person focus on an internal agenda in a way that is more difficult with the spouse in attendance. Even though many people will proclaim that it makes no difference whether their spouse is present or not, in fact there are few people who are totally able to "look the same" with their spouse as they do alone. This is particularly true in the emotional times surrounding the revelation of the affair.

There does not seem to be any clear-cut advantage in either beginning with a couple session and later including individual sessions, or vice versa. Usually the person who makes the initial call will have a preference, and it seems to establish a certain amount of trust to honor that initial preference. If the caller has no preference, beginning with a couple session can help to establish the systemic approach from the very beginning. If the caller chooses to begin with an individual session, it can be helpful to schedule an individual session with the other spouse prior to the first couple session, as a way of balancing the relationship that began to develop with the first partner. Once underway, there are treatment goals for both types of sessions that are important to cover.

Couple Sessions

The beginning couple sessions after the revelation of an affair are generally fraught with confusion, anxiety, chaos, and urgency.

The involved spouse frequently is unable to terminate the affair, and can be equally unable to consider terminating the marriage. He is usually depressed and anxious, and he may be unable to perform as usual at work and home. The noninvolved spouse will probably be feeling some combination of anger, rejection, inferiority, and the related anxiety and depression. In many instances, the noninvolved spouse is more intent on "saving the marriage" than is the involved spouse. This can be expressed in a desire to discuss the problem, perhaps excessively, with the involved spouse, and also in a desire to be very actively involved in therapy.

The goals for the couple sessions will reflect the needs of both people. Although the noninvolved spouse may have a great need for closure on one subject, the involved spouse may be unable to reach closure. Where the involved spouse may desire certain agreements on other subjects, the other may be reluctant to come to the agreement. Much of this will be a therapeutic juggling act. The heightened emotionality of the crisis also diminishes both of the partners' ability to truly hear and integrate interpretations or other forms of insight. The initial stages of the therapy cannot be based on the hope of a cognitive type of integration. Despite the general unrest, there are six treatment goals that can be identified as having the highest priority at this stage.

Explore and Define Expectations between the Spouses; That Is, Will the Marriage Continue?

In spite of the inevitable confusion about the future of the relationship, some definition about the future will be a critical treatment goal in the first few sessions. It is possible that both people will be able to firmly establish their conviction to continue the marriage and improve it. Sometimes this is presented with no prompting from the therapist. Either one or both will report that he realizes that there are significant problems in the marriage, but both partners have decided to work them out rather than get out of the marriage.

There are many times, however, when either one or both spouses will be cautious, uncertain, and unwilling to commit to a future in the marriage. There are, of course, the expectable times when the involved spouse is ambivalent about the marriage and refuses to rule out the possibility of a divorce. This situation is rather expected, in view of the attachment to the lover.

Conversely, there are times when the noninvolved spouse will be more focused on the possibility of the marriage ending than is the involved spouse. This preoccupation can be related to the injury felt as a result of the affair. When the focus is not on the affair, the crisis of the affair may have exposed a fundamental problem in the marriage that has been felt for some time. In instances when the ramifications of the problem had been considered, the noninvolved spouse may have considered a divorce well before the affair happened.

Since the therapist cannot begin to establish the goal of saving the marriage if the couple is unwilling to do so, the therapeutic goal has to acknowledge the ambivalence about the future of the relationship and establish a suitable goal. If the question cannot be answered, answering the question becomes the goal. This establishes a contract for future sessions, acknowledges the side of the ambivalence leaning toward terminating the marriage, and acts on the side of the ambivalence willing to explore the continuation of the marriage.

Establishing a goal to answer the question about the future of the marriage does not mean that the couple session will be totally dominated by asking that question over and over again. Both partners have probably been tormenting themselves individually and collectively with that question and have been unable to answer it. The best way to answer the question is to begin working on the following treatment goals.

Take a History of the Preceding Year

It will be necessary to develop some working hypothesis about the dynamic etiology of the affair. The couple will be unlikely to understand and digest it initially, but the therapist will need it as a base for the therapy. Taking a history of the preceding year offers clues about the emotional balance in the relationship and the evolution of that balance leading up to the present time. If the affair is new, the balance will reflect the precursors to the involvement. If the affair is a longstanding one, the history will reflect the forces that prompted the decision to seek treatment.

The history gathering is standard therapeutic practice, and as such needs little specific development here. It should pay heed to the emotional distance in the couple, crises such as deaths, and developmental changes such as births and job changes. Although the year preceding the affair usually will be the most important time to cover in the initial session, a detailed history of the couple from the beginning of their relationship will be an indispensable overview of the relationship, and it will offer valuable ideas about the dynamic etiology of the affair.

It is quite impossible to collect all of the relevant history in any one session. In fact, it would be unwise to focus entirely on history gathering in the first session, to the exclusion of an attention to the emotional trauma that is engulfing the two people. History gathering continues throughout the therapy as an integral part of the therapy. It is not an isolated chore that precedes the therapy.

For purposes of the initial session, a brief history can be augmented with a question about any major changes in the family that may have some bearing on the current situation. Sometimes the answer will be that there have been none. Sometimes one or the other partner will offer that the marriage has been in trouble ever since a certain event that happened many years ago. Although there is nothing that the couple will be able to do with that information at the beginning of therapy, it signals the need for the therapist to place that event on the top of a mental "to do" list, and look for opportunities to explore the dynamic meaning and impact of the event.

Establish the Systemic Nature of the Crisis

There is an inevitable pressure to identify villains and victims during a crisis. Interestingly, it is not always the involved spouse who is identified as the villain, despite the affair and the implications of a transgression. Sometimes the involved party may point the finger at the spouse and suggest that her inadequacies forced the involvement. There are times when the noninvolved spouse will assume responsibility for the affair, even though the involved spouse denies that premise. That type of maneuver inevitably is significant to the dynamics of the system.

The task of the therapist at this point is to de-emphasize the concept of blame and begin to establish with the couple the notion of a systemic interplay in the marriage. The history gathering can, by way of attention to the emotional climate, usually unearth preexisting tension. This frequently will be presented as a growing alienation and isolation between the partners. The crucial task for the therapist will be to develop both partners' involvement in that alienation. It usually happens, for example, that if one person was retreating into work, the other person was partially pushing, with incessant demands and insensitivity to other's needs. Or if one spouse was quiet, sullen, and uncommunicative, the other person, while trying valiantly to communicate in any one exchange, was really delivering contradictory messages from one time to the next. This then left the first party confused.

The assumption underlying this treatment goal is that both partners had some part to contribute in the evolution of the crisis of the affair. If in fact the contribution of either one of them is hidden or unacknowledged initially, the treatment strategy is to comment on the lack of understanding of that person's contribution to the problem. Just identifying that as a goal helps to create an expectation of a systemic model of the crisis.

There are times when a couple has colluded in the development of an image of the relationship that identifies one of them and not the other as the cause of the problems in the marriage. This type of polarization can be understood dynamically as being related to the basic level of fusion in the relationship. This can mean that both deny any problems with one of the partners. Tactically for the therapist this suggests that the identification of the contribution of the "good" partner will be done more during the history gathering, when the data is collected as neutral information rather than as problems identified.

Another tack indispensable to regarding the systemic nature of the crisis is the identification and assessment of triangles. Obviously the full range of triangles in the system will not be accessible in the first one or two sessions, but strategic questions regarding other relationships that may be significant will help to unearth the key triangles to develop in the treatment.

Begin an Exploration of Multigenerational Dynamics

Although the couple may see little relevance to the affair, the multigenerational triangles will certainly be a critical area of the emotional system. This tack is begun with the simple expansion of the family genogram to include the families of origin of the respective parents. An understanding of sibling positions, the emotional context of the families, and their perceptions of their parents' relationships will begin to reveal the critical triangles in the system.

Along with the broad-brush view of multigenerational patterns in the family, very specific family patterns can be tracked with remarkable impact on the therapy. Take, for example, a common "coincidence." The initial history taking revealed tension over a job change in the year prior to the affair and later revealed a job change in the involved partner's family of origin. Exploring the perceptions about the feelings in the family of origin regarding the job change, and comparing them with the feelings related to the recent job change, begins to reveal the multigenerational process in families in the vein of coping with stress and change.

At some point, the multigenerational pattern of extramarital affairs in each of the families will need to be explored. The timing of this tack is delicate. If there is strong, unresolved affect associated with the memories, and a lack of willingness to discuss the situation, it will be met with considerable resistance, and will need to be postponed until a bit later in the treatment. Likewise, if there is an urgent preoccupation with the current crisis, there may not be an ability to distract attention away from the crisis and truly focus on the multigenerational patterns.

The most powerful integration of the multigenerational themes usually will not happen in the early stages of crisis resolution, but they must be developed close to the beginning of the therapy. The therapist will need the dynamic insight for treatment planning during the crisis. Even if the couple is unable to use the information, it will begin to establish the foundation of the emotional system model.

Moderate the Affect

The high level of affect stimulated by the revelation of the affair generally impairs both spouses. This affects their level of performance in the session and throughout the day. Some combination of interventions designed to moderate the affect will help. It will improve their general performance at home and work, help with their capacity to do the therapeutic work that needs doing, and strengthen their trust in the therapist. Specific interventions for controlling individual affect, such as relaxation exercises, can be more effectively implemented in the individual sessions. There are, however, interesting types of affect-oriented interventions available in the couple sessions.

The words blame, guilt, remorse, and love are heard frequently in the early stages crisis resolution. "Who's to blame?" "Do you feel guilty?" "You should feel guilty!" "I'm sorry!" "Do you love me?" "Do I love you?" These are interesting and very confusing words at this point in the crisis. They are interesting because they sit on the border between cognitions and affect. The concept of blame, which might be considered a cognitive experience, actually becomes so powerful that it takes on affective characteristics. The concept of remorse, which would seem to be an affective experience, may only be an idea about a feeling that a person thinks she ought to feel. Love takes on the same complications. As discussed in Chapter 3, people think about love, and what it "should" be, and try to make decisions regarding the relationship based on this confused conglomeration of thinking and feeling.

This interface between the affective and cognitive dimensions will need to be addressed in the couple sessions. Developing the systemic nature of the crisis will minimize the blaming activity and, in turn, lessen the tension regarding guilt and remorse. It is true that people can and should take personal responsibility for behavior, such as extramarital affairs. It is also true that the emotional correlates of the behavior need to be examined for the systemic significance. So if the involved spouse refuses to acknowledge any personal responsibility and the associated feelings of guilt, that refusal may signal a personal resistance to "getting in touch" with those feelings, and must be explored.

On the other hand, if she (as the involved spouse) becomes preoccupied with guilt and remorse, it also has meaning in the emotional system. It sometimes acts as an unconscious ploy to distract the spouse and cut off his expression of anger. Likewise, if the noninvolved spouse remains preoccupied with the need for hearing expressions of guilt and remorse from the "guilty one," it is likely to suggest a lack of understanding of the systemic nature of the crisis or an unwillingness to assume personal responsibility for his contribution.

Part of the intervention strategy that will be effective with these cognitions/affects is in the very structure of the couple sessions. In the classic model developed by Bowen, each person in turn talks to the therapist rather than to the other. This establishes a level of control between them and defuses the emotionality. As each listens to the other talk to the therapist, each one is able to assume a position of detachment that is quite impossible when they are involved in the heat of the discussion. Later in the therapy, after some progress has been made in the resolution of the crisis and some beginning understanding of the systemic balance has been established with the couple, there will be opportunities to encourage the couple to talk with each other. The direct dialogue between them at that time will have a higher probability of being controlled and helpful.

The detachment that is developed generalizes and becomes part of the ambience of the discussions outside the therapy sessions. As the discussions continue, the couple begins to realize the complexity of ideas such as love, which they had taken for granted as simple and generally understood.

Establish Expectations for the Immediate Future and Daily Life

The brouhaha accompanying the revelation of an affair leaves the couple rather uninterested in the theoretical and philosophical predispositions of the therapist. They came in for therapy because they are in pain, emotionally and possibly physically, and because they want to alleviate that pain. They are likely to have only a mild interest in how their relationship with their parents is related to the pain they are now experiencing. They are, on the other hand, likely to look eagerly to the therapist for immediate help in alleviating that pain.

The spot with the highest potential for pain, and highest priority regarding day to day life will be the quantity and quality of the interactions between the spouses. The first level of decision regarding that interaction is the broad question of separation. Although there are couples who wouldn't consider a separation, and are determined to rehabilitate the marriage, there are others who are sufficiently traumatized that they have decided to separate. The task of the therapy then becomes one of defining the nature of the separation. Although some clients may intend to make the separation a permanent one, it is rarely wise to make permanent decisions in the midst of this level of a crisis.

A temporary separation, on the other hand, can offer respite from the emotionality of the crisis. The temporary separation is structured with an agenda of gaining individual time and space. The separation *is not* designed to offer people an opportunity to develop other relationships, or to have time for a retaliatory affair. If the option of a temporary separation is needed, clear expectations for the amount and type of interaction between the two should be established. This would include phone calls, "dating" opportunities, and other contact through the week.

People who opt to remain together will also benefit from some attention to the expectations of daily life. The crisis has impaired judgment and increased anxiety to a point that too much discussion can make the situation deteriorate. The noninvolved spouse, in particular, can display an overwhelming need to discuss the affair, which can effectively put her in the role of the pursuer at a time that the involved spouse is likely to be distancing.

Not only is the quantity of discussion open for negotiation, but the subject matter as well. Many times the noninvolved spouse will be preoccupied with "what happened" with the other person. She will want to know times, dates, places, activities, and so forth *ad infinitum.* Discussions of this sort are almost always contraindicated. Some discussion of it in the therapy will be useful as a vehicle for developing an understanding of previously unrecognized and/or unmet needs. The practice is dangerous if it takes on the flavor of who is "better" than whom, and as such should be strongly discouraged.

Individual Sessions with the Involved Spouse

The individual sessions with both the husband and the wife early in treatment are likely to be more relaxed than the couple sessions. They provide both parties an opportunity to shed their protective outer crust of hostility and general agitation and to become more introspective about the crisis at hand. Although the most important and productive work during the individual sessions will be focused on the person in the room, the absent spouse will be a natural and frequent topic of conversation. Occasional, limited focusing on the absent spouse can be useful if it helps to gain access to the inner life and concerns of the person in the session. It won't be helpful if it is used to avoid the personal work that needs to be done.

The separate agendas that are typical of couples entering therapy are particularly disparate during this crisis. This leads to different therapeutic agendas with the two people. We begin with the work with the involved spouse, designated here for simplicity of language as the husband.

Explore the Relationship with the Lover

The relationship with the lover has meanings in the life of the involved spouse that are more easily approached individually. Indeed, the involved spouse may be craving the opportunity to discuss this relationship in a therapeutic setting, without the complication of the spouse's reaction to consider. This topic can be extremely productive if the material is framed with attention to the whole system and the individual characteristics it can reveal.

The involved spouse generally proclaims that he "gets" something from the lover that he is not getting from the spouse. This could be a sense of less-critical acceptance, a sense of spontaneity and romance, a sense of orderliness and control, or any number of other qualities. In addition to what he gets, he also insists that he is able to be more free, and develop parts of himself that had been either unknown or buried prior to the affair. This could be a reciprocal sense of openness, a sense of playfulness, or a recapturing of an old sense of self. This can easily be seen as him "giving" something different to the lover than he does to the spouse.

The process of identifying the qualities that have been elicited in the extramarital relationship provides important clues about the unidentified and unmet needs of the involved spouse. This is not an opportunity to justify the affair and condemn the noninvolved spouse for her deficits. The involved spouse has actively colluded in not attending to those needs either by denying their existence entirely, or by minimizing their importance. Thinking about the overall emotional system, and contemplating the constellation of systems pressures that led to the current unhealthy balance in the marriage, relieves the burden of blame/guilt thinking and offers new perspectives.

This will quickly develop into an exploration of the definition of self of the involved spouse, as covered in Chapter 3. He has developed a certain limited image of himself in the marriage. Perhaps the image is one of a person who has given up some valuable personal activity, such as an artistic outlet, as one of the accommodations that seemed necessary "to make the marriage work." One of the exciting elements then identified in the other relationship—regained, perhaps is how it is experienced—is this long-neglected self. A distinction emerges between who he is with his spouse and who he is with the lover. This distinction is a split between two different elements of his self in the sense that he has been unable to integrate both elements into one person functioning in one healthy relationship.

The question this scenario raises pertains to the emotional process that developed in the marital system. It is impossible that the noninvolved spouse was "the villain." She could not unilaterally have suppressed these elements in her husband. It is unlikely, moreover, that she is as deficient as the husband believes. The original distinc-

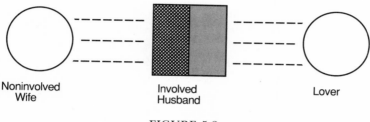

FIGURE 5.2

tion between the noninvolved spouse and the lover then becomes an external metaphor or representation of the internal split in the involved spouse.

The figures for the noninvolved spouse and the lover are intentionally blank in Figure 5.2. Although the qualities that the involved husband sees in the two women may have some basis in reality, the assumption is that the husband's perceptions of them are very much related to his own internal psychological makeup. The goal of treatment with the involved spouse is to develop an awareness of this process with him. This will entail him "letting go" of his perceptions of the two women that are either his own projections, projective identifications that they have colluded in developing, or some other systemic process of self-definition in the relationship.

The resolution of this split will bring about a termination of one of the two relationships. If it is the marriage that is terminated, this precipitates all of the complications and turmoil of divorce. If, on the other hand, the relationship with the lover is terminated, there will be profound repercussions that need to be monitored. There is likely to be a grieving process, first of all for the loss of the relationship with the lover and second for the perceived loss of the elements that the lover brought into the life of the involved spouse. In keeping with the emphasis on an internal integration, pursuing the possibility of fulfilling those needs in the marriage will be crucial to the therapeutic process.

Explore the Relationship with the Spouse

The individual time with the involved husband offers an opportunity to explore his relationship with his wife in a different way than the work that gets accomplished in the marital sessions. One of the trends among people who get involved is an inability or reluctance to identify openly problems in the marriage. Instead, the dissatisfaction gets channeled into covert distancing, such as the affair. The individual sessions provide a forum for the involved spouse to begin to identify and understand problems in the marriage and in his spouse in a way that can be productive. He can develop skills necessary to communicate these ideas productively at home. The emphasis, however, is not on displacing blame onto the absent spouse. Again the focus is on the identification of needs and understanding the inhibitions that have prevented those needs from being expressed and fulfilled in the past.

In keeping with the thrust of not blaming the spouse for all of the problems, perceptions need to be assessed. Exploring the accurate and distorted perceptions of the noninvolved spouse serves to develop a more realistic image of that person. For example, there may be a perception that the noninvolved spouse was cold and disinterested in romance, when in fact the discussions in the couple sessions and with the noninvolved spouse alone reveal a strong desire for more romance in the marriage. This does not suggest a wrong/right scheme. It again reveals the working of the system.

It is entirely likely that the couple did manage to communicate a disinterest in romance to each other to a certain extent. It is also likely that there was a distortion of perceptions. Either one or both may have misperceived the other's needs and intentions. The dynamic basis for this problem lies at the interface of the individual and couple systems. The individual work provides the forum to explore it from that angle.

Explore the Family of Origin

This theme is ongoing and pervasive. There is always enough relevance to the developmental issues to provide perspective during both the marital and individual sessions. The particular blend of family of origin work with attention to the other matters will depend on the relevance to any given topic being discussed. There will be times when the discussion is predominantly focused on developmental themes and other times when they are ignored.

Monitor and Assess Stress-Related Symptoms

The level of agitation common in the early stages of working out an extramarital affair can frequently lead to any number of stress-related symptoms, including some that may benefit from medication. Careful monitoring of these symptoms in the individual sessions can reveal indications for the use of the appropriate medications. Properly used, they will not mask problems or disrupt the therapeutic process. Quite to the contrary, they will alleviate the symptoms such that the therapy becomes more effective. Integrating this element into the therapy, for the nonmedical therapist, will depend on the ability to assess indications for medication and a referral to a collaborating psychiatrist or general practice physician.

Mild anxiety can interfere with the therapeutic process and interfere with daily life, yet it is not sufficiently developed to indicate medications. These symptoms can be modified with any of the widely used relaxation-training models. Generic exercises such as deep breathing, deep muscle relaxation, and imagery can be most effectively taught and encouraged in the individual sessions. Many clients have reported finding considerable usefulness in the commercially available audio cassettes designed to help relaxation.

Individual Sessions with the Noninvolved Spouse

These sessions are founded on the same principles as the sessions with the involved spouse. They offer an opportunity to work on material that may be highly guarded—but crucial to the therapy. The different agenda reflects not only the different position in the crisis, but the different emotional positions in the dynamics. Five broad goals can be identified. In keeping with the pattern established, the noninvolved spouse will be designated as the wife, for linguistic simplicity.

Coach Regarding Pursuing and Distancing

Along with feelings of anger and confusion, the noninvolved spouse is likely to want to "fix" the problems that led to the affair more quickly than is realistically possible. This can be expressed in excessive efforts to be sexually responsive and attractive, excessive efforts to prepare favorite meals or to offer special gifts, and excessive efforts to discuss the situation and resolve the problem. All of these activities can be categorized under the heading of emotional pursuing.

Meanwhile, the involved spouse is cautious at best. If he *has* agreed to continue in the marriage, he is sure to express a need to renegotiate those expectations of the marriage that were the *status quo* prior to the affair. Or he may be even more ambivalent. He may be unsure whether he can recommit to the marriage and may be considering a divorce. This gets expressed with an aloofness that the noninvolved spouse can find very threatening. He is cold in communication, and if he does participate in sex, it is with a markedly different presence. Categorize this behavior under the heading of emotional distancing.

This pattern of pursuing and distancing can escalate to a point where the pursuer eventually moves away in reactive distance, the distancer makes tentative and temporary attempts to move toward the spouse, both attack and counterattack, then both occupy rigid and unsatisfactory positions at a distance (Guerin et al., 1987). The goal in the individual sessions with the noninvolved spouse is to interrupt this cycle and to coach the person to adopt a calm, neutral position. This can be accomplished by a combination of education and encouragement.

As the noninvolved spouse becomes more aware of the meaning of emotional pursuing, she will become more able to discontinue the pattern. This generally leads to a decrease in tension with a corresponding improvement in the interactions in the couple. With this type of success, dropping the role of emotional pursuer becomes a self-reinforcing strategy and is further developed as time goes on. The noninvolved spouse may decide that she was often in the role of the pursuer prior to the affair and that the revelation of the affair had initially prompted her to do "more of the same."

One of the fundamental principles of systems theory is that it is easier to tone down the functioning of the overfunctioner in a relationship than to bring up an underfunctioner (Bowen, 1978). The noninvolved spouse acting as an intense pursuer at a time of crisis is the overfunctioner in the relationship. Limiting the pursuing behavior and disrupting the cycle follows one of the time-honored principles of systems interventions.

Develop a Systemic Understanding of the Crisis;
Explore the Family of Origin

These two goals continue and elaborate the same themes that are being developed simultaneously in the couple sessions. The noninvolved spouse is usually slower to recognize her role in the evolution of the crisis than is the involved spouse, who typically is painfully aware that his extramarital involvement is a major problem. The noninvolved spouse, in contrast, is likely to be feeling victimized and confused about her role.

The critical dynamic to explore initially will be her need for distance in the marriage. The emphasis is on her need for the distance rather than a need for her husband to have sex with someone else, or a need for an affair. Few people recognize or consciously admit to needing an extramarital involvement between their spouse and another person. But they often can recognize the benefits accrued from the distance that has developed as a result of it. In this way they begin to understand one of the emotional functions of the affair in their emotional system. Understanding this function doesn't necessarily translate into magnanimous acceptance of the affair, but it does diminish the highly charged negativity so prevalent in the early stages.

As the family of origin is explored, the multigenerational factors get revealed. There will be times that this material can be useful when developed alone initially, then repeated in some form in the couple sessions for the benefit of the spouse. Reviewing and interpreting the ideas in the individual sessions provide an opportunity for an understanding and integration. These processes also open up material that may have remained withheld in the couple sessions.

Provide Support through the Healing Process

There will be times when the noninvolved spouse is able to understand and work through many of the affair-related issues more quickly than the involved spouse. This is particularly evident when there is a reluctance to discontinue the affair. One common scenario has the involved spouse making an emotional and provocative pronouncement during a couple session that he will discontinue the affair, only to have the noninvolved spouse stumble on some type of undeniable evidence later that the affair is still active.

The noninvolved spouse is going to need support at that time. Along with reviewing ideas related to pursuing and distancing, encouragement regarding the length of time necessary for resolution of the issues, and a focus on the function and meaning of the continuation of the affair, will all be invaluable. The noninvolved spouse is likely to become incensed about the behavior of the lover and to see her as the enemy who needs to be conquered. Reviewing the systemic nature of the crisis can make it clear that she is not in competition with the lover.

One final theme prevalent throughout the healing process is trust. Trust will not be rekindled in the marriage quickly or easily. The noninvolved spouse will probably be slower to develop trust than will be the involved spouse. She may recognize this disparity, and she will need support regarding the length of time necessary.

Monitor and Treat Stress-Related Symptoms

This work is done in the same vein as with the involved spouse. Assessing the usual symptoms such as sleep disturbance, weight change, mood, and so on, establishes the need for medications or other anxiety-focused interventions. Frequently, the symptoms of anxiety will be expressed as emotional pursuing. That intersection can be explored in the therapy, with the advantage of addressing two different therapeutic targets plus illustrating the rich interconnections in the emotional system.

Sessions with the Lover

The lover is a significant component of the emotional system. Approaching the problem as a system in crisis, rather than as an individual or even just a couple who has problems, may offer an opportunity to transcend the limitations of a restrictive structure on the types of interventions possible. There are times when the involved spouse and lover may come in for some work. Frequently this relates to a desire in the involved spouse to terminate the extramarital relationship. There are also times when the lover has requested the opportunity to be involved in individual sessions.

The more classic, and certainly less complicated response to this type of request is to refer either the involved spouse/lover couple, or the lover individually, to another therapist. Experimental, uncontrolled clinical trials have demonstrated that one therapist, thinking and intervening systemically, may offer a useful overview of the situation and may be very effective at accomplishing the work that is needed. If everyone in the system in crisis understands that the others are all involved in the therapy, it creates a common point of reference. One patient expressed the notion that "at least one person seemed to see the whole situation and have some idea about what was going on!"

If the lover comes in for a joint session with the involved spouse, the therapeutic agenda is generally set by the couple. Questions of the relationship between the therapist and the lover need to be considered and monitored so as not to result in any negative impact on the couple. If the lover comes in for individual sessions, the same basic treatment goals can be developed as were outlined earlier. The special emphasis with this person can be on her emotional need to be in a relationship that has an uncertain future and an incomplete present.

TREATMENT PLANNING: A FINAL WORD

There are times, especially in the work of students learning family therapy, that there is a desire to reduce anxiety by establishing goals prior to a session. Indeed, some students have even developed an outline, written it down, and carried it into a session. The treatment goals developed in this chapter were intentionally not reduced to one eye-catching figure that could be copied and carried into a session. The personality and presence of the therapist cannot be overemphasized. And the need for careful individualization of these themes is a constant. Look to the next chapter for a typical example of how these goals develop in real life.

CHAPTER 6

Allen and Elaine: Successful Brief Treatment

The romance, intrigue, and emotional chaos found in extramarital affairs has provided endless material for drama. Stories about the psychotherapeutic treatment of people involved in affairs, on the other hand, are not frequently found on best seller lists or on Academy Award nominations. And when psychotherapy is viewed dramatically, it is frequently based on the dramatic development possible with the device of a flawed therapist and problem therapy. One might wonder whether the type of human drama which is to be found in responsible, high quality psychotherapy is sufficiently compelling to sustain dramatic development.

This story makes no pretensions to be compelling drama. It is developed with the belief that the process of change in human life can be dramatic, and seeing that process in others' lives can be inspiring. The drama is primarily seen in the courage of individuals to understand their lives and establish a new, healthy balance. Although the actions of the therapist certainly contribute to that process, and are of interest in a study of the treatment process, ultimately the work is done by the couple in treatment.

Allen and Elaine will be the protagonists in this drama. Their story is typical of the problems experienced by the couple and the therapist in the early stages of therapy. There is such commonality, in fact, that many readers will think they are looking into a mirror. This saga, however, does not reveal the details of an actual clinical record. For all the usual concerns of confidentiality, Allen and Elaine are fictional characters. Any similarity there may be between their story and actual lives merely reflects the universality of these dilemmas. Whereas Allen and Elaine do represent a typical course of treatment that ended successfully after a brief course, the themes are also typical of the beginning stages of treatment that continue into long-term therapy.

Couple Sessions 1 and 2

Allen and Elaine entered treatment together after Elaine revealed to Allen her affair with a co-worker. When Allen called for the initial appointment, he expressed a strong desire for an appointment as soon as possible. They came to the first session looking and acting tired and "stressed out," as Allen described it. Much of the fatigue had developed during marathon talk sessions, conducted into the early hours of the morning, over the preceding several days.

The focus of the discussions was, as could be expected, the meaning and implications of Elaine's affair. Allen volunteered his understanding of the meaning of the affair at the outset of the session.

> *"First, you gotta understand that this situation is just a nightmare for me. I've always maintained that an affair was the one thing that I simply could not tolerate in a marriage. I even vowed that I would absolutely not remain in a marriage if an affair happened. But now, look at me. Here I am, a total emotional wreck, and still talking about keeping this thing together. I don't know exactly what that means."*

> *"But I do have a little more understanding about the affair, after all this talking we've been doing. At least I think I understand it a little. It seems to have something to do with the fact that Elaine felt too tied down at home, between the kids, and going to work. But ya know, I feel tied down too. Life ain't easy when you've got little kids. I don't know if that's enough reason to have an affair. It doesn't seem to add up."*

Allen's graphic description of his current status is a powerful example of the discrepancy between cognitive and emotional functioning and the corresponding awareness. Cognitively, Allen has begun to understand some of the primary factors involved in the affair. But emotionally, his pronounced anxiety, confusion, and depression have destroyed his capacity to grasp the ideas in a useful way.

Even the one idea he had developed, about pressure from home responsibilities, was in truth a valiant attempt on his part to provide some cognitive structure to an overwhelming situation. He didn't really believe or understand the idea.

Elaine, meanwhile, was the picture of quiet pain. She spoke after Allen had finished. She tried to be firm in her resolve to emphasize the idea that her needs had not been met and that was how she had ended up in an affair. She seemed to waiver in her resolve to assert that position, suggesting that she, too, found it hard to believe that there had been some understandable reason for her involvement. It seemed much more natural to think that she had behaved badly and that she needed forgiveness from Allen while she herself was filled with remorse.

> *Even though Allen and Elaine were obviously well into their discussions about the affair, I needed to verify their initial impressions about their desire to maintain the marriage and to find out how long Elaine was admitting to being involved with the other person. I used Elaine's comment about her needs not being met, and I asked her if she had considered getting out of the marriage because of that. She quickly and firmly denied any desire to get out of the marriage, saying that she really wanted to make things work with Allen. Allen chimed in with strong agreement, without my asking him.*
>
> *I went back to Elaine and asked her to explain her sense of how she had gotten involved with someone else, and how long it had gone on. She proceeded to tell the story of innocently having had lunch with a new fellow at work and having been so struck with the need to talk with someone that one lunch quickly became a series of lunches, which finally culminated in a sexual relationship. She strongly emphasized that it was the conversations over lunch, and not the sex, that was the most meaningful part of the experience.*
>
> *She spoke of recognizing at the time of the sexual involvement that she was very confused, unsure, and guilty about the sex. She said that the total involvement was about two months—at which time she began to feel so confused and guilty that she told Allen about the affair. Allen indicated at that point that she had told him the same story.*

It was obvious in this first session that Allen and Elaine had made an effort at beginning to understand the affair in the discussions at home. The emotional chaos that had prevailed had sabotaged an

effective grasp of the ideas, however, and had contributed to significant depressions in both of them. The first therapeutic goal, then,
addressed the need for emotional stabilization. The interventions that
I chose focused largely on the emotional chaos more than on the
dynamic meaning of the affair. I found myself using statements with
a humorous/paradoxical edge.

> *One comment I made to Allen was, "You probably need to talk more*
> *about this situation with Elaine."*

This triggered a big grin from Allen, because it came on the heels
of my earlier observation that they were wearing themselves out
talking. Allen's grin suggested to me that he understood the paradox
that I was addressing. They did indeed need to talk more about the
situation. But they also needed to talk less than they had been talking.
The conversations would need to be developed over more time.

Another comment to Allen that elicited a smile was again quite
paradoxical. Following his brief description of some of the pressures
they had experienced over the past year I said to him:

> *"I'm impressed that you've remained so calm and cool through all*
> *of this."*

Since Allen's description had been laced with unspoken tension,
frustration, and anxiety, Allen's grin again suggested to me that he
immediately recognized the reverse intentions of my comment and
that he also was able to be more conscious of the tension than he had
been previously.

The interventions with Elaine were geared toward acknowledging and detoxifying the affect as well. I sensed that she was hiding
many feelings of confusion, depression, and general unrest. Despite
her more even outward presentation, I sensed that she was even more
upset than Allen. She was not acknowledging any emotion, and she
was avoiding many subjects, such as her feelings about Allen, and her
feelings about her lover, which I knew were central to her well-being.

> *In deference to this greater vulnerability, I chose to be less pro-*
> *vocative and humorous with her than I had been with Allen. The most*
> *powerful intervention, was, nonetheless, somewhat paradoxical. "It's nice*
> *of you to be so strong through all of this, since Allen is having such a hard*
> *time," was a comment I made to her in a very gentle tone, which instantly*

elicited pent-up tears. Allen was a bit taken aback that Elaine was able to express that much pain, while Elaine was able to indicate that she had been holding too much inside. Their homework for the first session was to decrease the amount of discussion they were having about the meaning of the affair and to put more time and energy into developing ideas individually about the situation.

They returned for the second session looking somewhat better than in the first session, but it was obvious that they were both still distraught and depressed. They had followed the homework assignment to the extent that they were no longer "pulling all-nighters," the marathon discussions from earlier. But they still were very preoccupied with the subject and were drawn to frequent discussions. The abundant amount of time devoted to discussion afforded them the opportunity to explore the entire range of issues that affected them, with some of those inevitably having some relevance to the affair.

I took advantage of the decrease in tension to begin to develop the family genogram. I had sensed during the first session that they were in need of a stronger focus on the current crisis and had chosen to wait until a more relaxed time to develop the historical emphasis in the treatment. Allen provided an opening when he mentioned talking to his brother between sessions about the fact that he and Elaine were having some difficulties. Following that comment, I asked him about the rest of his family and went on to get the same information from Elaine (Figure 6.1).

Allen is the oldest of three sons, with both parents alive and well. Elaine is the second of four, with two sisters and a brother. Her

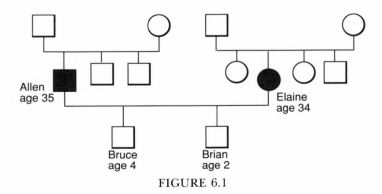

FIGURE 6.1

parents are also alive and well. They had been married eight years prior to beginning treatment and had two boys, ages two and four. While they were cooperative in relating this information, it was also clear that they had a need to refocus on the more immediate tensions. Allen, as could be predicted, reintroduced the topic of the affair in the form of the lack of attention the boys had been getting as a result of the preoccupation with these discussions. Respecting their need to continue working on the current crisis, I set aside the genogram and continued to listen as he began to develop his newest thoughts about the situation.

Although his thinking was more redundant than new, I continued to listen. My goal was to listen for the miscommunication as it appeared, such as one hearing the other incorrectly, or one misstating an idea. More importantly, I was listening to the images of reality each was struggling to create so that the other would be able to understand "where he was coming from." Elaine, for example, was quite unable to acknowledge the meaning of her relationship with her lover.

Allen, from his vantage point, was somewhat fixed on the sexual part of the relationship. Elaine did field questions from Allen about the sexual meaning of the affair, in the spirit of reconnecting with him. Allen wanted to know whether sex was "better" and whether different things happened.

Elaine emphasized that she did not have the affair to "have better sex." She chose to answer a few questions directly, but she emphasized the lack of importance of that line of thinking and refused to answer all of the questions. Although she responded very effectively to Allen's questions about sex, she was far less able to identify and communicate to him about the emotional attachment with her lover and what it provided that she hadn't gotten from Allen. I sensed that part of that "miscommunication" was semi-intentional withholding. Elaine did not want to hurt Allen's feelings. Part, also, was a possible fear. There was the sense that Elaine was so angry with Allen that she feared that if she did express the anger, it might come out with more force than either she or Allen could handle. And finally, I had the hunch that Elaine did not understand the full meaning of her feelings for Allen, nor did she fully grasp the extent of her displeasure.

I asked her a couple of questions about what she had gotten from her relationship with her lover that she hadn't found with Allen, and she drew a blank. Since Allen was somewhat preoccupied with the notion that the

major benefit was sexual, I developed a line of thinking with Elaine that
helped to take the emphasis off sex. I asked her how she would compare the
conversations she had with her lover with the conversations she had with
Allen. She was able to realize that she had been more comfortable and had
felt more accepted by "him" than by Allen.

Although there were rather narrow limits to Elaine's capacity to
develop these comparisons, enough was done to establish in Allen's
mind the concept that the affair was not primarily a sexual event. This
can be seen as a typical example of an intervention designed to impact
both partners, while ostensibly working with just one partner. The
fact that the limits were quite narrow for Elaine provided the opening
to suggest the need for individual sessions to which they both agreed.

Allen: Individual Session 1

Allen came in for his individual session looking at least as depressed as he had in the first two sessions, and possibly more depressed. He had begun to realize that whatever had caused this affair
was extremely complicated and that these problems were not easily
fixed. He said that he had really known this all along, but somehow
the situation was getting more overwhelming rather than less.

I used this time to steer Allen away from thinking about the affair,
which had been his sole preoccupation over the past several weeks. I
initially concentrated on his depression. He was not sleeping well, had
been eating too much, and had not been concentrating well at work. As he
became more aware of the extent of his depression, he began to realize the
need to restore a balance to his life and reestablish an internal equilibri-
um. I mentioned that there was the possibility of medication, if the
depression did not lift fairly quickly. I preferred, however, to wait at least
a couple of weeks to see how he progressed without medication. He
strongly agreed with the idea of postponing any use of medication, agreed
to increase his exercise and physical activity, and agreed to make a
conscious effort to decrease his preoccupation with Elaine's affair.

The idea of consciously controlling thoughts can be somewhat
mystifying. After all, if Allen were truly capable of controlling his
thoughts, it would seem as if he already would have done so. This

would seem to make the agreement to discontinue the thoughts rather implausible. Actually, calling attention to the thoughts brings them to a level of conscious awareness that facilitates more conscious control. At that point, cognitive/behavioral techniques similar to thought-stopping can be used quite effectively. Anytime Allen found himself preoccupied with his concerns about the affair, he knew he needed to stop that line of thinking, and focus on something else.

This type of intervention is closely related to the broader treatment goal of defocusing the affair for both members of the couple. Although the thought-stopping techniques help at any given moment, they will not unhook either one emotionally from the affair. Cognitive energy, in the form of thinking, and behavioral energy, in the form of talking, can build on itself to create another level of emotionality.

That emotionality can lead to "the affair," as a focus of energy, being triangled into the relationship. In other words, whereas the extramarital relationship is itself a triangle, the cognitive preoccupation with it is another level of triangling in the system. The preoccupation can serve to distract attention away from important dynamic and historical material in the therapy. In a sense, obsessing about the affair can be a form of resistance to a helpful therapeutic focus on other material. It becomes the therapist's job, then, to overcome that resistance, and encourage a focus on other pertinent points. That goal can be developed several ways, including exposing some of the painful emotional precursors to the affair.

We then moved on to an exploration of Allen's family of origin. He had a distant relationship with both of his parents, but more distant with his father than his mother. He had a cool but acceptable relationship with his younger brother, who was married with one child. Both of his parents were alive, and all of his grandparents were deceased. Allen had no knowledge of any other affairs in the family. The strict religious code of the family was such that any incidents of this nature would be denied and certainly not discussed.

The most useful pattern to emerge in this exploration had to do with dominance and control. Allen began to see that his mother had been the dominant person in his family and that his father's quiet manner may have disguised unspoken resentment. He began to realize that he had been the dominant one in his relationship with Elaine.

Unlike his father, however, Elaine had regularly expressed her dissatisfaction with this controlling style. Her complaints, however, had seemed to him like a manipulative ploy to gain control, rather than any type of expression of her feelings.

Allen's realization of this struggle for control between them became the first insight Allen was able to grasp both cognitively and emotionally. Whereas earlier ideas about Elaine's dissatisfaction with home responsibilities truly amounted to grasping at intellectual straws, this perception of the power struggle between them gripped Allen. He immediately saw the relevance to the development of the affair. Allen left his first individual session with a new awareness of important patterns, an acute appreciation of his own emotional well-being, and several ideas about addressing these problems.

Elaine: Individual Session 1

Elaine came to her individual session because she had felt obliged to come and not because she really wanted to come. I began with her just as I had begun with Allen, with a focus on her mood. She, too, was still quite upset. Focusing on her mood initially created a self-awareness in her that helped her effectively avoid some of its impact on her thinking. Although she was depressed, she was not as depressed as Allen, and generally, she was more aware of the various factors in the marriage that had led to her involvement.

> *Her level of objectivity and composure changed dramatically when I asked her about the status of her relationship with her lover. She immediately became tearful and quiet. When she still had not answered the question after several moments, I gently asked her if she could tell me what she was thinking and feeling. She merely shook her head no, and proceeded to dry her tears. When she finally was able to speak, she told me that she still cared very much for Tim, her lover. He offered a gentleness, understanding, and acceptance that she did not find in Allen. She knew that she needed to stop her relationship with him if the marriage was going to work, but she has been quite sad about the prospects of not seeing him.*

Elaine felt compelled to withhold these feelings from Allen. She was sure that he wouldn't understand. At the same time, he was able to sense some of her sadness and would ask her about it from time to time. She was left in the undesirable position of needing to offer somewhat dishonest answers to Allen's questions about these feelings. Elaine expressed great relief at my reassurance that her feelings of loss regarding Tim were quite understandable and acceptable to me. With that acceptance Elaine was able to talk more about her feelings and perceptions of Tim.

> *Tim, it seems, although married himself, was on the verge of ter-minating his second marriage. Much of the relationship between Tim and Elaine was founded on their mutual dissatisfaction with their spouses and the support they received from each other while discussing these problems. But the image of Tim started to shift. When Elaine no longer felt a need to defend him, she began to see him as an untrustworthy person. She began to recall some of his comments about his first wife, and began to compare them to comments about his second wife, and quickly began to consider the possibility that many of the problems were in Tim more than in the women.*

A broader perception of Tim, which incorporated views of him as a flawed person, was quite useful to Elaine. It helped to shift her perception of Tim away from being idealized, which helped her begin to let go of him. With that flexibility, I proceeded to turn her atten-tion toward what she would be giving up in her life when she let go of this relationship. Along with asking her a question quite directly focused on this theme, I also developed a variation on this theme. Who is she when she is with Tim, and how does this compare to who she is when she is with Allen?

Her first answer to these questions was to consider the possibility that she was less guarded with Tim than with Allen. She also seemed less guarded now, in the session with me alone, than in the first two couple sessions. That gave me a first-hand experience of the guarded-ness, and I assumed the critical factor was her distrust of Allen more than me. I was sure there was much more to understand about this guardedness in her, which would have to be developed in future sessions. It was, nonetheless, very productive for the first individual session, and a useful step in the broad goals for the overall therapy.

Couple Sessions 3 and 4

Elaine and Allen came into the third couple session with an interesting mixture of the old and the new. They still were struggling with the meaning of the affair to their relationship. Allen still was depressed, and Elaine was still upset, but both of them seemed to have a new objectivity toward the situation and their respective roles in the drama. Intellectual understanding of the situation was beginning to cut through the affect that had previously gripped them.

The progress made in the individual sessions had a clear impact on the interactions between them at home, and their ability to explore cogent material in the couple sessions. Both had expressed an interest in the other's individual session, but both had respectfully acknowledged any reluctance to reveal content. There was no reference during the couple session to any concern about secrets and confidentiality. I interpreted that to suggest that their mutual experiences in the individual sessions had assured them that the focus of the work was going to be on internal aspects of the situation and not on the "absent partner."

> During this session, and the next one, which was also a joint session, we had the opportunity to review the full history of their relationship. I had collected a brief sketch of the family genogram in the second session, but I had not taken time to develop it in detail, since their respective anxiety and preoccupation was with the turmoil of the affair. At this stage of the therapy, the affect had subsided considerably, and they both had unanswered questions about the meaning of the affair, which could be addressed with a more complete history. This more complete history included a detailed review of their history as a couple, along with a look at their respective families of origin.

My role in this process is quite complex. On the one hand, I prompt them to report the facts as they know them and encourage them to consider the meaning and importance of various experiences at different points in their history. But more than that, I monitor their reactions through this process, both to their own ideas as well as to those of the other. For example, Allen and Elaine were able to learn that they each had different perceptions of the emotional climate between them at the beginnings of their relationship. At that time, Allen remembered feeling jealous and insecure about his relationship with Elaine and worried that she would be more attracted to someone else. This feeling persisted well into the first years of their marriage.

Elaine, conversely, remembered feeling quite attached to Allen in those years and was surprised that he questioned her loyalty to him.

My role, which can't be summed up with some dramatically labeled intervention, was to validate each person's perceptions and to highlight the elements of each perception that had dynamic relevance to the ultimate development of the affair. In this instance, I made mental notes to check the possibility that Allen's jealousy translated into a type of emotional pursuing from which Elaine unconsciously pulled away.

The question that balanced this one had to do with Elaine's behavior and attitude toward men. Was she so naturally engaging, seductive perhaps, that she was unaware of her nonverbal communication to other men, and in turn to Allen? And if this was true, what were the dynamic and genetic roots of this behavior? Both of these questions were far too complex to address quickly or easily. A cursory treatment of them would yield a cursory answer at best, and at worst elicit denial that would carry over into future work, making future exploration that much harder. For these reasons, I avoided direct confrontation with them about these questions.

Allen: Individual Session 2

The second round of individual sessions followed these two joint sessions, with Allen's session being scheduled first. I noted to myself that he seemed to be the one to express more pain outwardly and thus was the one to be more eager for an individual session. He came to the session appearing much less depressed than earlier but still quite obsessed with the "whys" of the affair. I assumed that he was continuing his preoccupation because he had been unable to effectively process ideas earlier, when he was quite depressed. Also, I believed that he was taking much of the blame on himself in the form of feeling inadequate. Some of the preoccupation, moreover, was a diversion away from anger that he was suppressing at Elaine and himself, in the vein of triangling.

Given that series of hypotheses, I was faced with a choice. Do I accept his question (why the affair?) at face value and assume that he needs to have an intellectual understanding before he can drop the preoccupation? Do I assume that the intellectual understanding will come in due time and that the potential for self-blame and suppressed anger was strong enough to warrant some exploration? Or is there some other, unconsidered track that would be far more useful than any of these? All of this thinking, obviously, must be done in a few seconds. Since I didn't see one theme that was clearly more crucial or clearly more accessible than another theme, I looked to Allen to help to define the most useful thread.

Instead of answering his question of why did the affair happen, I commented on his preoccupation with the affair and asked him why he was preoccupied with that question.

That question took Allen quite off guard. The obvious was just too obvious. His facial expression spoke quickly, before he uttered a word. My reading of it was, "What kind of stupid question is that?"

I responded to his nonverbal question with a humorous, self-effacing disclaimer. Laughing, I said, "I know, sometimes I just can't help but ask stupid questions."

The humorous edge appealed to Allen, who was able to verbalize a similar thought, but this time with humor, since he had understood that I was challenging him to think about something that was less than obvious. But before moving on to a serious consideration of my question, he couldn't resist a humorous barb in return, with a laughing comment.

"Wouldn't you like some answers if your wife had an affair?"

He was satisfied with a return grin from me, with both of us understanding that his question was semirhetorical, and certainly was not going to be answered.

This brief exchange is a typical example of therapeutic work that is not infused with the aura of clinical importance but carries a critical role in the ongoing success of the work more pointedly directed at the dynamics. It is in part a way of enhancing the therapeutic relationship, in part an opportunity for comic relief in the midst of the primary drama, and in a very fundamental way, an opportunity for a person-to-person connection that transcends the therapist–client roles and enhances the possibilities for accomplishing the therapeutic work.

Following this exchange Allen returned, with a serious attitude, to the original question about his preoccupation with Elaine's affair. He went on to repeat his opinion expressed in the initial session—that an affair would have been the one thing that he would never tolerate. He saw that as being important to understanding his preoccupation, since that feeling had been with him so long. Allen began to wonder whether he had somehow forced Elaine into having an affair, almost by some mysterious power of suggestion.

We spent the rest of the session exploring different nuances of this question. The basic theme was a close variation of the second hypothesis that I had considered at the start of the session, that Allen's preoccupation was related to self-blame. It was developed by Allen's choice, indicating that he was ready to work on that idea. The other hypothesis about anger was still viable and could wait for another opening.

Elaine: Individual Session 2

Elaine appeared very comfortable when she came in for her second individual session. Along with that sense of relaxation came a reluctance to contemplate her own role in the current crisis with Allen. She began by relating her exasperation with Allen over his incessant need to continue discussing the affair, and his preoccupation with talking about their relationship.

I was faced with a dilemma. I could confront her and tell her that we were here to talk about her, not Allen. I could sit quietly and wait for her to develop a series of associations leading her to her own complicity in the situation. Or I could try to develop some association from her initial point of departure in the session that would open up a productive line of thinking about herself and her role in the balance of the system. Given the early stage of therapy, the cooperative nature of her first individual session, and her overall naiveté regarding therapy, I chose the third alternative. Choosing to start with a simple and obvious type of question, I asked Elaine if she had expressed these feelings (of exasperation, which she had just described) to Allen. Her answer was no.

> *"Why not?" I asked.*
> *"I just figured that Allen deserved to ask me questions, since I was the one who created this whole mess," Elaine responded.*
> *"Do you usually let Allen know when he is annoying you about something?" was my next question.*
> *"Well, probably not very often," Elaine admitted.*

That admission opened a crucial door. The implications for Elaine individually, her ability to recognize and act appropriately on negative feelings such as annoyance, aggravation, or anger were quite important, and they were made accessible with that admission. Additionally, her ability and willingness to express those feelings to Allen was now defined as inadequate. I took the turn down this path when I chose to focus on Elaine's lack of ability to identify and express negative feelings, rather than by focusing on her feelings of guilt, which she also had expressed. I avoided the focus on her guilt because I had the sense that she and Allen were both in strong agreement that she was the guilty one and that she needed to be punished. By avoiding that same tack, I avoided reinforcing their unproductive line of attack and established a beginning look at dynamics that had predated the affair.

In continuing this line of pursuit, I assumed that Elaine was going to contend that she was rarely bothered by Allen. More precisely, I was assuming that Elaine would be denying to herself, and to me, the extent to which she was bothered by Allen's behavior and attitudes. My job was to help her break through this denial. And I wanted to do this in a way that avoided shifting the blame entirely over to Allen. I wanted to have Elaine understand her contribution to this process and, hopefully, develop some beginning understanding of the origins of her style. The focus, in other words, was not on the fact that Allen was to blame after all, but on the pattern of Elaine's inability to identify and express negative feelings to Allen.

> *The remainder of the session was focused on the question of negative feelings. Questions about Elaine's perception of her ability to tell Allen negative feelings in the early years of the relationship were laced in with questions about the style of identifying and expressing negative feelings in Elaine's family of origin. Elaine's perception of her internal reactions began with her original assertion that she rarely felt negative, then proceeded to shift rather quickly. She amended her position to the assertion that if she did feel negative, it wouldn't do any good to express it. She then coupled that with her desire not to hurt anyone's feelings by "being negative."*

As Elaine reviewed her ambivalence about expressing her feelings to Allen, I was listening and thinking about the array of theoretical concepts that could address these concerns. The question of differentiation between self and other, feelings in self, feelings in other, and the mutual interaction of these feelings with complications such as projection all ran through my mind as I was listening to Elaine. It was obvious that Elaine was poorly differentiated, in the sense that her level of anxiety was quite dependent on her perception of Allen's level of anxiety. It was also obvious that the affair had been an attempt to distance herself from that uncomfortable closeness.

Elaine, however, was not yet prepared to grasp that type of abstract complexity. The more productive line of development was the more mundane question of identifying and expressing negative feelings. By the end of the session, Elaine had reviewed situations with Allen, including the most recent series of conversations about the affair, in which she realized that she had felt more negative than she had admitted. She had begun to understand that she had developed that style growing up in her family, and she was ready to experiment with a newly developed willingness to attempt to use these feelings productively in discussions with Allen.

Couple Sessions 5 and 6

Each couple seems to establish its own patterns in therapy, and Elaine and Allen were no exception. The next two sessions were couple sessions. Although the ostensible reason for that was one of scheduling constraints, it continued the symmetrical pattern that began at the outset of therapy, with groups of two couple sessions alternated with a round of individual sessions. I could not attribute any profound meaning to the pattern, and I assumed that Allen and Elaine were not even aware of the pattern, but I did track it for future reference if it should become meaningful in the context of some other pattern that emerged.

These two sessions were noteworthy for the shift in emphasis away from the affair as a point of discussion. The central theme appeared originally under the guise of a disagreement about child-care arrangements. Allen wanted Elaine to take charge of picking up the children at the day-care facility at a time that was usually "his responsibility," and Elaine was unwilling to make the change. Since Allen initially presented the subject for discussion, he offered the first statement of the problem. From his perspective, this was yet another in a growing series of incidents in which he had a very reasonable request, since he needed to reschedule work time, and Elaine was being selfish and unreasonable, since she would only need to reschedule a more optional activity with a friend.

Allen's definition of the problem sounded reasonable and could be convincing in its slant that characterized Elaine as unexpectedly unyielding. When compared with the "other side of the picture," in the form of Elaine's definition of the problem, it takes on a radically different meaning.

Elaine chose to highlight a much broader pattern in her description. She initially acknowledged that she could look somewhat selfish in her refusal to pick up the children, but she needed to break away from expectations from Allen that she believed were excessive. Specifically, she felt as though Allen was "always trying to run her life." If she agreed to pick up the children in this instance, there would be another problem soon enough in which Allen expected her to forfeit her individual time for something that he wanted her to do.

Elaine's description expanded the field of observation. Instead of focusing on the isolated incident of transportation for the children, she was focusing on a pattern of exchanges between them that she characterized as Allen's excessive expectations. Although the redefinition in terms of patterns was useful, it was lacking in balance. My strategy, then, was to clarify the definition of patterns involved, and help develop a balanced view and understanding of them.

The themes that cried out for development were the familiar ones of pursuer–distancer and autonomy–connectedness questions. Obviously, in my mind, these themes were critical to the dynamic evolution of the affair. The therapeutic work would entail developing that same awareness in the couple and beginning to explore possibilities for new patterns. I would begin with the current tiff over transportation, since that was the focus for the emotion at the moment, and then use it to establish more generalized patterns.

The conversation continued with a quick review of the facts pertinent to the transportation question, including their respective schedules, and quickly broadened to include their perspectives on patterns of expectations between them. This conversation, as could be predicted, did not have any easily identifiable victim or villains. Both Allen and Elaine had examples to support their contention that the other was a problem, and neither one was ready to acknowledge personal responsibility.

With the session nearing an end, I asked them if some interim solution regarding the transportation was possible until we learned more about why the problem has been so difficult to resolve. With that they arrived at a solution that effectively split the duties. I refrained from offering a solution. I sensed that they had the capacity to arrive at some type of compromise themselves, and I believed that the solution would be more effective if they personally developed the plan.

They began the next session with an enthusiastic report on the success of the compromise they had developed. The success seemed to establish a reservoir of good will and self-confidence that opened up several new themes. Both of them were more willing to acknowledge new understandings about the pressure their previous stance had put on the other. And both were ready to look critically at the question of balancing individual needs with the needs of the couple and the family.

While Elaine and Allen were celebrating their newly developed principle of a healthy balance between individual and family needs, I was aware of the difficulty that comes in translating this into everyday patterns. One small, and relatively short-lived compromise is sufficient to bolster their confidence in the process of therapy, but it does not demonstrate a broad ability to arrive at compromises, or to understand the dynamics that make them difficult.

My therapeutic strategy was to exploit the strength gained from this small victory in the sense that I wanted them to feel stronger, encouraged, and optimistic. Simultaneously I wanted to open up themes of unresolved pain, confusion, and mistrust between them in a way that would give me therapeutic leverage. It is these feelings, and not any abstract concern over a lack of differentiation of self, that would provide the impetus for further therapeutic work.

The lingering questions about the affair provide a ready and obvious source of these feelings. Allen opened up these questions. He said that he still found himself thinking about the affair, and he still did not have a satisfactory understanding of it. Elaine grimaced at the mention of the affair, but she did not say anything.

I believed that a review of the affair might be useful at this stage, because I wanted to gain therapeutic leverage, because Allen wanted to explore it further, and because I was sure that the issues were unresolved and in need of further work. In the time left, which was about half a session, Elaine reviewed her need for a stronger sense of independence. She was unable to express her need for more acceptance.

Allen talked about his concern that Elaine had too much independence and that she seemed to be reluctant to connect with the children and him. Essentially, there was little evidence of movement on either side. Allen was unable to understand the relief that the affair provided for Elaine, and he was unable to understand the pressure he put on her with his expectations. Elaine was unable to verbalize any dissatisfaction with the type of emotional connection she felt between them, and it was unclear whether she was even able to identify it for herself.

The pattern of two couple sessions followed by a round of individual sessions would be continued. Elaine reported a problem with scheduling because of impending work demands, and Allen expressed a desire for an individual session. I agreed to the plan, after finding a time for Elaine to come in alone. I wondered while the plans were being made whether I should be more insistent about a joint session, since there had been a noticeable lack of resolution about the affair in this session. But I assumed that we would be able to get back to it in a future joint session and felt that any work we accomplished in the individual sessions would probably help loosen up some of the sticky points.

My decision not to focus on that type of therapeutic process detail as a therapeutic strategy reflects a belief that the most helpful process to develop is the systems process in daily life events, rather than a strong focus on the process of the therapy. If, indeed, Allen and Elaine were "resisting" another joint meeting, I could more effectively use their energy to explore related topics rather than confronting this level of process resistance.

Allen: Individual Session 3

Although this was only Allen's third individual session, the fact that he had been involved in six couple sessions clearly put him at a more advanced point in therapy. He was still distraught and confused about the affair, but his distress was under considerably more control than when he began therapy. His success in working out several different problems with Elaine had bolstered his confidence, and he had a more objective view of the possibility that the affair was the result of some type of interaction between him and Elaine.

When he began, yet again, with questions about the meaning of the affair, it was clear that he was more rational, more clear-headed, and more thoughtful than he had been when he first asked those questions. Sensing this, I chose to adopt more of a role of educator, with the focus being emotional triangles. The educator role in therapy is a complicated strategy. Long and intricate explanations are generally ill-advised, yet the content, of triangles for instance, is complicated and not amenable to short and complete explanations. Allen, like most clients, was able to understand enough in a very brief introduction of a few sentences, to begin to understand the meaning and significance of emotional triangles. I was sure that I would have other opportunities later to expand on some of the nuances of triangles. For this session, it was more important to help Allen develop a personal grasp of the meaning and implications of triangles in relationship to Elaine's affair.

To accomplish this goal, I offered this explanation to Allen.

> *"There's an idea about how family systems operate that may be useful to understanding this situation, and it has to do with triangles. It is possible to see families breaking down into a series of different triangles, based on the types of emotional connections people have. Any three people in the system can make up a triangle, or we could put people in different groups on various ends of the triangles. Triangles frequently are a way for people to help diffuse tension between them and someone else, in the sense that they may become closer to a third person if they are having some kind of problem with the second person. In this sense, an affair is really one specific type of triangle in an emotional system."*
>
> *"Triangles usually can be thought of as having different shapes, with the length of the lines suggesting something about the relative closeness of the people involved,"* I continued, *"and generally they change shapes at different times, depending on the situation."* With that brief introduction, I asked Allen to go to the board and draw a triangle that would illustrate the relationship between him, Elaine, and the children. Allen quickly went to the board and drew a triangle that indicated his

basic understanding of the idea, in which he was further from the children than was Elaine and in which they were closer to each other than to the children (Figure 6.2).

After he finished drawing the triangle, I asked him if he had any thoughts about the triangle. He stepped back, looked at the triangle, and said that it was obvious that he had left too much of the child care responsibilities to Elaine. In order to check his understanding of the triangle pictured with my own interpretation, I told him my understanding of the triangle as I detailed above. After he agreed with that description of the triangle, I moved on to the loaded triangle of the affair.

I asked Allen if he had any idea about how he might draw the triangle of the affair. His initial reaction was to squirm and look uncomfortable. He regained his poise, however, and said that it seemed that he should put the "other guy" in his spot, and put himself in the place of the children (Figure 6.3).

Allen instinctively chose the common strategy of retaining the first, successful triangle that he had developed and changing the people occupying the different corners. He fixed the triangle and stepped back to look at it.

Always aware of the distinction between thinking and feeling, and sensing that Allen was reacting more emotionally to this triangle than to the first one, I asked Allen how he felt as he looked at that triangle. He replied that it was obvious that he was more distant from Elaine than he should have been. I responded with the observation that his response was more of a thought than a feeling, and that I was interested in how he felt about the triangle. He said he felt upset, confused, and sad. With that, I invited Allen to sit down, and we continued to explore the meaning and implications of the triangle he had drawn.

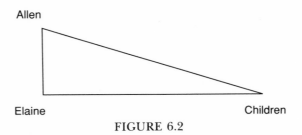

FIGURE 6.2

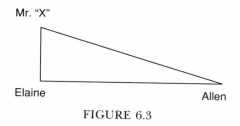

FIGURE 6.3

My first move was to "detriangle" the children, in the sense that I didn't want Allen preoccupied with the idea that Elaine was simply distancing from her parenting responsibilities. I wanted to get Allen thinking about the aspects of their relationship, and his behavior, which contributed to her distancing by way of the affair. I steered in this direction by asking him to think about what, other than pressures from the children, might have prompted Elaine to move away in this way. He responded by saying that she had been telling him lately, in all this talking they had been doing, that she feels as though he tries to run her life, and that perhaps that is what she was pulling away from.

I remembered that Allen had admitted that he was initiating most of the conversation about the affair, with Elaine asking for respite. I took that bit of self-awareness that I knew that Allen had and injected it at this point, comparing it to what Allen was describing as his control over Elaine. I asked if she might feel pressured by his insistence in talking about the affair. His eyes lit up with agreement.

With the principle of Allen's emotional pursuing in the relationship firmly established in his mind, I moved on to the prospect of creating some homework for Allen. I wanted to create an expectation that he would greatly diminish his role of emotional pursuer and give Elaine enough emotional territory to begin to reconnect with him in her own way. I wanted to give her the chance to be the pursuer. I simply reviewed the ideas we had developed, noting that he seemed to be the pursuer between them and wondered if it would be possible for him to discontinue pursuing as an experiment, to see how Elaine would respond. He agreed, and after a bit of development of that idea, we stopped the session.

Elaine: Individual Session 3

"What did you say to Allen? He's been a different person ever since his last session!" Elaine blurted out her question as she walked in for her

third individual session, even before she got a chance to sit down. She was indicating her amazement, and she was also indicating her approval by way of a big smile on her face. Obviously, the last session with Allen had resulted in some type of shift in his approach to her.

I chose to respond to the second part of her statement, and asked her how he had been different. She said he had been more relaxed, was not insisting that they talk about the affair the way he had been, and generally seemed easier to get along with. My next question moved the focus off of Allen, and onto Elaine. I asked her how she had responded to his change. She said that in some ways she liked it, because he wasn't annoying her by his constant demands. In other ways she was uncomfortable, because she found that she was thinking more about herself, her problems, Tim, and what she was going to do with her life.

Elaine had responded to my question with a willingness to look at herself and her life in a way very typical of the work that evolves with the strategy of simultaneous conjoint and individual sessions. She was ready to look at her contribution to the problem and did not need to continue focusing on Allen as an avoidance strategy. I sensed that Elaine was receptive to developing any line of ideas that might be helpful and pertinent to her situation. She had covered a wide range of ideas in her reference to the problems she had been thinking about, and it was unclear which of these would be the most helpful.

To help answer this question, I asked her which of "her problems" she had been thinking about. She replied that she had realized that she had not been very nice to Allen, despite his new approach, and that she believed that she didn't like him very much. Moving to further clarify her thinking about the locus of the problem, I asked her why this was her problem rather than his.

She went on to develop several ideas, ideas which she clearly had been mulling over for some time, given their complexity and the amount of supporting incidents she could report illustrating them. The general thrust of her thinking was that she was not sure how to be close to Allen without feeling trapped. She gave several examples of her attempt to be close to him to which he had responded by doing something that she saw as controlling. She then proceeded to balance this with a series of incidents in which his behavior had been "just fine," yet she still felt uneasy being close to him. This most recent shift on his part brought out this theme rather dramatically.

I continued to develop the line of ideas she had begun. In my mind, this was the other part of the pursuer–distancer loop that had been explored with Allen. We talked about her feelings about being close to Allen, what it felt like, how she saw herself behaving when she was close to him and when she was more distant, and any meaning she could develop about these patterns. She could report observations about the patterns, but she was quite unable to develop any ideas about the meaning of the patterns. With this block in her thinking, I chose to "move up a generation," the time-honored strategy in Bowen Systems therapy in which the present day problem is explored in the previous generation.

> *In response to a question from me about her recollections of similar patterns between her parents, Elaine lit up with recognition as she began to talk about her mother's frequent complaints about her father's domineering habits. She admitted that she did see her father as overbearing, and remembered wishing as a teenager that her mother would stand up to him. She also remembered her chronic disappointment that her mother would never confront her father, but would frequently complain to her (Elaine), about the problem.*
>
> *Although I could see the potential for transferring that pattern to Elaine's marriage to Allen, I wanted a stronger connection in her mind before bringing the conversation back to her marriage. I asked her to elaborate on her perceptions of her father as domineering. She talked about his style of making all of the decisions around the house, ranging from children's privileges to household maintenance and financial planning. She remembered how he was aggravated and out of sorts when people disagreed with him, and how everyone in the family tried to avoid upsetting him. Following those memories, Elaine spontaneously made a connection to her current situation. She offered, without prompting, the comment that she obviously had been seeing Allen in the same way she used to see her father.*

We continued developing this theme for the duration of the session. She found it most obvious to see her involvement with Tim as a way of getting away from Allen, and she was also quite ready to consider the idea that she may have been unconsciously distancing from her father as well. Regarding her relationship with Allen, she began to consider how she might be able to reach out to him in ways that would be comfortable for her. Regarding her father, she began to contemplate the possibility of some type of conversation with him regarding her memories of his dominance in the family.

Couple Sessions 7 and 8

The tone of the next two sessions was dramatically different from the initial two sessions. Each person's level of anxiety was greatly diminished, with the corresponding level of relaxation higher. Both looked and acted more rested, more confident that the marriage would survive, and were less focused on the affair. The emotional crisis of the affair had, for the most part, passed. They had moved on to a stage of concentrated attention to the dynamics in the relationship that had brought about the problem.

There were two main areas of emphasis in these two sessions, the pursuer–distancer pattern in the marriage and their respective families of origin. The pursuer–distancer dynamic was the most salient to them, especially in light of Allen's recent shift away from the role of constant pursuer. This shift only served to highlight the more longstanding pattern and to whet both of their appetites to know more about the workings of the emotional distance between them. These sessions were typical of sessions following periods of relative calm. With no recent crises to report and dissect, the session can be used to explore the evolution of their understanding of the systems dynamics at work in their relationship.

Since I had seen Elaine last, I began session 7 with a question to Allen, asking him what he had been observing between them since our last meeting, and what he had been thinking about. I took the time with him to develop his perceptions of the distance between them, with Elaine listening attentively all the while. Allen began with a report of his recent attempts to avoid controlling Elaine and, generally, to avoid pursuing her.

He continued by telling of his disappointment that she did not seem to recognize his efforts, nor did she reach out to him. He saw that as a typical pattern, which he had noticed but had not acknowledged to himself prior to this time. Following a fairly thorough development of this theme by Allen, I invited Elaine to join the conversation by way of comparing her perceptions of the emotional distance between them to Allen's perceptions.

I specifically chose to keep the focus on a cognitive rather than an affective level because I sensed that neither one was reacting so strongly that it would "get in the way" of the ideas. And the ideas were, indeed, important to have understood and developed for both of them. Elaine was able to agree with Allen's report that he had changed his style and also agreed that she had neglected to tell him that she had noticed. She admitted that she probably should have said something to him and admitted that the lack of acknowledgement was a problem.

As the conversation evolved, my role was to continue the focus on the systemic meaning of the distance between them and to avoid the tendency to focus on one person's inadequacies. They each had opportunities to listen to the other's perceptions. Elaine began to hear Allen's perception of his pursuing behavior as evidence of his insecurity and his need for her. This was in sharp contrast to her own perception of that behavior as controlling and insensitive. Understanding that difference in perception gave Elaine considerable insight into Allen's needs—and seemed to give her some relief.

Allen, in turn, was able to hear Elaine describe her need for independence and acceptance in a way that was not threatening to him. Her description of her relationship with her father, and her views on her parents' relationship with each other, offered him some perspective on the role which he had assumed in their relationship and Elaine's role as well. Elaine compared her need for independence and equality to Allen's need for her. She was beginning to understand both sets of needs as their respective vulnerabilities.

By this stage of treatment, my role has begun to change. Allen and Elaine have learned "how to behave" in the sessions. They are not likely to interrupt each other, and they have learned the distinction between thinking and feeling. They have a general sense of how the conversations will flow, understand that one person may speak briefly or continue on to develop long and complex ideas. In either case, they will have an opportunity to compare, contrast, agree, or generally develop their own ideas. With the process of the sessions more established, I am free to focus more thoroughly on the process of the emotional system in the couple and family network. This focus is not usually something that I choose, but rather one I hear being offered in a tentative and undeveloped way by one of them. My input is in the choice of developing one idea rather than another.

Allen: Individual Session 4

By this time Allen was solidly in the middle stages of therapy. He had continued to do considerable thinking about the sessions in between meetings and had surveyed his relationship with his parents, brother, Elaine, and his sons. He had prepared himself for this meeting and had wanted to focus on two related ideas, his control of his brother, and his control of Elaine. He had even written down a few ideas that had occurred to him, ideas he wanted to remember to develop in our session.

> He began with his thoughts about his brother. He reviewed how his parents had expected him to watch out for his brother, four years his junior, while they were growing up. He related several stories of how he had carried out that function to an extreme, and ended up being disliked by his brother.
>
> He guessed that he probably felt jealous of his brother while they were growing up, because it seemed as if his parents were easier on his brother than on him. He wondered if his excessive control of his brother was his attempt to balance that situation. After developing that idea a bit more, Allen made an easy comparison to his relationship with Elaine. He admitted that he had been more and more impressed with how much he tried to control her, in ways he had never noticed.

Allen was doing an excellent job of developing his ideas, and really needed no help from me at this point. Instead, I chose to restate what I heard Allen developing, using some of the language and concepts from systems thinking. I began by telling him that I was thinking about how nicely he had been developing the importance of the triangle between his brother, his wife, and himself.

That simple, supportive, compliment, turned out to be an unexpectedly useful "intervention." Allen's previous work with triangles had prepared him, but he had not generalized. On hearing me use the word triangle, however, he immediately saw the relevance, and he was able to go much further in developing his thinking about control in the two relationships. Allen did not exactly need help, in the sense that I needed to confront him on areas he was defending against. More simply, I was restating to him what I was hearing him say. That provided a counterpoint that accented certain themes and propelled his own thinking.

Elaine: Individual Session 4

Like Allen, Elaine also was showing signs of being deeply engaged in the therapeutic process. Her focus continued to be different.
She still was prone to reviewing her relationship with Tim, and trying
to make more sense of it for herself. She came in to the session with
the report that Tim had called her on the phone. She admitted that
she had not told Allen and was afraid to do so.

I could sense considerable ambivalence from Elaine about the
call, coming from her tone of voice. I knew that ambivalence could
provide therapeutic leverage, if I was able to find the most effective
way to use it. I did *not* want to bury the ambivalence artificially by
chiding her for having contact with Tim, or threaten her with the
prospect of raw, open disclosure to Allen. The long-term goal was to
help Elaine understand the emotional meaning of her relationship
with Tim, which meant allowing the positive element of the ambivalence to be expressed and explored.

I assumed that the positive part of her ambivalence had to do
with emotional needs that had been tended to, which had not been
tended to in the relationship with Allen. I did not assume that Allen's
deficiencies were the reason they were not fulfilled, though that may
have played a part. The more important point of focus for the
moment was that Elaine had allowed something to come into her life
by way of Tim that she had not allowed into her life by way of Allen.
Elaine herself was not entirely aware of what it was, or why it was. The
goal was to clarify that piece of the puzzle.

> *Just as every long journey begins with a single step, so too did the
> complicated exploration of all of this ambivalence begin with a simple
> step, finding out whether Elaine recognized the ambivalence. This was
> accomplished with a simple question, asking Elaine how she felt about
> receiving a call from Tim. Her initial response was to say that she wished
> he hadn't called. After she developed that idea for a while, which basically
> amounted to a mini-lecture on the negative side of the ambivalence, I
> asked her if she had any other feelings mixed-in about his phone call. She
> said she didn't exactly know what I meant and continued to avoid
> commenting on the positive side of her ambivalence.*
>
> *Given her reluctance, I chose to open the subject myself. I told her
> that I was watching her eyes when she had told me about the phone call,
> and that I saw a glitter in her eyes that made me think that perhaps she*

was just a little bit glad to hear from him, even though there were all those
negative things that she had just talked about. She lit up at my observa-
tion, agreed, and went on to develop her thinking about her understand-
ing of the positive elements of that relationship.

She was able to recognize that she had been warmer and more spontaneous with Tim than she had ever been with Allen. She wondered whether she had been hampered in the early days of her relationship with Allen by her anxiety over whether it would "go somewhere," in other words, whether they would marry. Since she had totally dismissed that possibility with Tim, it seemed easier to be another type of person, a type of person she couldn't allow herself to be in the marriage.

Elaine made it quite clear that the reluctance to be "free" in her marriage was something she had seen in herself long before meeting Allen. She had had similar ideas in a serious relationship she had been in prior to becoming involved with Allen. That insight on her part effectively diminished Allen's role in her feelings and pointed sharply in the direction of her family of origin. With that in mind, I steered Elaine more toward thinking about her parents. She considered a few ideas, including her image of her mother as being quite unemotional and unspontaneous. She wondered whether she had thought that she, too, needed to be like that in a marriage.

Time ran out in the session before Elaine could go very far in developing ideas related to her family of origin, but there would be more opportunities for that in future sessions. Elaine left this session with an understanding of one of the emotional facets of her affair that had previously been quite hidden from her. She concluded the session with a semihumorous comment that it was fortunate that Tim had called. Her smile told me that she now understood that it was "good" because it appealed to the positive side of her ambivalence and because it gave her the stimulus to do an important bit of work in her therapy.

Couple Session 9

"Things have been going very well."

Allen began the next couple session without any prompting, immediately after sitting down. Although I recognized the potential to explore the dynamic implications of Allen beginning the session, as opposed to Elaine, and without any cues from me, I chose to continue to listen to his report. He went on to elaborate on the different things that were going well.

> *"We're talking more. Or should I say, Elaine is talking more, and I am listening more. And when I do talk, I am more aware of my potential to try to control Elaine. We've also had a couple of disagreements come up that we were able to talk about and come to a solution. All in all, we should have been doing this a long time ago, and maybe we wouldn't have gotten into this fix in the first place."*

Allen was clearly enthusiastic and positive in his opening statement. Elaine's demeanor suggested solid agreement with his position, but I wanted her to articulate that herself and add whatever perspective she might have. When Allen finished, I turned to her, and in a casual tone said,

> *"Well, Elaine, what do you have to say about all of this!?"*
>
> *Elaine said she agreed with Allen that things were going much better between them, and she went on to say that she was feeling much better herself. She related a conversation between the two of them in which she finally was able to tell Allen that she didn't feel accepted by him and had pointed out a couple of instances in the past week to prove her point. She saw two important things happen in that conversation, besides the fact that she had raised the issue in the first place.*
>
> *First, she saw Allen listen to her in a way he had never done before, and she believed that he understood her better. Second, she was able to get a new understanding of him, since he had explained to her that he wanted to be able to disagree with an idea she may have, without being concerned that she took the disagreement as rejection or not being accepted. They both went on to review the differences between their families of origin. Allen's was typified by outspoken discussions about opinions, with frequent disagreements, whereas Elaine's was characterized by unspoken tensions and disagreements frequently handled by extended periods of silence and emotional cut-offs.*

It was clear that they were more aware of the rather extreme styles which typified each of their original families. They also were demonstrating a new-found resolve to temper those longstanding tendencies in themselves. They were intent on developing a system that would work better for them.

As the session neared the end, Elaine took the initiative to raise the question of continued treatment. She pointed out that upcoming business trips would make scheduling difficult in the next several weeks and that they had been discussing the possibility of "trying it on their own" for a while, anyway. Their conclusion was to schedule the next appointment for one month hence, if I was in agreement. Before indicating any agreement, I turned to Allen to ask if he had any more he wanted to add, and he simply said he was in total agreement and didn't have anything to add. With that I indicated my agreement.

I left unsaid my sense that much of the progress was rather new, and many of the habits they had brought into the marriage from their original families were likely to continue. Overriding that hesitation was my desire to encourage and support the positive thrust of their plan and my basic belief in the importance of giving Allen and Elaine control over their own process of healing.

Couple Session 10

They returned in a month looking quite cheery. The conversation was quite similar to the one in the previous session, with each of them commenting on positive exchanges they had seen and reporting new things they were learning about themselves and the other. Obviously, the progress had continued over the past month, and their idea to lengthen the time interval between sessions had been sound.

Fairly early in the hour, Allen mentioned that they had discussed the possibility of not scheduling any future appointments, with the understanding that they would call if there was a problem. Elaine was nodding in agreement. I addressed Elaine, partly to acknowledge her unspoken agreement and partly to explore her sense of the resolution of the initial crisis—the affair. Since Allen had asked for my opinion about the plan to terminate, I used his question in my question to her.

"Elaine, maybe you could help me decide whether this is a good idea. Could you review for me your sense of where the two of you started, and where you are now? And where does the affair fit into the picture?"

"I feel so different now, it's hard for me to remember how I felt before I got involved." Elaine began with an acknowledgment of the affair but declined, in a typical fashion, to use the name of the other

person. "I see now that I was very vulnerable to the emotional comfort that I found in that other relationship, because I was feeling so dissatisfied with us. But I can definitely see that whatever I got from that relationship came with a pretty high price tag. I felt so confused and depressed about it that it made the whole thing not worth it."

Elaine went on to talk about how much she had learned about why she was unhappy in the marriage and how pleased she was with the progress that she saw between herself and Allen. She also included an observation that she had been thinking quite a bit about her relationship with her parents lately, and she had been contemplating the possibility of discussing some ideas with them. She concluded with an optimistic statement that she thought they were ready to stop regular sessions and was sure that they would call if something came up.

With that, I again turned to Allen and asked him how Elaine's description compared to his sense of the crisis and the work that they had done in the therapy. He began with an emphatic exclamation, "Well, I sure don't have any trouble remembering how I felt. I felt horrible. And I hope I never feel that bad again!" He went on to talk about his view that he had become less depressed as he finally understood why the affair happened and what part he had played in bringing them to that point.

He reviewed his perception of the confusion between them about control. He now understood that part of that was because he had been too controlling, but part of it was Elaine's sensitivity to feeling controlled even when he had no intentions of controlling her. He concluded by anticipating that they might have more difficulties between them in the future, but he felt confident that they could work them out themselves. And he would call if they couldn't work it out.

I reinforced their perception that they had, indeed, come a long way, and that they had turned the crisis of the affair into an opportunity to develop a better relationship. I mentioned being impressed that they had begun to think about some of the influences their respective families may have had on their relationship, and the evolution of the affair, and anticipated that they might find themselves discovering more and more about those influences as they continued to think about them. I finished by agreeing with the idea of not scheduling any more appointments. As they were leaving, they both offered their hands for a handshake, which I warmly returned.

EPILOGUE

The story of Allen and Elaine concluded with the same characteristic that it had throughout the story, its typical nature. Allen and
Elaine were satisfied with the treatment, and their lives were significantly better after therapy than before the crisis of the affair. Both of
them learned some dynamic ideas that helped to clarify their understanding of their relationship and the meaning of the affair. Both
of them developed new behaviors that reflected this new understanding, and in turn, this eased the level of tension between them.

They also had an experience of the potential of a psychotherapeutic process that was sufficiently positive that both indicated that
they would make use of it, if need be, in the future. This type of
potential, at its worst, could be criticized as a type of revolving door
mentality. But at its best, it can be seen as discreet and judicious use of
a helpful process. Indeed, this type of termination is becoming more
the rule than the exception in the marriage and family therapy field.
Some therapists have compared it to the concept of the family physician, being available for help in times of crisis.

Another element of this case that is typical, especially of brief
therapy, is the clear implication that there was a lack of resolution of
some of the dynamic pressures that probably contributed to the crisis.
In this case, the unresolved pressures coming from the respective
families of origin are in question. Although there was some attention
to them in the therapy, and indeed some shift in the emotional
balance in the couple as a result of those insights, there is considerable
reason to believe that neither one of them grasped the full implications of those pressures. Without begging the age-old questions
about the need for insight, and the subsequent impact on insight in
everyday life, it simply can be noted that the potential for deeper
understanding in these areas may be one area of exploration if there
should be any further call for therapy.

In a follow-up phone call to Elaine and Allen approximately one
and a half years after termination, both reported that they were doing
well. They indicated that they had been happy with each other and
strongly believed that they had put the crisis of the affair behind
them. They believed that they had learned valuable lessons about
their respective roles and needs in the marriage in the therapy and
were alert to shifts that could indicate a relapse into their old, unhelpful habits.

CHAPTER 7

Themes and Variations: Long-Term Intensive Treatment

Some couples live for years with extramarital affairs. Sometimes it is a relationship with one other person that quietly and steadily exists over years of a marriage. Sometimes it is a series of relationships that exist for brief-to-moderate durations. The longevity of both of these patterns stands as a testament to the powerful forces in the emotional system that coalesce to maintain them. It is consistent to think that at least at some point in the development of this type of pattern, the people needed that pattern to exist. If that need did exist, it was, as suggested earlier, a rather unconscious need.

It happens that those needs change, the balance in the system changes, and people can strongly desire to alter the *status quo*. Both the noninvolved spouse and the involved spouse recognize the pattern, appreciate the unhealthiness that it signifies, and have a desire and commitment to altering the pattern and establishing a healthier lifestyle. As honorable as those desires may be, it soon becomes apparent that it is more difficult to do than was initially realized. Ingrained patterns of emotional distance and intimacy in a relationship are not changed by brief examination and reshuffling.

The process of change, whether viewed philosophically as distinct from, or intrinsic to a related cognitive understanding, takes time. It takes time to experiment with alterations. Inevitably, some of the alterations will be less successful than hoped for, which then requires time to recover from ideas that didn't work, and time to understand why they didn't work. This, then, creates the necessity to develop new ideas, which takes time. The new ideas will likely include

184 HUSBANDS, WIVES, AND LOVERS

several that are helpful, but it will take time to know which ideas work the best.

Even the best ideas will be tested by the powerful forces of the system, and there will be the inevitable regressions. It then takes time to recover from relapses to old patterns in the system. With continued work, change is possible. It will take time, however, to know that the decided upon changes have taken root and time to solidify the changes.

All of this comes under the category of "Rome wasn't built in a day" and compels the consideration of long-term intensive treatment. The very concept of long-term intensive treatment is rather ambiguous in the field of marriage and family therapy, with its strong emphasis on brief treatment. But the concept of long-term affairs is not ambiguous, and the concept of people being caught in lifestyles that are highly resistant to change is not ambiguous. This chapter will develop the complexities of the emotional system and process of long-term change.

Multidimensional Change

The broad-based focus of the therapy is one of the most radical distinctions between brief therapy and long-term therapy. The affair may be the major organizing theme during brief therapy, with other elements of family life and levels of the system used primarily in a way that makes sense of the affair. In intensive long-term therapy, on the other hand, the affair will step to the side and become a supporting theme, with the issues of self, differentiation, intimacy, and the full range of family and individual life becoming the focus of the therapy. The work of the therapy will be on multiple levels of the system, with multiple levels of change, and multiple levels of meaning.

This creates a host of problems that are never encountered in brief therapy. The tension and emotionality typical of early treatment translate into emotional pain and discomfort that pose a challenge to the therapist. Ironically, in some ways it makes the job easier. The couple is desperate for relief and willing to become committed to the therapy. This commitment usually translates into increased flexibility and willingness to disrupt unhealthy patterns in the relationship. As a result, change can more easily be seen by the therapist and experienced by the couple in the early stages of treatment.

As this change accumulates, whether it is in the form of consistent efforts by the couple to communicate, renewed and improved sexual interaction, vows to discontinue the affair, vows to spend more time together and leave the children with a babysitter, or vows to change problem-creating work habits, the subsequent focus of treatment becomes more difficult to define. Not only are the treatment goals for the couple more subtle, but the process of change decelerates in pace, and the role of the therapist changes substantially.

On the Efficacy of Long-Term Marriage and Family Therapy

Indeed, the therapist's role shifts so markedly that some concern has been expressed about the possibility that the therapist loses potency with a couple if the amount of contact with them is too long or too frequent. Dell (1982), for example, in developing the notion of coherence, explores the possibility from a theoretical point of view. He begins by posing the concept of coherence, a concept that implies a congruent interdependence in functioning whereby all the aspects of the system fit together. This fit has a basic impact on the functioning of the system, in that every action alters the subsequent nature of the system. "A system cannot behave without altering itself" (Dell, 1982).

Dell asserts that the change in an individual has a coherent, systemic impact on both the individual and the system. As the individual changes, and as the changes become part of the system, the change is no longer "change" but is part of the system. Through this process the impact of the therapist becomes neutralized, and the corresponding pace of change slows down.

Whereas Dell's hypothesis may be one of the more elegant examples of the concern over long-term marriage and family therapy, it is but one of a chorus of voices that express similar concerns. Paul (1976), as another example, refers to a "gnawing impatience" with traditional models of psychotherapy. This impatience prompted him to experiment with cross-confrontation techniques and various types of stressor stimuli to help accelerate the process of change.

Paul developed these techniques to overcome what he described as a "halting pace" of change. He was assuming that the halting pace was a result of the techniques, or lack of techniques, of the therapeutic process. Paul and Dell identified therapeutic technique, and systemic properties, respectively, in their articulation of problems inherent in a progressively slower pace of change over the duration of long-term psychotherapy. Although they represent only two viewpoints on long-term change, they are representative of the wariness with which long-term therapy has been viewed among marriage and family therapists.

Session Frequency

Closely related to the questions regarding the pace of change, and the therapist's role in this pace, is the question of the frequency of contact between the therapist and clients. Bowen (1971) reported scheduling monthly sessions with a multiple family group in the late 1960s, initially because of scheduling constraints. The results were so strikingly positive that he began to schedule most of his family psychotherapy at monthly intervals. He speculated that the progress was related to the fact that monthly intervals left families more on their own, which made them more resourceful and less dependent on the therapy.

Years later, the Milan group came to the same conclusion, for some of the same reasons. In discussing the long time interval between sessions, Selvini Palazzoli (1980) again noted the amount of change that was seen with monthly intervals. Her speculations emphasized the process of change that was unfolding in the family and the relationship with the therapist. Monthly sessions aided the process of change, she concluded, by allowing the particular emphasis of any one session to develop over an adequate amount of time, rather than being distracted by the focus of a subsequent session.

Also, the therapist was less likely to become part of the "solution" the family was incorporating into its system. When the therapist becomes part of the family's solution, she speculated, the family may be resistant to improving, lest the therapist decide to terminate. The Milan team limited the therapy to ten sessions as a solution to the possibility of the therapist's decreased and/or negative impact on the family after the initial stages of therapy.

The Speed and Efficiency Mentality

Along with pioneering clinical research and eloquent theoretical formulations that were pushing toward fewer and more infrequent therapy sessions, broader social forces were having an impact on the practice of marriage and family therapy as well. Insurance companies, HMOs, and other third-party payers were limiting the amount of therapy that would be subsidized. Usually this came in the form of limits on the number of sessions, or limits on the amount of benefits paid during a calendar year. Although there were some plans that subsidized generous benefits, many of the plans subsidized only short-term courses of therapy.

Clients, as consumers, have brought considerable pressure to bear on the field of marriage and family therapy. In an era that includes jet travel, instant food, microwave cooking, and computer-aided living, speed and efficiency are highly valued—and frequently taken for granted. That the type of change that is desired may take longer is not considered. The expectation is that the new and improved technology (perhaps with the help of computers) can make it possible to accomplish the goal quickly.

There are indications that the treatment of extramarital affairs reflects these complicated forces that push toward brief therapy. Humphrey (1986) reported statistics indicating an average of nine couple sessions, six sessions with the wife, and two to four sessions with the husband, as being the typical course of treatment with couples in treatment related to affairs. These sessions were spaced over a time period of six to nine months, thus suggesting the probability of long intervals between the sessions.

ON BEHALF OF LONG-TERM THERAPY

There are times when ten sessions spaced over ten months is not enough therapy. Therapy is not a game, like golf, in which winning is defined as having the least number of swings at the ball, or the fewest number of sessions. Change, and the process of therapy which contributes to that change, is more accurately compared to a journey. The definition of winning will evolve over the journey. Although speed may have some relevance at certain points, it is but one of many considerations.

There are times when the work with a couple can last as long as two to four years, with a session frequency ranging from once a month to three sessions per week. The three sessions would include one couple session and one individual session with each of the spouses. This is not simply an example of an unhealthy mutual interdependence between client and therapist. It is not necessarily an example of an inability to change based on the therapist being incorporated into the family system.

In the best of circumstances, and even in circumstances that are almost-but-not-quite the best of circumstances (in other words there is room for occasional human failings), intensive long-term therapy can offer an opportunity for reflection, exploration, and support that can promote steady and solid change in the lives of the clients, and most probably in the life of the therapist as well. The parameters of the therapy will be diffuse and therefore more difficult to define than short-term therapy. The goals will be less tangible and, therefore, less accessible to empirical measurement. And the demands on the therapist will be more personal than in the early stages of treatment.

In view of the broad history of modern psychotherapy in the twentieth century, it would seem a bit incredulous that long-term intensive therapy should be in the position of benefiting from any type of restatement of its value. Yet it seems that the evolutionary trends have indeed created this potential, especially in the realm of family and systems-based psychotherapy. The emphasis on speed, efficiency, accountability, and therapist involvement have combined to establish a persuasive argument in favor of brief treatment. This does not need to be abandoned, but neither should long-term intensive treatment be abandoned. It offers a viable, necessary, and powerful model of psychotherapeutic intervention that has a different, but no less complex set of challenges than brief therapy.

A Definition of Long-Term Intensive Therapy

Defining long-term therapy is a bit like defining an affair, there are many different images and opinions that are possible. For example, the Milan team described their approach as "long brief therapy" (Tomm, 1984). The treatment was brief because of the restricted number of sessions, long because of the extended time between sessions. Although the juxtaposition of "long" and "brief" is rather catchy, it still doesn't add up to much contact between the therapist and client, and it still doesn't really cover much time in the clients' lives. It is not an intensive engagement between the players in the project.

Intensive long-term treatment is characterized by an open-ended contract between the client and the therapist. The contract specifically acknowledges a commitment to continue the therapeutic relationship for a substantial and initially undetermined amount of time. In that time, the frequency of sessions will be established in response to the needs at any given time. In the early stages of treatment, intensive involvement between the client and the therapist is quite difficult if sessions are less than weekly. Although the duration of the therapy is uncontracted initially, in practice there are trends that suggest that average long-term therapy continues for one and a half to three years, with some therapy continuing even longer.

Affairs and Long-Term Treatment

As was mentioned earlier, the long-term existence of a pattern of extramarital involvements is one indicator for long-term therapy. This is not fail-safe, nor is it the only indication for long-term therapy. There are, as usual, going to be occasions when the dynamic pressures that led to the affair may be responsive to brief intervention, and the situation can be resolved quickly. Additionally, there are times when the affair may have been a brief involvement that was but one of a long series of problems with a couple. The long history of poor relations may prove to be more of a problem, and more of a therapeutic focus, than the affair. Thus the therapy continues longer.

Indications for Long-Term Intensive Therapy

What, then, can be the indications for long-term therapy? It is a two-sided phenomenon. One half of the picture is the couple and one half the therapist. In the couple, there must be a willingness to continue with the project of therapy for an extended period of time. This is not something that can be taken for granted, since there are many couples who simply would not consider the process valuable and would therefore not consider being involved. If these couples have any interest in therapy, it may be limited, in which case the more pointed interventions of brief strategic therapy will be indicated.

Second, there needs to be the ability to develop a cognitive understanding of the crisis the pair find themselves in as well as solutions for alleviating the crisis. A lack of interest or ability in this area would again suggest a course of brief treatment. Although this trend toward a cognitive approach to problem solving is not found in every couple, it would be simplistic to associate the trend with any other variables, such as socioeconomic class. It is possible to find both groups of people in any socioeconomic class.

One final indication is the presence of some type of problematic symptom in the couple. This could come in the form of a continuation of the affair, a problematic depression in either one of the spouses, serious disharmony in the marriage, or symptoms in the children. The presence of this type of symptom can be seen as a need for continuing therapeutic work. Whether or not these symptoms are perceived, acknowledged, and interpreted in this way is a function of the therapist.

Other specific indications in the couple are characteristically vague. Essentially, the structure of "indications–contraindications" is a carry-over from a medical model of disease that is only partially useful in the realm of emotional and psychological healing. It is quite impossible, for example, to arrive at a diagnosis indicating the treatment of long-term therapy in the same way in which a lab test would indicate the treatment of a certain medication with a certain physical illness.

The therapist variables pertinent to the indications for long-term treatment are equally as important as the client variables. Even if a couple has the interest and the cognitive ability to engage in long-term intensive treatment, if it is outside of the therapist's belief system, the project simply won't happen. The primary therapist variable is an interest and belief in the process. A lack of interest is sure to reduce the therapist's field of vision in a way that any indications for long-term therapy would be ignored or reinterpreted to fit into another belief system. Beyond an interest, there are several factors that are relevant to the therapist, but they will be considered later as they relate to broad concerns during long-term treatment.

Establishing the Contract

In most marital and family therapy, the contract for long-term therapy will be made sometime after the initial session, or sessions. Most couples enter therapy with hopes that the problem can be resolved quickly, and they have very little awareness of the potential for longer work. Soon after the initiation of the therapy, the possibility of a longer course of therapy begins to emerge.

Frequently, the contract will be made between the fourth and eighth sessions. If the sessions are held weekly, this suggests the contract will be made some time during the second month of therapy. By this point, the breadth of dynamic material pertinent to the situation has been glimpsed during the sessions, the potential difficulty in altering the patterns has been experienced during daily life at home, and the therapeutic relationship with the therapist is strengthened to the point that its potential usefulness in the process of change has been established.

Contracting usually includes the agreement of an open-ended period of involvement, a discussion of the frequency of sessions, and an initial comment about the process of termination. There are no magic formulas that apply to any of these issues. An open-ended commitment in time is related to the question of termination. The indications that the time for termination has arrived usually are evident to both the clients and the therapist. On the clients' end, they frequently report feeling confident that they have their lives under control and are ready to terminate. The therapist agrees with these assessments in a high percentage of cases.

Other times clients may report a desire to discontinue treatment because of fatigue with the process, rather than a sense of completion and resolution. This calls for an exploration of the dynamics of the fatigue and a decision to build in a vacation from the therapy, or some continuation with modifications. This concern can more accurately be understood as a midtherapy concern rather than a termination issue.

The contract for the frequency of sessions reflects real world concerns more than it reflects any magical thinking about perfect formulas for the frequency of sessions. The amount of material, and the level of detail relevant to the everyday life of the couple, that can be explored during sessions scheduled weekly, are different than when sessions are scheduled every other week or monthly. Simply put, the more frequent the sessions, the more detail can be explored.

During crisis periods such as the time around the revelation of an affair, and for several months following that revelation, most couples can benefit from the amount of detail that can be examined during weekly sessions. In fact, weekly couple sessions and weekly individual sessions can be used very productively, making a total of three hours

per couple per week. As the crisis subsides, as the cognitive understanding of the system develops, and as the family patterns change,
the usefulness of weekly sessions diminishes, and the possibility of
recontracting for every-other-week sessions arises. This same process
repeats itself for later stages of treatment, moving to monthly sessions
and even less frequent sessions.

EXPLORING UNCHARTED TERRITORY

One of the typical comments from clients as they move past the
beginning stages of therapy that was initiated by an affair was a
feeling of surprise. They note that the affair *does* seem to be over and
that they are pleased with that, but they still don't feel secure about
the marriage. They are surprised because they had always assumed
that if the affair was finished, they would feel good and everything
would be "back to normal." They are not able to identify precisely
what is wrong, it is more of a feeling than a specific problem. This
nagging feeling of something being amiss will be the stimulus for
continued work in the therapy. Logically, since they don't know
exactly what is wrong, they don't exactly know what the goal of
therapy would be. But they are willing to try to figure out the problem.

There is an internal change in the therapist at this stage of the
treatment as well. The lack of definition that characterizes the later
stages of therapy can evoke feelings which are reminiscent of being
on a long trip, with no itinerary, no time limit and only a vague notion
of a destination. To further complicate the venture, the maps of the
territory being traversed are vague and imprecise.

In many ways, it is an exploration of uncharted territory. The
maps of psychotherapy are the theories and belief systems about
change and about human nature. Although there are some specific
theories, techniques, and strategies, they pale in comparison to the
unending details of daily living that are fodder for the therapy. But it
is in the details of everyday living that the broadly powerful, but
abstract dynamics of the system, and the individuals in the system, can
most vividly be seen and experienced. Consequently, some alterations
in these details will be necessary to alleviate the pain and to disrupt
the unhealthy patterns that initially brought the couple to treatment.
It is in the later stages of this project that the need for flexibility,
creativity, and improvisation by the therapist is most obvious.

The Foundations of the Therapy

The working phase of long-term intensive therapy usually begins after approximately fifteen to twenty sessions. Assuming a schedule of weekly sessions, and a contract to continue the project for a substantial period of time, it is at this point that the therapeutic relationship has deepened to a level of trust that permits the exploration of subject matters, feelings, and patterns in a way that was impossible early in treatment.

The treatment up until this point has been punctuated by a series of rather predictable phases. This first phase, which usually lasts *the first six to eight sessions,* was focused on crisis resolution, controlling the affect, and beginning work on the array of goals developed in Chapter 5. If the revelation of the affair itself was the crisis, it probably triggered anxiety and depression. If the affair was known, whatever stimulus prompted the initiation of therapy destabilized the system such that a process of change was begun. Any time a system is destabilized in that way, it creates some level of crisis for the people involved. The crisis, however, is not a permanent phase for the couple. Generally this phase will pass within the first half dozen sessions. At that point the clients are experiencing more control in their lives and are more optimistic about the future.

The second stage of treatment continues from around *the eighth session through the fifteenth session.* Greater clarity in the definition of the dynamics has yielded continued usefulness in daily life, as patterns unseen early in treatment are identified as being problems and subsequently modified. There is, in effect, another perceptible improvement in the overall level of functioning of the individuals and a corresponding improvement in the level of functioning of the system as a whole. The involved spouse is likely to be more capable of recognizing the implications of the two relationships in her life. The noninvolved spouse has begun to understand the types of emotional pressures he had contributed to the marriage and the types of emotional pressures to which he had reacted negatively from his spouse as well.

Moving On

As the second phase draws to a close, several factors coalesce to propel the treatment into the later stages of therapy. One of the more powerful motivating forces frequently comes in the form of a *regression*. Generally, some gain made early in treatment is suddenly called into question. The most provocative regression comes when the noninvolved spouse discovers either a new involvement, or a renewal of an old involvement by his spouse. This is upsetting anytime it happens, but is even more upsetting when there had been some type of promise from the involved spouse earlier in the treatment to quit the relationship. The "promise" is then exposed as empty rhetoric that probably was never acted on.

The regression does not need to be limited to the involved spouse. At this stage of the therapy, the eruption of some type of symptoms in either the noninvolved spouse, or perhaps even the children, is quite possible. The noninvolved spouse is particularly vulnerable to depression, which frequently manifests itself at this stage of treatment. The symptoms common in the children can include oppositional behavior at home and school, and other types of disruptive behavior.

A second factor that pushes the therapy into the later stages at this point can only artificially be separated from the question of regression. It is at this point in the process that a new awareness of the dynamics engenders a new level of respect for the pervasiveness and depth of the problems and for the necessity of change. It is at this point that the subtleties of the problems of intimacy, and the pertinence to the level of differentiation in the family, begin to emerge. In other words, the couple becomes aware of the serious lack of intimacy, and corresponding emptiness, in their relationship.

Demands on the Therapist

The technical demands on the therapist, in the form of conducting the session, and the personal demands, in the form of being aware of personal reactions to the therapeutic process and content, become increasingly complex in the later stages of long-term intensive therapy. There is a continuation of the possibility of reactions based on the therapist's personal experience with affairs, as was discussed in Chapter 5. But in the same way that affairs become decentralized in the therapy, so too does the therapist's personal experience with affairs become decentralized as a factor of his reactions in the therapy.

The basic questions about connectedness in families, including intimacy, separation, and differentiation cannot help but strike a chord in the therapist. As the couple explores the meaning, repercussions, and possibilities of these areas in their lives, it is impossible for the therapist to avoid resonating to the relevance in his own life. This resonance can be conscious, controlled, and perhaps helpful to the therapy, or it can be unconscious and operate in ways that retard and disrupt the therapy.

The common wisdom suggests some type of process designed to increase the level of awareness of the therapist's own individual and family patterns and emotional agendas. This has been articulated in the family therapy community as becoming more aware of patterns from the therapist's family of origin. The psychoanalytic community addresses the issue with a standard training analysis. The family therapy community has been divided in opinion as to whether a "training therapy" is necessary and how it would be done. It is clear, however, that some effort to develop this type of awareness will make the therapist more effective—and probably more relaxed.

The Therapist's Current Life Circumstances

The crisis intervention stage of therapy is emotionally easier on the therapist. On a very human level, helping others out of a crisis is a pursuit that does not expose the *self* of the therapist in the same way as it is exposed in a long-term relationship. Certainly there is some personal involvement, but the emotionality in the system, and the general upset with the clients at the outset of therapy, greatly overshadows the nuances of the personality of the therapist. The crisis resolution phase of the therapy is such that there probably are far more similarities than differences between one therapist's work and another's, even if they pledge allegiance to different schools and belief systems.

This commonality is less likely in the working stages of long-term intensive therapy. As suggested above, patterns from the therapist's family of origin will have a considerable impact on the therapist and thus on the therapy. Patterns that relate to the therapist's current life situation will impact the therapy as well. To pass these off as less meaningful than the influences of the family of origin is a mistake. The types of therapist life circumstances that have an impact on the therapy range from the profound questions of marriage, divorce, death, and sexual orientation, to the mundane and almost invisible patterns of daily life. Included here would be patterns such as work and career balances in the therapist's primary relationship, power distribution in the relationship, parenting styles, and so on.

As therapy continues over a long period of time, these questions inevitably confront the therapist. Whether they are denied or acknowledged, they will influence the course of therapy. The logical conclusion would be to advocate more therapy for the therapist for purposes of examining the interaction of his current life and therapy. Although this can have a helpful impact in certain situations, it also creates yet another step in the process. In other words, there now exists the question of how the therapist's therapy is influencing the therapy the therapist delivers. It can begin to look like a dog chasing its own tail. At some point in the chain, the therapist needs to assume an independence, maturity, and self-critical awareness as a personal basis for the long-term intensive therapy.

Confidence and Humility

Both spouses recovering from the crisis of the affair are vulnerable to feeling a severe lack of confidence. Despite growing sophistication and understanding about systems, the blame/guilt thread is so deeply ingrained that most people carry it with them and experience a corresponding lack of confidence. The involved spouse may lack the confidence that she can live without engaging in another extramarital relationship, or lack the confidence that her spouse is going to be receptive, forgiving, and sensitive to her needs. The noninvolved spouse may lack the confidence that he can fulfill her needs and lack the confidence that she will continue to be faithful.

The therapist will need a level of personal confidence that is able to fortify his belief in himself and the process of change. This, of course, is fairly standard for any therapeutic endeavor. And in this way, the treatment of affairs is standard psychotherapeutic practice. There is a demand for a confidence that the therapist, by way of knowledge about emotional system functioning, by way of therapeutic instigations, and by way of the therapeutic relationship, has a major but at times undefinable impact on the process of healing.

There is a demand for a level of confidence that a connection with the family is possible without the therapist being "swallowed-up" in a type of unhealthy emotional fusion with the family as he establishes a healthy level of intimacy and rapport. The fear that too much contact with the family will render the therapist powerless and undifferentiated from the family must be confronted and overcome. If the therapist, as an outsider, is unable to stay unhooked from the emotionality of the system, it is difficult to expect the clients in the system to do as much.

There is, on the other hand, a demand for humility. Part of the humility will accompany the realization that any one therapeutic instigation has but a minimal impact on the overall process of change. This is the reverse perception of the temporary feelings of power that accompany the "perfect" intervention of the early stages of therapy. The possibility of a lack of a helpful degree of humility is not limited to any one category of therapists. Where the junior therapists fall prey to an understandable desire to overcome feelings of inexperience related insecurity, senior therapists can fall prey to a need to believe their many years of experience have honed their skills to such a degree that each sentence they utter is impeccably perceptive and powerful.

A sober, honest appraisal of the therapeutic process, and the process of change, challenges most claims to therapeutic wizardry. Change inevitably happens in a context of so many variables that it is unlikely that one simple factor can be isolated as being *the* cause of the change. Indeed, for a systemically oriented therapist to profess that one single intervention was accountable for a therapeutic success directly defies the very systemic theoretical foundation of the intervention. It harkens back to a level of linear causality that supposedly has been abandoned in systemic thinking.

Therapist Errors in Long-Term Therapy

The humble acceptance of the basic powerlessness of any one statement or intervention does fit nicely with one other major consideration for long-term therapy. It is quite impossible to conduct long-term intensive therapy, with its never-ending parade of unanticipated situations, and avoid making an occasional mistake. Sometimes the mistake has to do with unresolved personal agendas, as was mentioned previously. Sometimes it might be an error in judgment, and sometimes it might be more benign and is related to fatigue or some other situational distraction. These situations demand a humble acceptance of the humanity of the therapist and a creative ability to fashion a potential for learning and a potential for furthering the

healing process in spite of the mistake. The healing process continues
in the sense that all of the parties involved, the therapist as well as the
couple, have the potential and the opportunity to learn and grow.

Clients can be quite forgiving, and can learn a new level of
acceptance of their own imperfections, when they have the opportunity to see the therapist realize, admit to, and recover from a mistake.
Even if the learning does not extend to that level of awareness by the
client, the therapist who is able to modestly accept the lack of power in
"good" interventions, will be able to appreciate the corresponding
lack of power in not-so-good interventions. It is unlikely that occasional minor mistakes by the therapist are going to impede the healing process seriously.

It must be acknowledged that the entire concept of therapist
error is one that is likely to be inflammatory and controversial within the community of mental health professionals. This is partially
related to the rash of malpractice litigation and the resulting insurance premiums. It has been fueled by the grievous problems of
sexual contact between therapists and clients, which is increasingly
in the news. And it is inevitably related to a natural desire to command the respect of clients and colleagues and to offer high quality
service.

The types of errors that are going to be the most common in
responsible long-term therapy are going to be of a rather insignificant
order, compared to such problems as sexual contact between therapist and client. They are going to include scheduling errors and other
mechanical problems, perhaps with billing. They are also going to
include problems related to the therapist's level of concentration at
any given time. There will be times when the therapist's concentration
wanes, and facts may be missed that will be needed later. It is this level
of human error on the therapist's part that is not only inevitable, but
can be useful in the overall course of the treatment, if the therapist
can acknowledge it and use it well.

Systemic Vicissitudes in the Later Stages

A less pompous title for this section could be "Who has the ball in
his court?" There are three primary loci of change that are co-
evolving as the therapy continues—each spouse as an individual, and
the couple as a unit. The children, extended family, and the social

network are more peripheral to this process. Looking exclusively at the two spouses and the marriage, the change that is developing in one is meshing with whatever change is developing in the other two. But it is not a symmetrical or predictable rate of change. Both people are changing in different ways, at different times, and at different rates of speed. Speed of change is rather impossible to measure, but it can be initially considered in terms of some quantity of change over a certain period of time.

There are times throughout the therapy, but more so in the later stages, when one person's behavior or emotional posture is "more of a problem" than the other's. When one person's behavior or emotional posture *is* more of a problem than the other's, the "ball is in his court." In other words, some type of change is necessary from them before further progress can be made with the couple. This is *not* meant to challenge the assumption of a systemic interplay, and it is *not* meant to propose the reintroduction of linear causality. It is, instead, a report of the process of long-term change and the pattern of interaction of individual change in the couple.

The ball looks different in different courts at different times. Sometimes this can come in the form of the involved spouse saying one thing and doing the opposite. For example, she could give some indication that she wanted to develop the marriage after she terminated the outside relationship and then proceed to distance by way of some type of activity outside the home such as work. The marriage can't be developed if she is hiding outside the home. Sometimes this can come in the form of the noninvolved spouse increasing the level of distance in the relationship by way of pushing the other away with emotional demands. Although he may be well intentioned, the emotional force of the demands creates problems in the relationship. In either case, it will be necessary for one person to make an emotional shift before the other one is capable of responding.

In the early stages of therapy, even the most feeble systemic assessment of dynamics in a relationship will identify areas of change necessary in both of the individuals. And furthermore, it is rarely critical which change is made in which order, since it is quite possible to have simultaneous change. For example, if the noninvolved spouse is unable to put a damper on her need to pursue in the middle of the initial crisis, the involved spouse may still be able to focus on the personal meaning of the extramarital relationship, which would effectively continue the process of change in the couple. In the early stages of therapy, if the change is not simultaneous, the ripple effect of any change destabilizes the system sufficiently to stimulate a beginning of the process of change.

The Point of Necessary Change

While the initial change in the therapeutic process will precipitate some change in both people, that process will eventually stop. In one way, the image of a train becoming derailed comes to mind. Sometimes it can feel like the journey of the therapy has slowed to a halt. The difference being emphasized here is that the process sometimes stops because one person is resistant, rather than stopping because the vehicle is broken down. The metaphor of the ball being in one person's court suggests that that person needs to take action before the action can continue. When this happens, the other necessarily waits for the move.

One of the classic examples of this phenomenon is an affair. The affair has at times been defined as a flagrant problem that barred any further progress in the relationship. The classic therapeutic intervention based on that assumption was to refuse any treatment until the affair was terminated. Although the notion of pressuring one point of change in order to free up other possibilities for change is valuable, a stronger conceptual model is needed to provide a basis for the decisions.

Individual Vulnerabilities and the Multiple Levels of Systems

This point of derailment can be traced to the intersection of two different variables, the specific vulnerabilities of the individual and the multiple levels of experience in the emotional system. The multiple levels of the system can begin to be identified formally with the integrated model of Chapter 1. Since it is designed to be economical in form, it is by nature limited in the concepts it names and can easily be augmented. Whether this is done with concepts from other models, or common sense concepts from daily life, there is ample room for elaboration. Ideas such as career roles, daily biorhythms, and sexual/physical needs can be appropriately fit into an expanded model of the emotional system.

The level of trust, rapport, intimacy, and overall fit between two people in a relationship will be a culmination of their respective definition of self as well as the resulting negotiations and perceptions on all of these various dimensions of the system (Figure 7.1).

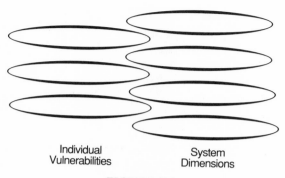

Individual   System
Vulnerabilities   Dimensions

FIGURE 7.1

These negotiations will be profoundly influenced by each partner's individual sense of vulnerability in the various dimensions. This sense of vulnerability is not some abstract intellectualization, it has continuous impact on daily life. For example, while one spouse may wish to engage in love-making two or three times each week, the other spouse may have complicated feelings about sex related to traumatic childhood memories, and may be reluctant to engage in sex at all. The effect of this is to lower drastically the frequency of contact.

Whereas one spouse may have very strong ties to his family of origin, and wish to have considerable contact with them, the other spouse may have a more distant relationship with her family of origin. That person, in turn, may see the corresponding time spent by the other as an infringement on time spent as a couple. Where one spouse may have a desire or need to discuss feelings, daily events, and a wide range of business pertinent to the couple, the other spouse may be unskilled in verbal communication or may be frightened to address many of those issues on a conscious and verbal level.

The interaction of individual vulnerabilities with the multiple levels of systems culminates in an emotional balance in which each person has certain strengths and certain weaknesses. For example, although one person may spend a disproportionate amount of time with her family of origin, and truly detract from the time spent with the spouse, she may be more adept at communication during the time actually spent with the spouse. A second example would be the person who is comfortable communicating sexually but uncomfortable and inadequate with verbal communication.

As the need for change in various areas becomes more clear in the later stages of long-term intensive therapy, the strengths and weaknesses of each individual will become more clear as well. Although there will be reason to see potential for change in both people, they won't be able to respond equally. In any given situation, the person with a higher level of vulnerability, leading to less strength, will be less able to respond. That person will be more of a problem and will be the person who has the ball in his court.

The systemic perspective is maintained with the understanding that is founded on the broader view of the relationship. Neither person is totally responsible for the function/dysfunction of the relationship, but either may be more responsible for certain areas, or at certain times in the process of change.

More than Just a Friend

One of the more interesting and ambiguous examples of this concept, as it relates to the later stages of therapy with affairs, has to do with relationships outside of the marriage. The affair was a relationship that detracted from and threatened the marriage. Generally, both spouses agree on this point. They may not agree, however, on what type of relationships outside the marriage are appropriate.

Frequently, the noninvolved spouse will be reactive to any relationships the spouse has outside the marriage. Although some of that reactivity could understandably relate to a fear of reinvolvement, many couples report that this reactivity existed prior to the affair and was one of the points of contention in the relationship. The involved spouse felt overly constricted, and the noninvolved spouse was behaving in an overly possessive style. Observed from this perspective, the need for the noninvolved spouse to understand and perhaps diminish the reactivity to other relationships can be explored in the therapy.

There are, however, two points pertinent to the involved spouse that offset this vulnerability in the noninvolved spouse. First, the involved spouse has demonstrated a capacity for developing outside relationships to a point of danger for the marriage, thus validating the other's original concerns. And second, the involved spouse is frequently unable to establish a level of intimacy, and an atmosphere of trust and rapport in the marriage, which would help to create security in the face of the other relationships.

This provides an interesting and delicate example of which ball is in which court at which time. The noninvolved spouse has an unhelpfully low threshold of fear of outside relationships. The involved spouse has a capacity for letting outside relationships become more than just friends, and a corresponding tendency to avoid intimacy in the marriage. Both people need to explore the meaning of their own individual contribution. It is not enough for the noninvolved spouse to accuse the involved spouse, or vice versa.

Two clinical examples can help demonstrate this point. Ed and Laura had begun therapy after Laura had confessed to an affair with a co-worker. Approximately six months after the affair, they attended a party where Laura was busy dancing most of the evening with several different men. After the party, Ed expressed his considerable displeasure with Laura's "flirtatious" behavior. He admitted that he was not interested in dancing as much as Laura was, but he was uncomfortable with her behavior.

Exploration of the event with Ed led to more ambiguity. He suggested that he might not be as reactive to Laura's dancing if he believed that she was giving a clear message of a lack of availability to the other men. Laura, in the meantime, maintained that Ed needed to be more relaxed and less threatened by her innocent fun with other men. She emphasized her need for a greater sense of freedom in the marriage.

Al and Cathy offer a more complicated example. They entered therapy after Cathy discovered Al's involvement with one of his employees. Although that affair had been over for more than a year, the couple remained in therapy to work on a basic lack of intimacy in their marriage. Al spent much time at work, and although the woman whom he had been involved with left the company, the time away from Cathy still created problems. Cathy, as part of her contribution to the lack of intimacy, was significantly disinterested in sex.

In addition to the sexual problems and general problems with intimacy, the question of their respective relationships with other people was a bone of contention between them. Al contended that Cathy was against his having any relationships with any other women. He offered as an example an episode in which he was traveling with Cathy in a distant city. They coincidentally encountered a woman that Al knew through his business. Although Al said that he was simply cordial to the other woman, Cathy became noticeably jealous. Another time, Cathy became enraged when she discovered that Al had gone out for dinner with another woman associate. It was later discovered that Al had indeed developed that relationship into yet another affair, although the sexual involvement did not come with that first dinner to which Cathy had reacted; it came later.

The Motivated Partner

One of the fundamental strategies Bowen developed for changing a system was to work with the motivated partner. This meant that his therapeutic energy would be focused on the person who was most motivated to work in the therapy. The strength of the assumption could be seen when one partner refused to come into treatment, and the therapy continued with the partner who was willing to come. The assumption was that any change would precipitate other change, thus creating a new balance for the overall system.

The previous examination of the interface of individual vulnerabilities with the overall system raises questions about the limits of that strategy. It is highly likely that each person will be most motivated to change in areas that are less threatening, because of a different level of personal vulnerability. Both Al and Cathy were motivated, as were Ed and Laura. But each person was motivated to do different things, in different ways. And both viewpoints had some validity.

Implications for Therapy

The model that evolves from the concept of individual vulnerabilities and a "ball in one person's court" has conceptual implications and operational implications for the therapist. On the conceptual level, it refines the notion of systemic interplay and alters any suggestion of total symmetry in the system. Looking specifically at the topic at hand, whereas an affair may represent a need for distance in both members of a couple, it may not represent the perfect solution for both partners. It may provide distance in ways that are more suitable to the involved spouse than the noninvolved spouse. Conversely, where one partner may be receptive to intimacy and mutual involvement in decision making, the other may be more receptive to sexual intimacy. The symmetry of the system can be seen in the overall level of differentiation of the partner.

As was noted earlier, Bowen (1978) postulated that people choose spouses of equal levels of differentiation. If this is understood as choosing a partner with a basically similar level of reactivity to the dynamics of emotional connectedness in a family system, rather than totally identical vulnerabilities, the symmetry of the needs in the system can be seen as operating at the level of emotional reactivity rather than at the level of specific daily needs.

This refinement also suggests a new conceptual perspective on the notion of resistance to change in the system. The resistance to change comes from the person who is most threatened by the specific dimension of connectedness that is being provoked. Since each individual has a slightly different set of vulnerabilities, each individual will, in turn, be the more resistant partner at various points in the therapy.

This somewhat dry conceptual point is more than intricate theoretical footwork. It has profound clinical implications. In the later stages of therapy, the therapist is going to be more often in the position of "agreeing with" one spouse about the problems of the other. Not only will it be necessary to agree, but it will be necessary to address the identified problems in the therapy.

This can become a juggling act, attending to two different positions with two different people. With Al and Cathy, for example, Al was willing to address the problems of reactivity to outside relationships. He could see clearly that Cathy's reaction to his encounter with his business colleague was inappropriate and was anxious to discuss it as "a problem." But he was less capable, and even somewhat unwilling, to address the problems of a lack of intimacy in the marriage. Cathy, on the other hand, was anxious to discuss the problem of outside relationships becoming too close and was reluctant to see her reactivity to a chance encounter as being anything other than justified indignation at Al's behavior.

This type of situation occurs continually in the later stages of intensive, long-term treatment. Each person will be identifying problems in the other that are legitimate problems and need to be changed. It places difficult demands on the therapist to make clinical judgments and to maintain a focus on the multiple layers of experience. Clinical strategy, again subject to improvisational modification, would be based on:

1. Agreeing with each person when she accurately identifies areas of vulnerability in the other. This must be done in a way that validates the initial perception, but doesn't diminish the other;
2. Refocusing the person who made the observation on her own areas of vulnerability, which are probably different.

3. Watching for opportune moments to address the specific areas of vulnerability with the appropriate person.

This maneuver is best accomplished without confronting one partner with the wisdom of the other. Both people inevitably offer some discussion in the therapy that reveals their own vulnerabilities. They can be focused on those deficiencies quite easily by way of their own reports rather than by way of the spouse's reports of their problems. This tack also diminishes the potential for opportunistic attacks in the therapy. If one partner is allowed to "prove" that the other is wrong, this can set up an unhealthy competition in the therapy.

The element of clinical judgment cannot be overestimated in this process. The question that will need to be answered time and again will be, whose vulnerabilities are more basic to the resistance? Does one person need to change before the other can change? If one person refuses to change, are there other dimensions of the system that can be focused on to further the process, and perhaps make the point of resistance more accessible? The specific answer to these questions will be a function of the individual style of the therapist. The broad answer to the question will reflect the treatment goals in the later stages of the therapy.

TREATMENT GOALS

Treatment goals in the later stages of therapy are by their nature vague. Generally, they become an amalgam of the various points developed throughout the book. They are further confused by the structure of combined joint and individual meetings. Over time, the continuation of this structure leads to a powerful intermingling of what is "individual business," and what is "couple business." This intermingling really reflects the integration of these two dimensions in everyday life, and it can assist in a healthy integration of these two levels of experience in the couple.

Although specific goals become vague in the later stages of therapy, there are a number of themes that are prevalent in the treatment of affairs. These themes can be pursued in both the couple sessions and the individual sessions, and they can be developed into specific therapeutic strategies and focal points. The themes to be expected are:

Length of Time in Therapy; Length of Time Needed for Healing

There are concerns that change is taking too long and that there may never be any real, permanent change. Sometimes this theme emerges around the 10th month of therapy, soon after the commitment to long-term therapy has been made and in the time after the second burst of change has been integrated into the system. There may be a plateau evident in the process of change, or there may even be some form of regression. Either of these can stimulate feelings of fatigue, discouragement, fear, and defeat.

Anniversaries also trigger these types of fears. The anniversary of the initiation of therapy, anniversaries of deaths, of the marriage, and so on, all serve as benchmarks in life that naturally call into question the *status quo* and the ideal goals. The therapeutic responses to this theme as it unfolds are to provide support by validating the feelings of discouragement, offer encouragement by providing perspective on the length of time needed to resolve difficult problems, and begin to explore the meaning of the situation that stimulated the feelings and the corresponding thoughts about the length of time in therapy. This leads to a cognitive understanding of the dynamics of the problem, which is the second major theme that can be expected in the later stages of therapy.

Systemic Interpretations

The goal of making the couple experts in their own emotional system continues throughout the therapy. Sometimes this entails an exploration of the particular problem that has arisen, but this will be most helpful if it is developed into a broader look at the abstract dynamics at work. The broad systems forces such as distancing, definition of self, multigenerational patterns, and other dimensions of the integrated model provide the structure for the interpretations.

The Use of Daily Events

Early in the therapy, it is quite likely that each partner will come to sessions and want to address different agenda items. This is partial-

ly related to the fact that early in treatment there are many issues that
need to be addressed and partially related to differences in perception. What one person sees as being critical, the other person sees as
being insignificant and may have even forgotten. As sophistication in
therapy develops, both people will begin to recognize the critical
events and be able to distinguish them from the incidental events. As
this happens, both people are more likely to come to sessions with
intentions of addressing the same, critical incidents.

These critical incidents, which have developed since the previous
session, can be used to enhance the understanding of the dynamics
relevant to the couple. For example, a solid appreciation of the
significance of the themes of distancing and pursuing to such "insignificant" events such as a chance encounter with a friend in a
distant city, as happened with Al and Cathy, establishes a clear and
usable link between everyday life and fundamental dynamics. Clients,
like therapists, need reassurance that there is a link between theory
and practice. The practice, of course, is not the practice of psychotherapy, but the practice of living.

Daily events can be used in a proactive as well as a reactive
fashion. The reactive use of daily events is in the analysis of events
that already happened prior to the session. The proactive use of daily
events comes in the form of instigations for behavior and exchanges
between the couple as developed in Chapter 4 on technique. The
basic approach links theory and practice. Homework assignments are
developed that put pressure on the dynamic balance in the relationship. Usually the homework does not become a permanent solution
for the couple to incorporate into their lives, but it can accent dynamics in a way that prompts a shift.

Continued Exploration of Themes Discovered Early in Therapy

A woman client once made this observation about the process of
long-term intensive therapy:

> "The therapist made things happen by asking questions. Some were
> so tricky and came so fast, in answering I felt as if I were trying to
> keep my footing in a log jam. Others required reflection. After
> attending the sessions many hours, I realized many questions were

repetitious. It was as if I were climbing a spiral stairway inside a lighthouse, and being told to look out at the same seascape each time I passed a seaward window. I was surveying the same thing over and over, but each time from a slightly different perspective. The view from the top was worth the climb."

This metaphor is so lovely that it belies the difficult work involved in the process. All of the dynamic issues identified early in the therapy, as well as themes unearthed later in the process, will be found in different images, conflicts, and concerns in the later stages of therapy. The familiarity of the themes leads to a lower frequency of new, profound, and invigorating insights. Indeed, there are times when the material is so redundant that it becomes tedious. The work will be most effective, however, if the burdensome nature can be reshaped into ideas and feelings that are more interesting and compelling. Attention will be focused on variations and permutations of the basic themes, as well as how various themes interact.

Use of Self of the Therapist

Although the deepening of the relationship through long-term intensive therapy does not necessarily neutralize the therapist's effectiveness, it does suggest the need for an ongoing process of self-evaluation and scrutiny. The familiarity and congeniality that can develop between therapist and clients in the couple sessions combine with the one-to-one intimacy of the individual sessions, and they put the therapist in the position of being known by the clients more fully than he might in other treatment models. This can be very powerful and beneficial, if the therapist is able to acknowledge and use his own humanity in a way that is beneficial to the healing process.

The therapist will need to consider the usual questions about which interventions are the most appropriate for himself and the client, but he will also need to consider a personally comfortable approach to addressing topics that may not be strictly related to the therapy. These topics can include birthdays, holidays, and other celebrations. Obviously these topics can be presented in a way that demands therapeutic attention, but it is also possible that they simply can be acknowledged in a more casual way.

TERMINATION

The conclusion of long-term therapy usually comes on the heels of a gradual slowdown of the work and is not a sudden and radical change. The primary indication for termination will be a perception, usually shared by therapist and clients, that the functioning of both of the individuals separately and together is stable and satisfying. This can include the expectation that there will be occasional conflict that will be productively resolved as well as occasional individual problems that will not seriously impair the functioning of the individual or couple.

Lest these ideas sound like a series of platitudes to be packed away with motherhood and apple pie, it should be understood that subjective feelings about the likelihood of this course are the rule rather than the exception. Prior to termination, clients regularly report feelings of satisfaction but uncertainty. This usually comes in the form of an unsolicited comment that many of the complaints that had brought them to therapy are noticeably changed for the better, but there is a nagging sense of distrust and a desire to continue therapy a while longer. When the couple reaches the point of confidence in their mutual ability to continue without therapy, it is time for termination.

There are, as usual, complexities to consider. One of the most common fears in the treatment of affairs is the possibility of another extramarital involvement. If the therapy has continued long enough to allow for an in-depth exploration of the dynamic significance of the affair, there usually is a strong belief in the spouse originally involved in the affair that the usefulness of an outside relationship as an emotional solution is gone. It is seen as an unhealthy solution to a series of individual and system problems that are now understood and solved in other ways.

At the conclusion of treatment, neither the involved nor the noninvolved spouse is able to derive the same emotional benefits from an extramarital affair as were gained prior to therapy. The potential, therefore, of another affair is drastically reduced, and probably eliminated.

If, on the other hand, the couple decides to terminate therapy after the initial crisis has been quelled, but before any fundamental change and understanding has been developed, the chance of another involvement is higher.

The concept of termination in marriage and family therapy, and this model in particular, is quite relaxed. Even in situations marked by agreement between therapist and clients that termination is appropriate, there is the anticipation of the possibility of future contact with the therapist, in the event of unforeseen crises. Although this "open-door policy" could be challenged as an ambiguous separation between client and therapist, it can also be understood as a more humanistic approach to the usefulness of the therapeutic relationship over extended time.

The element of clinical judgment again steps forward as the critical factor. If the therapist and/or client is unable to terminate and uses the open-door policy as a way of maintaining a nonproductive pseudotherapeutic relationship, there is a problem that needs to be understood and resolved. The most productive use of the open-door policy will be seen when the boundaries are clear, the relationship has been helpful, and there is a reasonable desire to contract for a termination.

CHAPTER 8

Fred and Marie:
Long-Term Therapy

This saga of Fred and Marie is developed in the same mold as the story of Allen and Elaine. It presents a fictional but typical course of treatment. It will be different in that much of the therapy will be viewed through a wide-angle lens rather than a high-power lens with a narrow field of vision. Like life itself, long-term therapy is not a continuous "highlight film." Intrinsic to long-term therapy is the potential to be preoccupied with the unending minutiae of life. Much of the work is redundant and occasionally even dull. In the way that the therapist needs to cull the material presented by the client, so too will this vignette sift through the course of therapy and present a general flow of the work rather than a step-by-step account.

Fred and Marie are "therapy veterans." They had been in therapy individually and together prior to commencing work with me. It is possible that they remained with me rather than leaving for another therapist because there was a better "fit" between me and them. Or perhaps if they had seen me first, they would have left me for another therapist. It is possible that they had come to realize by the time that we had begun working together that the problems that needed to be worked out were within and between themselves. That speculation focuses on the process of healing in the individuals and the system rather than on the notion of a particular fit between therapist and clients.

This type of therapy is not undertaken with the goal of saving the marriage. The client's high level of ambivalence regarding that idea, which has been developed several times previously, makes that an

212

inappropriate therapeutic goal. The most effective tack is to explore the emotional chaos created within and between the individuals resulting from the structure of a triangled-in outsider. The assumption is, then, that resolving the need for that structure will be the most viable and effective goal.

The Opening Moves

Fred and Marie were referred by their family physician. They had been in therapy with another therapist and were dissatisfied with the progress they were making. Fred made the call to me and said that they were interested in a consultation. He indicated that, because of their previous experience, they were somewhat skeptical of the efficacy of therapy. That skepticism, however, was overshadowed by the tension and strife created by Marie's recent discovery of Fred's involvement with another woman. They needed help. Our initial contract for meeting was with the understanding that it would be for assessment and consultation.

> *The first meeting was typical of many clients in that situation. They described the problems in language that was a mixture of words and ideas from their first therapy, concepts from popular books they had read, and their own personal ideas about the problem. But, simultaneously, they gave poignant and convincing accounts of the continued problems between them and their feelings of frustration and bewilderment about being unable to change the situation.*

My initial agenda was twofold. Along with getting an initial sense of their personal history, and the evolution of the problem, I was equally interested in their previous history in therapy. This included what they had learned, what had changed, what had not changed, what had been satisfactory, and what had been unsatisfactory.

> *The point that both of them made most strongly was that their previous therapist simply did not talk enough and did not help them figure out what was happening to them. They described session after session in which the therapist said little more than "and how do you feel about that?" and then went on to encourage them to talk to each other. Their impression was that the sessions deteriorated into free-for-all ventilation sessions,*

with them feeling worse after the sessions than before. After relaying this
experience to me, they went on to say that they had informed that therapist
that they were not interested in continuing the work with him, and then
asked me if I would be willing to work with them in therapy.

The question in my mind, of course, was whether they were
genuinely looking for a different type of therapeutic experience, or
whether they were bolting from an adequate therapeutic experience,
and would eventually do the same when I challenged them later in
therapy. I posed just that question to them, following my usual guide-
line of open communication with my clients. Being the "knowledge-
able consumers" of therapy that they were, both acknowledged my
concern, indicated that they had discussed it with each other and the
other therapist, and had concluded that there simply was insufficient
structure in the other therapy. Indeed, they would welcome being
challenged, and it wasn't happening in that work.

They had seen the other therapist for about ten months, and
their dissatisfaction with the process had been growing for the last
four of those months. In fact, it had been a regular topic of the
therapy during the final two months and had culminated in Fred's
contact with his physician asking for a recommendation to another
therapist. I had heard Fred and Marie's experience from numerous
other couples and had appreciated their need to try something different, so I agreed to continue to work with them.

If there had been any interpretations about dynamics made in
their first therapy, Fred and Marie had not heard them in a way that
prompted them to understand themselves differently and try different behaviors. The primary insight centered around their mutual
awareness of Fred's inability to express his feelings to Marie. They
understood that to mean that they needed to talk more than they had
in the past.

The question of Fred's extramarital involvement had prompted
them to begin therapy in the first place, and Marie's recent discovery
of the continuation of that relationship had triggered another crisis
between them. Neither one of them had any solid ideas about the
meaning of the affair, or the dynamics that may have contributed to
its evolution. Marie had taken to a strategy of demanding that Fred be
home promptly after work, account for his whereabouts when he left
home, and talk to her on a frequent basis when they were home
together. Fred, on the other hand, was looking and acting confused

and depressed. He talked about his desire to remain in the marriage and his confusion about his attachment to Margaret, his lover.

A Brief Family History

Fred and Marie were both thirty-eight years old and had been married for sixteen years at the outset of our work together. They had been college sweethearts, marrying soon after finishing their undergraduate degrees. Fred had continued on to graduate school in business after they were married, and Marie went to work as an elementary school teacher. Their oldest child, Jennifer, was now twelve. She had been born shortly after Fred had finished graduate school and had begun working. Andrew, nine years old, was the middle child, and Elizabeth, at seven, was the youngest.

Fred was the younger of two children. His sister, Beth, was three years his senior. His father was still alive and well at seventy years of age, and his mother had died six years earlier at the age of sixty-five. Marie was the older of two girls. Her sister, Barbara, was four years younger. Her father, also, was alive, though in failing health, at the age of sixty-seven. Marie's mother had died three years earlier, at the age of sixty-two (Figure 8.1).

Fred and Marie had, in many ways, a history that was very successful. After beginning his career with a big corporation, Fred went on to start his own business with a partner. That partnership proved to be very successful. Marie had begun the marriage working as a teacher but had discontinued that when the children were born,

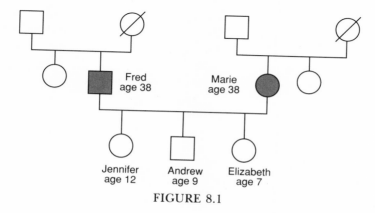

FIGURE 8.1

and she had not worked out of the home since then. The relationship, over the years, had been relatively free of conflict, though Marie remembered recurring feelings of jealousy when she would sense that Fred was showing interest in some other woman. She had first felt this when they were in college, and Fred had shown interest in her roommate. Over the years, she would occasionally wonder whether Fred was involved with another woman, since he was away so much, but she would usually dismiss this possibility.

Fred recalled the early years being characterized by his sense of obligation to Marie. He had been shy in college and had depended on Marie to keep him socially involved. After they were married, he experienced a serious depression, and he had relied on Marie even more for support and reassurance. He admitted that he had been involved with another woman near the end of that depression. He believed that he had needed that involvement at that time to help pull him out of the depression.

The four years preceding therapy had been characterized by Fred avoiding Marie, ostensibly because of work pressures. This was now acknowledged to be a function of his involvement outside the marriage and of his desire to avoid what he saw as Marie's controlling manner. Although he had needed Marie's support when he was recovering from his depression, he had come to feel a need to be more independent from her. He had never been able to express that need to her.

Marie, meanwhile, was only partially satisfied with her life. Since she had stopped teaching, she felt a chronic emptiness. She had enjoyed taking care of the children when they were younger, but now that they were in school, she was aware of a need to have more in her life than she had. She saw the last four years from a very different perspective than did Fred. For her, it seemed that Fred had abandoned her at just the time that she felt a greater need for him. Between the loss of her mother and the house that was left empty with the children off at school, Marie was depressed herself. Like Fred, she had been unable to talk about her feelings.

The Beginning Stages of Work

The early stages of therapy with Fred and Marie were quite similar to the therapy with Allen and Elaine, though the history that was developed by the couple suggested problems that had been much longer in their development than were the problems described by Allen and Elaine. Fred was more dependent on his outside involvement than Elaine had been on hers, and so he was less inclined to discontinue that relationship. He admitted to having had a relationship with Margaret for approximately the last five years. He had met her through his business, although they did not work in the same company. So, even though many of the topics of discussion, and many of the ideas, were similar to the work with Allen and Elaine, even in the early stages of work with Fred and Marie there were hints that this therapy was going to take longer.

In his early individual sessions, Fred tentatively began to develop ideas about his need for his relationship with Margaret. Actually, it would be more accurate to say that Fred gave me ideas about his need for Margaret. He was not ready to understand the ideas or to process them in a way that freed him from the triangle with Marie and Margaret. He talked frequently about his need for independence from Marie and his sense that Margaret depended on him for support in ways he never saw from Marie. He was unable to see Marie's need for support over the past few years. In fact, he relayed a contrasting picture of her as someone who was continuously able to be strong, no matter what problems she encountered.

Another theme that I probed in the early work with Fred was his relationship with his mother. I noticed that he dated his involvement with Margaret to within one year of his mother's death. Fred reported those two events at separate times, with no connection in his own mind. I made the connection and watched for an opportune time to explore it. My hypothesis was that Fred's involvement with Margaret may have been part of an emotional shock wave in the wake of his mother's death.

Understanding his relationship with his mother, and the triangle between Margaret and his mother, was useful in uncovering Fred's perception of his mother as a strong, competent woman in the same mold as Marie. Margaret then stood out as a contrast to both of the other important women in his life. As is typical of the early stages of work, we eventually shifted away from a focus on his mother to other more immediate concerns. I was aware of the shift, but I chose to "file" the subject of his mother under the heading of "needing more work later" and assumed that we would find other opportunities to develop those dynamics.

The early individual sessions with Marie were quite typical of the work needed with the noninvolved spouse. We began to develop ideas about distancing and pursuing in the marriage, and she came to understand that she had been the pursuer in the marriage from very early on in their history. She became quite aware of how she pursued Fred in ways that she had never even considered, and she quickly developed alternative strategies which helped to release her from that position in the relationship.

The Transition to a Long-Term Commitment

By the end of the third month, the therapy had started to develop a routine, with the regular rotation of individual and couple's sessions. And despite the fact that both Fred and Marie seemed to be using the therapy time productively, there was no sense of resolution to the topics that were discussed. The ideas were new to them, and the problems were sufficiently ingrained that palpable changes in day-to-day interactions were minimal.

Since they had come to me because of a dissatisfaction with the progress they saw in their first therapy, I took the time to ask them to assess the work that we had been doing together and their satisfaction with the progress. They both agreed that they were pleased with the focus of the therapy, and although they didn't see the marriage as being the way they would have hoped it would have been by this time, they were beginning to understand how difficult it was going to be to develop it to that point.

The two factors that they saw as being the most critical were trust and communication. Although Fred had recently announced that he had terminated the relationship with Margaret, Marie was unable to believe that he was sincere and able to follow through on his intentions. Fred was rather glib in his insistence that his commitment was secure, which successfully created even more mistrust in Marie.

My reaction to this point was significant. Whereas I didn't feel "mistrust" in the same way that Marie was expressing it, I did share her hunch that Fred's resolve to abandon the relationship with Margaret was weaker than he was proclaiming. I did not, however, challenge him on that point at all in the couple sessions. In the individual sessions, I pressed on the feelings he was experiencing "now that he had left her." I avoided agreeing with Marie in the couple sessions because I believed that Fred would experience that as a collusion between Marie and me, which could alienate him. By exploring potential feelings of loss in the individual sessions, I could further cement my rapport with Fred while simultaneously unearthing emotions that would help clarify the dynamic meaning of his need for a lover. That strategy of relationship building with Fred contributed to his willingness to contract for long-term therapy.

Simultaneously, I was developing a relationship with Marie that would create the opportunity for long-term work. Although she had been more functional than Fred for most of their marriage, she would need to be convinced of the value of continued therapy that was designed to do more than simply get Fred to behave. She needed to be willing to see herself as a full participant and engage in a therapeutic process that would challenge her understanding of herself individually and in the marriage.

> *The opportunity to do this came in the form of the anniversary of her mother's death. Marie mentioned the anniversary in an off-hand manner during one of her individual sessions. Rather than letting the comment slip by unacknowledged, I prompted her to reminisce about her mother. This triggered a flood of tears, so much so that she was unable to talk about her mother. When the tears subsided, Marie quickly pointed out that she felt so lost and that she had assumed that she had been feeling bad about Fred, but now she was wondering whether she was also feeling upset about her mother.*

This brought Marie to a new level of awareness about her unresolved attachment to her mother and the unresolved grief about her death. She didn't understand the nature of these feelings and attachments, but she did understand that they were significant to her. Her desire to understand and resolve these feelings helped solidify her commitment to long-term therapy.

Months Four through Six

This stage of the involvement was turbulent and chaotic for Fred and Marie, and challenging for me. The rollercoaster feeling of the activity was typical of this stage of the work. It began innocently enough, with such basic issues as trust between the two of them and unresolved grief about Marie's mother being the two most obvious areas of work. Marie's powerful feelings of loss had subsided, although the memory was powerful enough that she still knew she needed to explore that relationship more thoroughly. Fred was functioning well at work and was focusing in the therapy on his need to communicate with Marie. All things considered, the general level of anxiety in both of them seemed relatively low, and daily life seemed more relaxed than it had been for quite some time. Despite the peacefulness, however, both of them expressed concern that life was not totally secure between them, and they had no desire whatsoever to discontinue therapy.

> *My strategy during this peaceful time was to make use of the low level of anxiety to prompt them to look at the many mundane and "insignificant" exchanges in their relationship that contribute to the overall level of intimacy and balance of power in the relationship. The question of money came up in the form of Fred's realization that he had misgivings about the way Marie spent money. In a familiar fashion, Fred had managed to "ignore" his misgivings about her spending habits throughout the marriage. As he became more attuned to the impact of differences between them, he began to let himself recognize longstanding problems such as money. Marie had come to understand the importance of being able to know and appreciate Fred's opinions about their relationship, and as a result, she was quite willing to listen to his ideas about money.*

Money is not a topic that can be thoroughly developed, let alone resolved, in one sitting. The pervasive impact and intricate nuances possible on both the concrete and the symbolic level offer fertile ground for many hours of discussion. Fred and Marie began by articulating their individual impressions of the various types of decisions each of them made. The initial difference in perception centered around Fred's belief that Marie made more decisions regarding the allocation of money than he did. Marie, conversely, was sure that she deferred to Fred most of the time.

The first foray into the topic of money concluded with no definitive image developed about the place of money between them and certainly no clear shift to a new equilibrium. With such a complicated topic, this type of conclusion is more the rule than the exception. But the luxury of long-term therapy is to be able to take the time to develop a solid, accurate understanding of a topic. When that is done, everyone involved can usually arrive at new possibilities for solutions.

Replaying an Old Tune

Further work on the money topic was not destined for this point in the therapy. Marie came to the next couple session with a grim, angry expression on her face. She announced that in the past week she had been told by a friend that she, the friend, had seen Fred out at a restaurant with Margaret. Fred's expression was a combination of sheepish regret and exasperation. Marie went on to say that although she was angry and upset, she really had absolutely no idea as to how she should respond and what the incident meant.

At that point I turned to Fred and asked him what meaning he saw in this incident. His initial response was to veer away from the problem of his association with Margaret and focus, instead, on his feelings of being perturbed with "the informer," who was not one of his favorite people. This added fuel only served to lower further his estimation of her.

I deflected his attention away from that element of the story, saying that there were more important concerns to be dealt with at this time, and asked him to look specifically at the question of what this meant for his relationship with Marie. Fred was quite unable to articulate anything sensible. When I asked him to guess about some type of meaning after his initial comment of "I just don't know," he was at a total loss for ideas.

My assumption was that the contact represented a type of distancing on Fred's part. I had no way of knowing whether he had actually been maintaining contact with Margaret during the time when he had "given up" the relationship. But whether it had been maintained or had been renewed, the fact that they chose to meet in a public place where the likelihood of detection was high suggested that Fred was, perhaps unconsciously, willing to risk being seen.

This translated, in my mind, into a bid for more distance between him and Marie. This need for distance, however, was juxtaposed with the recent spell of decreased tension and positive experiences they were enjoying together. I was quite sure that some part of his need to distance was in fact related to the increased closeness. With that formulation, I chose to push the conversation toward "encouraging," or at least validating, the need for the new distance. The entire conversation became a paradoxical intervention, with me asking whether it may be time to acknowledge the need to terminate the marriage, since they had tried long and hard and still there seemed to be a desire to get away from the marriage.

> *Marie responded to this proposition with a facial expression that suggested rather clearly that she was not in favor of that possibility. But I expected that from her. Steadfastly, she had been in favor of repairing the marriage. I prevented her from expressing that desire, however, by holding up my hand with a gesture that asked her not to talk, and simultaneously addressing a more specific question to Fred. I wanted to prevent Marie from jumping into the role of emotional pursuer at that moment.*
>
> *My question to Fred was designed to exacerbate his ambivalence about the fluctuations in distance between them. Specifically, I asked him how he felt about the idea of terminating the marriage. He said he felt very sad about it, and he really would prefer to try to make the marriage work. Marie looked surprised and relieved with that comment, and seemed to sense why I had prevented her from responding earlier.*
>
> *With that acknowledgment of the commitment between them established, I continued along the line of validating the need for distance between them that the incident was suggesting. Again, since their rapport was so fragile, they were more cognizant of the need for more closeness. But there seemed to be emotional dangers to the closeness between them, and these needed to be identified and modified before a safer type of intimacy could be established.*

Fred: Hearing New Sounds in the Old Tune

This theme continued for the remainder of that session and for the next several weeks of the therapy. In his individual sessions, Fred began to develop an understanding of his contact with Margaret from several different perspectives. He became aware of the fact that she had no one else in her life and had become very lonely as he had moved away from her. When he learned that, he felt a need to comfort her. As he explored the meaning of those feelings, he came to realize that his need to be needed was one of the important links in his association with Margaret. He saw Marie as being stronger, and expressing less of a need for him than did Margaret.

I remained aware of both elements of the triangle, with the move toward Margaret being complimented with a move away from Marie, and I focused Fred's attention on that dynamic. This was still more difficult for him to develop, in large part because of his capacity to deny problems between them. When he was unable to offer any ideas about why he might want to distance himself from Marie, I drew on our mutual experience of the history of the sessions and noted that we had been talking about the problem of money in the relationship in the session that had preceded his being discovered in the restaurant. I pointed out how difficult and essentially unresolved that topic was, and wondered if he might have any lingering feelings about the topic.

This type of intervention is common and increasingly useful in the later stages of long-term therapy. All three people, the therapist together with the couple, have a growing body of shared experiences. Patterns emerge in a way that can later be used to establish recognition and eventual modification of those patterns. I did not refer to case notes before or during the session with Fred either to "prepare" that type of comment or to validate it in the session. It was simply a person-to-person recollection of a shared experience that probably held some answers for the question at hand.

> *Fred's response to this line of thinking was positive. He admitted to feeling frustrated after the discussion about money. He noted that he had become aware of other areas in which he felt as if Marie were more powerful than he was, and he had been unable to shift that balance. He mentioned her stronger relationship with their son and her ability to "get her way" on a wide range of household questions such as decorating, and even the style of the family diet.*

This realization surprised and impressed Fred. He admitted that he would not have seen or acknowledged these types of differences earlier. We concluded the session without any further discussion of his relationship with Margaret. I did not want to put myself in the position of his jailkeeper by way of a demand that he refrain from seeing her. I doubted that he would be able to answer reasonably if I asked him if he thought he would see her again. And finally, I believed that the progress he was making in understanding his relationship with Marie would, in the long run, be far more effective in neutralizing that affair.

Marie: Reharmonizing the Old Tune

The focus with Marie through this period was more work on the familiar topic of emotional pursuing, in conjunction with attention to her contribution to the maintenance of distance between them. The work on emotional pursuing was particularly relevant, given Fred's recent episode with Margaret. Marie looked to me for specific advice. How should she handle him, and how should she respond?

In my response to her, I was juggling several different elements. First, I wanted her to understand the systemic implications of the situation as it was evolving. Secondly, I was willing to offer concrete suggestions, as long as there was some dynamic basis for them. And thirdly, I wanted to avoid her attempts to triangle me into a collusion in which she saw the two of us as trying to fix Fred. It was critical to establish and maintain her awareness of her own contribution to the problem.

I began the individual session with Marie reviewing the dynamic of pursuing–distancing by way of a comparison. I asked her to compare how she felt now with how she felt earlier in treatment, when she knew that Fred was involved with Margaret. Specifically, I wanted to know whether she felt inclined to reach out to him and prove that she was the "right" person for him.

The accent on current feelings was ideal for Marie, because she was indeed preoccupied with the thought of more closeness between the two of them. Focusing her attention on those feelings, and having her make the comparison to the earlier months of work, helped her gain distance and perspective on her tendency to pursue.

Moving from her feelings to her behavior, I asked her if she had any ideas about when she may have been "pursuing" Fred over the past week, and what type of behavior went along with that feeling. She responded that she had actually been feeling happier than she had been in a long time, because it seemed that life had returned to a more normal routine. At least it had seemed normal to her until she discovered Fred's continued involvement with Margaret. At that point, she became upset.

"Well, I guess that Fred's involvement with Margaret helps to make life perfectly normal, doesn't it?" I said to her with a grin. With that, she looked at me, and with tears streaming down her face, burst into a grin herself. She confirmed her basic understanding of my paradoxical suggestion by her retort, saying, "I guess it does, doesn't it?"

"Do you think we need to have someone else out there to make life normal for us?" Marie continued.

I chose not to answer that question in the yes/no format in which it was formed but instead encouraged her to consider how she would answer the question. This led to a powerful, and sensitive exploration by Marie of her somewhat confusing need to be close to Fred, confounded by her desire to be more independent from him. She was able to review her behavior over the recent weeks and talk about instances in which she was pursuing him in ways reminiscent of earlier in treatment. She knew that behavior was unhelpful and wondered aloud why she regressed to it. She also began to consider her own need for more distance from Fred.

Near the end of the session, I focused Marie's attention on the upcoming week. I chose to use the humorous/paradoxical approach that had been so successful in pulling her out of her tears earlier in the session. I asked her what she could do to create a "normal" week for the two of them. Marie responded by saying that she was beginning to think that maybe she didn't want a normal week and that she needed to pay more attention to how she was the pursuer.

Bringing the Pieces Together

Fred began the next couple session with a discussion of his thinking about the relationship with Margaret. He reported his new insight about Margaret needing him and his need to be needed. He also repeated his intention to get out of the other relationship, with the qualifier that he now realized that he may be having more difficulty doing that than he had realized. He distinguished between his own trouble letting go and Margaret's inability to let go of him. He said that the combination of the two had him stymied.

Marie, following the spirit of using the work done in the individual session to catalyze the work in the joint sessions, spontaneously said that she was now more aware than ever that she, too, may be used to having someone else in their relationship. She had come to the conclusion that she was now ready to work on their relationship without another person balancing their emotional needs. She was truly ready for Fred to give up the other relationship.

This triggered one of those intense, emotional moments that can happen in marital therapy, in which both people seem to allow their defenses to rest and to connect sincerely with each other. They looked at each other, Fred reached out with tears in his eyes, and took hold of Marie's hand. Marie, also with tears in her eyes, squeezed his hand and smiled at him.

Fred broke the silence with a rather startling proposition. He said that he had been considering the idea of having Margaret in for a session with him, to provide him with a forum for getting out of that relationship. He didn't seem to be able to do it when he was alone with her. Although he turned to me with a questioning expression on his face, obviously wanting my opinion about the idea, I chose not to respond with an answer but instead to look to Marie for her reaction to the idea.

Marie initially wanted reassurance that the object of the meeting was to terminate the relationship rather than repair it in the way they were working to repair their relationship. Fred offered that reassurance, and Marie then indicated that it would be agreeable to her. Not willing to accept her agreement without further assessment of the full range of possibilities, I questioned Marie on her thoughts about the implications of my contact with Margaret.

Would she feel uncomfortable with the idea that I was seeing Margaret?

What if we need more than one session to accomplish the task?

Would she prefer to be in the meeting, so she could know exactly what transpired?

She responded that she was not at all concerned about me seeing Margaret. She had total confidence that her relationship with me was secure and was not threatened by that type of contact with Margaret. She also trusted that whatever decision was made regarding the number of sessions would be appropriate and fine with her. And she believed that it would be wrong for her to be in the session, since this was something Fred needed to do. Fred strongly agreed with her on that point.

Although I agreed also, I chose to check it out in the form of a question with her rather than a command. I was willing to risk the unlikely possibility that Marie would have said "yes" to the opportunity to be in the session. I assumed that if that came to pass, I would need to explore the meaning of that decision rather than the decision not to attend.

So, here they were, six months into therapy, which followed ten months of initial therapy, and both of them were finally ready to acknowledge the previous difficulty in terminating the affair that had operated in their relationship. That both of them were able to ac-knowledge their own emotional involvement in that triangle was a powerful move toward neutralizing its function. That both of them were willing to allow the forum of a formal meeting here with Fred and Margaret was an equally powerful move toward terminating the relationship.

The Work with Fred and Margaret

The strategy of having a session with a spouse and a lover may be seen in some quarters as being unorthodox at best, and perhaps wrong-headed. The technique is certainly not for the therapist who works on cautious, concrete goals in marital therapy. The problems that are presented range from "What do I do?" to "Who am I going to be to the lover?" Despite the complications involved, the potential for having a broader impact on the extended emotional system (the couple in treatment plus the most significant triangled person) was most intriguing.

I was mildly surprised that Fred had made the proposal in the first place, and that Marie had agreed. I was just as confident as Marie that our relationship would not be threatened and that it would likely raise some helpful themes in the therapy. I was less sure about what to expect from Margaret. Certainly she knew that I was working with Fred and Marie to help them heal their marriage. And Fred had told her that he wanted her to come in to a session to discuss some difficult matters.

Could she anticipate the likelihood of his desire to terminate their relationship?

How do I handle the loneliness and neediness I have heard Fred describe in her?

Will it be possible for me to do anything to help this relationship end and perhaps to encourage Margaret to seek therapy for herself?

How do I juggle Fred's ambivalence about terminating this relationship?

As I prepared for this session by contemplating all of these questions and more, my own doubts about my ability to handle this situation occasionally crept through. Perhaps I should have taken the safer route and said that it would be inappropriate for me to see Fred with Margaret since I was "Their (Fred and Marie's) Therapist." Say-

ing it would be inappropriate sounds much more clinical, and maybe
even officious, than saying that it sounds too complicated.

> *The session turned out to be less complicated than the various
> musings that had occupied my mind prior to it. Margaret did indeed have
> an inkling that Fred's agenda was to terminate their relationship. She was
> also smart enough to know that an emotional scene would be futile and
> ill-advised, given the circumstances. Her tack seemed to be to suggest that
> she was accustomed to Fred's ambivalence about their relationship. Writ-
> ten between the lines was the inference that she would wait for Fred to
> return later.*
>
> *I spoke to that tacit suggestion, saying that she seemed confident that
> Fred would come back. Her reply opened the way to a critical intervention
> with her. She said that she had seen this with Fred before and that she had
> seen it with her father as well. The mention of her father, and the
> insinuation that he, too, had been involved in affairs, provided me with
> an opening to ask about her family. She revealed that her father had, in
> fact, left her mother for another woman. As the conversation unfolded, it
> became painfully clear that Margaret was ambivalent about being "the
> other woman" but partially believed that it was a safer emotional position
> to be in with a man than to be "the wife."*

As the pain and turmoil in Margaret's life came out, it became
easier to understand what my role with her needed to be. She was in a
relationship that was unhealthy for her, because she would never be
able to have a total relationship with Fred. His resolve to stay with
Marie was quite obvious. Given that certainty, I spoke to Margaret's
loneliness and her unresolved feelings about the loss of her father. As
she began to see her experience with her father as being significant to
her relationship with Fred, she began to take on a different physical
posture.

I didn't expect her to lose face by acknowledging any new insights about this during this session. I wanted her to be able to leave
with her dignity intact and with a positive image of the possibilities of
therapy. I mentioned to her that if she should be interested in pursuing therapy in the future, I might be able to help her find a therapist.
The session concluded by Fred restating that it was his intention to
stop seeing her. He said that it was very difficult for him, because he
was very attached to her, and still thought very highly of her. The
need to say this in a formal setting testified to that.

Fred and Marie: Months Six through Nine

The rhythm of the therapy is decidedly different at this stage than in the initial phases of work. There is an element of familiarity and trust between Fred, Marie, and me that allows for qualitatively different discussions about many of the same topics broached earlier. By this time we have passed through several holidays, at which times we exchanged pleasant wishes at the conclusions of the sessions nearest the holiday. We have jointly solved all of the problems of scheduling, no small task for three busy people. We have had the mutual experience of working around each other's travel schedules and have learned that all three of us occasionally can be the victim of the common cold or other, more complicated maladies.

Each and every one of these experiences weaves into the therapy. They serve to put the therapeutic work into the context of human lives. By acknowledging life outside the therapy hour, the conversations officially labeled therapy become more easily integrated into the areas of life where there is the most need for that integration. Put simply, the full range of life, including the many subjects that are not usually considered official elements of the therapy, have coalesced and have an ever-increasing and intangible influence in the later stages of the therapy.

There are, of course, specific focal points of the therapy. Fred's formal session with Margaret had all the earmarks of a major event. There was the potential for a substantive shift in the emotional balance in the marriage, if indeed Fred maintained his resolve. But Margaret's expressed skepticism regarding Fred's resolve actually was shared by Marie, and I was in the position of "wait and see." Marie did not ask for a report of the work between Fred and Margaret and was not offered one.

Despite the covert uncertainty regarding Fred's resolve, there was enough of a dynamic shift with his move that it resulted in a shift in distance between them. Fred was more involved emotionally in the marriage. He was trying to be communicative and affectionate in ways that were uncharacteristic of him, such as looking for discussions with Marie, and initiating more of all types of physical contact between them, ranging from casual hugs to sex.

Marie was trying to respond to Fred's overtures. In the first several sessions after Fred's session with Margaret, Fred and Marie talked about problems related to communication with each other and differing expectations regarding sex. If a still photo could have been taken of their lives and relationship at that point, it would have looked like two people reasonably comfortable with each other, ironing out a few minor difficulties.

One lesson of long-term therapy, however, is not to be fooled by any one slice of the process. About a month after the punctuation point of the Fred–Margaret session, Marie started becoming depressed. There were several immediate factors identified, including her decision to explore employment possibilities and the fatigue she felt in trying to juggle the basic family obligations along with the stress of working on her relationship with Fred.

Marie had decided not to return to her previous profession of teaching. Her uncertainty about her career path left her without a specific goal in a way she had never been before. She was ambivalent about reaching out to Fred for support, and he was uncertain and ambivalent about how to offer it. She investigated several different possibilities in the business world, but she was unable to make a decision to accept any position. Simultaneously, over the course of about three weeks, she slipped deeper into depression. The depression reached a point where she was unable to sleep, was loosing weight, and was restless to the point of agitation. At that time I recommended to her that she enlist the assistance of medication to help with the depression. She agreed, and scheduled an appointment with a psychiatrist for the prescription.

Along with encouraging the use of the medication, I monitored the effects, both primary and secondary. I assumed that the primary therapeutic relationship was with me, despite the fact that I was not the legal prescriber of the medication. I watched for side effects, kept track of dosage levels with her, and monitored the impact on her depression. She welcomed and appreciated my involvement, and she was reassured by the integration of the use of medication into the ongoing task of therapy.

In addition to the clinical management of Marie's depression by way of medication, there was the question of the dynamic meaning of the depression both for Marie individually and for the overall emotional system. Marie was following the same course as a number of previous clients, in which the noninvolved spouse became depressed shortly after the involved spouse made a move out of the affair and back into the marriage. I knew from those situations that the depression functioned as a type of emotional spacer in the marriage. If a person is depressed, she is not going to be emotionally available.

As Marie pulled up out of her depression, her mind started to clear, and she began to be more effective again in the therapy. At that point, I encouraged Marie and Fred, in a joint session, to consider the possible meaning and function of Marie's depression. Their first interpretation, which they agreed on, was to point to the recent stress surrounding Marie's return to a career outside the home.

I agreed with that factor, and questioned whether there was any connection with the progress they were making in their work together. Fred noted that he saw Marie in a new way, since she was usually so strong in his eyes. Seeing her impaired with a depression was very different. He felt as if he had more power in the marriage.

This was a keen, systemic-based insight from a man who, six months earlier, basically was unable to articulate any semblance of psychological awareness. Seeing that type of progress, and having a sense for the type of positive impact it can have in their lives, is one of the gratifying elements that sustains me through the more difficult times in the therapy. Even though I was very pleased with Fred's insight, I refrained from any comment. I wanted to see if Marie had any awareness of the shift in the power dynamic between them, and if she had any other observations about the impact of her depression on the relationship.

When I solicited her comments, she indicated that she was not able to see the shift in power in the way that Fred saw it, because she was not sure that there had been any imbalance in the power in her favor in the first place. Moving on to the topic of emotional distance, she commented that she thought perhaps she was less available to Fred now than she would be if she were not depressed. But she couldn't quite understand what all the implications were.

I asked her if she could sketch out her view of the evolution of the emotional distance between them, with the scope being the last three months. She easily talked about the month prior to the Fred–Margaret meeting being characterized by tension and distance between her and Fred, the time immediately following the meeting as being almost a second honeymoon, and the time around her depression as being a period of more distance. I went to the blackboard and improvised a shorthand schematic of her narrative to add a visual reference point.

This session had a rather pronounced sweet and sour flavor. The sweet taste was the newly matured ability in both of them to identify and articulate complex systemic insights. The sour flavor was the awareness that the question of emotional distance between them, rather than being solved by Fred's termination of the affair, had taken a new form and was begging for further development. That development was now changed by the role reversal in which Marie, by way of her depression, was the distancer, and Fred was the pursuer. The implications of that reversal were strong enough that neither Fred nor Marie were fooled into thinking that it would be "fixed" by Marie getting out of her depression. It was now obvious that there seemed to be some basic need for distance in the marriage that needed to be understood and modified if there was to be a lasting, satisfying intimacy between them.

The Conclusion of the First Year of Therapy

Again following a common pattern in the therapy, Fred and Marie began to take note of the passage of time as the one-year anniversary of our work together loomed ahead. Separately and together they expressed ambivalence about the passage of time. Both were glad that life between them was better than it had been a year ago, but they also were discouraged that it was not even better. They yearned for better times and wondered how long it would take to reach that goal.

My response to those feelings was as typical for me as the feelings were for them. I had used interventions that were "going opposite directions simultaneously." Some interventions were designed to make them less tense, and some were designed to increase their tension. The interventions that were designed to decrease their level of tension were aimed at minimizing their concern that they should have made more progress by this time. I accomplished that by reviewing with them, in more detail, the evolution of their relationship. This broad focused historical view helped to clarify the amount of time it took to reach the crisis point in the marriage.

Each of them was now able to see the seeds of discontent from the earliest years of their marriage. They both had developed an understanding of the insidious process of denial and fear that had developed between them. This process manifested itself in the form of silence and hidden tensions, which had mounted steadily for several years before the crisis precipitated by the affair. They were able to compare the emotional climate of their relationship at this point in therapy, seeing that there was substantial progress in some critical but intangible elements in the relationship. That developmental perspective significantly reduced their agitation about the length of time in therapy.

The other half of my response to their concern about the length of time in therapy was to search out the elements of their dissatisfaction. What were they unhappy about in the relationship? Identifying these factors became an avenue for developing therapeutic goals for this stage in the therapy. I assumed, though, that bringing that dissatisfaction to a more conscious level would have the effect of "making them feel worse," since they would see more clearly the problems in need of work.

Briefly summarized, the interventions at this point can be described as making the couple feel better and worse, simultaneously. The interventions are specifically aimed at different levels of the therapeutic process and different levels of awareness in the clients. On the affective level, the level of pain and agitation must be kept low enough that the clients don't get overly discouraged and bolt from therapy and high enough that they are motivated to continue. On the cognitive level, they need to be able to see the long-term process, and use that image as a backdrop for the image of the more immediate short-term process.

Marie was well out of her depression by this time. She had been able to think clearly in the therapy, had taken on a part-time job with an advertising firm, and had no further problems with any of the physiological symptoms of her depression. We decided that it would be appropriate for her to discontinue the use of the antidepressant medication, given all of that progress. She consulted the psychiatrist who had originally prescribed the medication in her next scheduled medication review, and he also agreed to the plan. As Marie regained her full level of functioning, the work of the therapy shifted back to some of the basic dynamics in the marriage.

The Return of the Power Motif

The dynamic that re-emerged in this process was power. It had made earlier appearances in the therapy, one of the more notable forms being the aborted discussion of money prior to the discovery of

Fred and Margaret. At this point in the therapy both Fred and Marie
were becoming more sophisticated about the dynamics between them,
and they were able to identify the question of power in many different aspects of their relationship, including money, child-rearing
philosophy, and time together.

*The question of power was initially formed as "Who gets to make the
decisions in these areas?" The initial answer was a clear statement from
both of them that rather decisively portrayed the other as being the one with
more power. Fred characterized Marie as making most of the decisions
about how to spend the money, and cited instances of daily expense
decisions such as food, clothing, and general household expenses. He told
several stories of incidents in which he had expressed his disagreement
with Marie's decisions, to no avail. She went ahead with her own plan.*

*He went on to develop the same theme regarding child rearing and
told stories of Marie's decisions about how their time should be used that
followed the same theme. He clearly felt quite powerless in case after case.
The one bright spot in his soliloquy was the clear improvement in his
ability to identify and articulate his feelings and perceptions.*

*Marie countered Fred's image of the power balance between them
with an equally convincing statement describing Fred's position of power
in the relationship and her fundamental inability to make any basic
impact on the situation. She described Fred's control over the money
coming in the form of investment decisions that allocated large per-
centages of their resources. She agreed that she, probably, had more of a
say regarding the children. But she had frequently asked Fred for more
help, and he had continually avoided more involvement with them.*

*As for the question of time, she agreed with Fred that she frequently
made decisions regarding their social plans, but in a much broader way
she had very little control over the time. Fred would stay away, ostensibly
because of business demands, for so much of the time that there was
precious little time for them to be together and socialize together. She made
a special point of emphasizing Fred's habit of "going to work" on the
weekends, usually without notifying her that he was leaving.*

These ideas were developed over the course of several weeks,
with time in both the individual sessions and the couple sessions being
used to refine the ideas. By this point in the therapy, Fred and Marie
had a well-developed ability to focus on themselves in the individual
sessions and to use those ideas in productive ways in the couple

sessions. The beauty of the process, from the therapist's point of view, is the therapeutic power emanating from the structure.

In addition to the opportunity to work on these issues from two different vantage points, the potential to learn about life in their system from two different perspectives helps to clarify the overall dynamics and define the basic problems in the system. If they were working with two different therapists, they both could be persuasive that the other was emotionally inept and resistant to change. Instead, in this structure, we have both images in one place and the obvious need for an understanding of a broad and complex emotional system.

Months Twelve through Eighteen

The process of change shifts at this stage of the therapy. It is tempting to say that it slows down, since the urgency of the crisis around the revelation of the affair has passed, and many of the insights are subtle expansions of earlier discoveries. The changes, however, are no less complex, and in truth seem to be the shifts that will establish the long-term, more healthy balance in the couple.

Both Fred and Marie convey a strong sense of trust in me, a comfort with the process, and a desire to continue the work, which adds to my therapeutic leverage. The differences that I see between them in the couple sessions and the individual sessions can be used in the treatment. Both, generally, are less guarded, warmer, and more willing to discuss their concerns about their own failures in the individual sessions, but they continue to learn the possibilities of bringing those ideas into the couple's sessions. There is, however, one topic that remains hot and remains difficult to structure in the couple sessions.

Marie came into one of her individual sessions early in this period of the therapy and immediately began relaying her fears that Fred was involved with another woman. Though she wasn't sure that it was Margaret, she couldn't decide whether she would be more bothered knowing it was Margaret or knowing that there was yet some other woman. Marie was unsure whether he had been involved all along, whether he was renewing an old friendship, or whether Fred had found someone new.

In any case, she was fearful that he was seeing some woman. She developed several different images that had prompted her to wonder. Fred was spending even more time "at work" than his usual excessive hours. He was acting more perturbed with her over small things, which was a pattern that Marie remembered from the time when he had admitted to being involved. And during lovemaking, Fred seemed distant and pre-occupied.

Marie recounted these points, with specific examples to support them, with a sense of belief in her convictions that was hard to deny. I was faced with a treatment decision—how do I handle this situation? I decided to break it up into the component parts, in my own mind, and to proceed to develop interventions that would address them as help-fully as possible. I began with Marie, since she was the person with me at that moment.

I needed to know how she was interpreting the situation and began to question her about that. She said that she was able to see that Fred was distancing from her, but she didn't exactly know why. In response to a question about her reaction to his distancing, she admitted that her natural instinct was to pursue him, but she was trying to be aware of that and avoid that role. She said she didn't think that confronting him with her fears would be useful, since she only had vague cues about a problem.

"I think it's good that you're being so thoughtful about your response to your fears," I said. "Avoiding the urge to pursue is probably the most helpful strategy for you. And along with that, it would be very helpful if we could come up with some type of understanding about the meaning of this situation. The way I see it now, on your side of things, we have your fears, which are very real."

"And on Fred's side of things," I continued, "we have the potential of his involvement, which may or may not be real. Neither one of us knows for sure. I am, though, willing to believe that he has been more distant lately. Whether his behavior is a reflection of involvement or not, we certainly need to understand his increased distance and get his perceptions of that distance."

My response to Marie combined support and validation for her perceptions and fears, a reminder that the situation involves both her fears and Fred's behavior, and encouragement to think about the enormous complexities of the emotional distance between them.

The focus on her fears turned out to be useful as a way of "detriangling" myself from the emotionality of the potential of the affair. In other words, rather than getting caught up in an alliance with Marie based on the "problem" of Fred and his affair, I was instead focusing the work in the session on Marie's feelings and an understanding of their meaning. A vital theme emerged with the examination of these feelings, trust. Clearly, Marie was *very* mistrustful of Fred. Just as clearly, this mistrust translated into increased distance in the relationship, *created by Marie!* Independent of the number of hours Fred was working, or was with Margaret, whichever the case might be, the fact that Marie was fearing that possibility put her in a guarded, mistrustful, and ultimately more distant position relative to Fred.

This was a stunning insight for Marie. Finally accustomed to seeing herself as the emotional pursuer in the marriage, the possibility that she, too, might have times in which she was emotionally distant was unsettling and provocative. Despite her earlier experience with depression, she believed that she was not temperamentally disposed to creating distance between them and that the depression was an uncharacteristic anomaly. She didn't deny it, however, and actually was able to develop vignettes in which she now, with hindsight, could see that she was being distant.

She remembered being short and abrupt with Fred when he called her from work, and later that day "forgetting" that she had promised to call him back later. She also remembered finding herself very tired on one evening last week when Fred had come home from work earlier than had been his habit in recent weeks. She, just coincidentally, retired early that evening and had very little interaction with Fred. Again, with hindsight, she saw this episode as an instance in which she obviously was distancing from Fred.

Marie left that session with a new perspective on the problem of distancing and pursuing in the relationship. She was more accepting of the possibility that Fred might be involved again with Margaret. She didn't *like* the idea and certainly wouldn't endorse it as her favorite strategy for establishing distance between them. But she now saw more clearly that the involvement with Margaret was one expression of a much broader problem of the dance of distance between them. The notion that she, too, took the lead in the creation of distance, helped to establish an entirely new image of the process for her.

The next session, in the rotation of the therapy, happened to be an individual session with Fred. I was now faced with another problem. What, exactly, do I do with the ideas generated in the session with Marie? Confronting him with the data laid out by Marie, regarding his excessive work hours, etc., was totally out of the question. That would put me in an adversarial position that would serve absolutely no therapeutic purpose. The issue of the emotional distance between them, though, was crucial. I decided to wait to see if Fred would allude to the issue himself.

> *Fred made my job easy. Just as I had found that the session with Margaret was much easier than I had anticipated, so too was the exploration of this subject with Fred. Fred began the session with a comment about how hard he had been working lately. As it turned out, he was using it as a preamble to developing his concerns about the episode in which Marie retired early on the one evening in which he had come home early. He used that episode as an example of his belief that Marie was insensitive to his needs. In this case, he had needs to be close to Marie and interact with her which she seemed to ignore.*

I found it most interesting that Fred focused on the same incident that Marie had focused on. I was certain that this was unplanned and decided that it was an indication of their increasing expertise at observing significant emotional negotiations between them. I now knew that I could proceed with the exploration of the question of distance between them. I didn't have any indication from Fred about any new involvement with Margaret, but I did have his acknowledgement of long work hours, which Marie had seen as a form of distancing, and the evening episode described, in which Marie seemed to have been the distancer.

I began with the evening episode. Fred had established that as his point of interest, and I assumed it was going to be easier for Fred to begin to see the dynamics of distance between them in an instance when he saw himself as the aggrieved party. So with all of these thoughts in the background, my intervention with Fred was a simple, understated question that basically requested more clarification. I asked him to tell me more of his thinking about the meaning of the evening episode in question.

> *He focused on his belief that Marie was, in many ways, incapable of knowing and fulfilling his needs. He described himself as making an effort to come home early to see her and, in turn, being rebuffed. I asked*

him how he had felt in that situation, and he indicated that he had felt angry with her and saw now that it was that type of situation that may have motivated him to get involved with Margaret.

I looked at Fred and raised an eyebrow. He had just handed me a direct connection between the level of tension between them and his extramarital relationship. The question was, however, did he understand that? And beyond that, I took great interest in the fact that Fred was raising Margaret's name after some months of not hearing about her. Although I could not then assume that he *was* reinvolved with her, as Marie had decided, it was clear that the triangle with Margaret, Fred, and Marie was more active now than it had been in recent months.

I saw several possibilities for points of intervention. On one side we had the dynamic of Marie's distancing from Fred, and his reaction to that. On the other side we had Fred's distancing from Marie, admittedly by way of his work hours, with the question of Margaret hanging in the air.

I chose to reiterate the point that Fred had just made, having to do with his dissatisfaction with Marie. "So, you get angry with her when you see her as not being sensitive to your needs! It almost seems as though she were avoiding you, doesn't it?" Fred's eyes lit up with that question. He, too, was aware of the ongoing assumption of his being the distancer in the marriage. To have an incident that suggested the opposite was just as significant for him as it had been for Marie.

Not content to allow Fred to focus opportunistically on the deficits of Marie, and her complicity in the distance between them, I moved ahead to refocus his thinking on himself.

"Do you have any ideas why Marie may have changed her style and decided to distance from you that night? Had there been any type of disagreement between the two of you. Or had she been upset with anything?" I was encouraging Fred to think systemically and be self-critical at the same time.

Fred was quite unable to identify any clear problem.

I referred to Fred's remark earlier in the session in which he indicated that he had been working a lot lately and asked him if he was under a lot of pressure at work. After a slight hesitation, he said that he had indeed been under much pressure at work and probably had been working even longer hours than usual. I asked him if he knew how Marie was reacting to those longer hours, and he said that she probably didn't like it, though she hadn't said anything to him directly.

I wanted to stay away from any type of victim/villain formulation with him on these examples of mutual distancing. I chose to focus on the emotional meaning and consequences of the distancing, and possible motivations for the distancing. He was able to see that his work hours probably could be interpreted as distancing, though he hadn't seen that before. He then reiterated his stand that there was not as much for him to come home for as he would like, and that was important.

Fred was returning to a definition of his situation that placed the "blame" on Marie. I saw this as being a common defense, especially in situations in which the affair was a long-term affair rather than a short-term one. My job had to be to refocus Fred on himself. I did that directly, asking him to look for reasons other than Marie's short-comings that could help us to understand his own tendency to distance.

"Well, I remember from some individual therapy that I was involved in many years ago that there was some question of whether I have some kind of fear of intimacy, *but I was never too sure about all that then, and I'm not any more sure about it now," Fred responded. "But I suppose that it could be considered as some type of answer to the question you're asking."*

Fred was genuinely looking for some type of explanation that would account for his contribution to the problems of distance in the marriage. His intellectual capacity, however, was developed well beyond his self-knowledge. The phrase of a "fear of intimacy" was more a handy cliche for Fred than it was any type of statement about his internal awareness.

"What do you mean, a fear of intimacy?" I said.

My simple response points directly to the problem that needs to be explored.

"I suppose that I really don't know what I mean," Fred admitted. "All I see is that when I come home, Marie doesn't want to sit down and

talk to me. And there are too many times when I am interested in sex that she just isn't interested. But then I'm supposed to be the one who has a fear of intimacy. I can't say that I buy that."

Fred's response cuts two directions simultaneously. He admits to not knowing and understanding exactly what a fear of intimacy is all about. He then goes on to point to Marie's avoidance of him as a way of deflecting the focus on him and perhaps excusing his behavior.

I went on to talk to him about his long work hours, which is where we began with the idea of his fear of intimacy. As we developed the topic, Fred became aware of his style of frequently avoiding Marie by way of not being with her and then expecting an unrealistically intense rapport when he *did* come home. The juxtaposition of excessive distance with excessive closeness struck Fred as a clear image of their entire marriage, and it became the central theme as the therapy continued through the second year.

The Struggle for Intimacy

Marie and Fred came out of the previous series of sessions with an acute awareness of both the overall problem of intimacy between them and the necessity of understanding each individual's contribution to the problem. With that backdrop, the exploration of intimacy proceeded to use the full range of life between them. In session after session, we were able to see recent events, both significant and insignificant, as being yet more data to illustrate the vicissitudes of intimacy in the relationship.

The first significant pattern that was developed emanated from the discussion with Fred described above. The pattern broadened in definition to be seen as one in which Fred established distance in the relationship in more of a passive manner, such as staying at work and not seeing Marie. Marie, on the other hand, was creating distance currently by avoiding Fred and being overly guarded when he *was* home. At this stage, there was no direct confrontation of Fred related to his possible involvement with someone else. Marie had decided that his continued interest in therapy and his continued interest in remaining in the marriage were sufficient indications of his commitment. If, in fact, he was involved with another woman, she was able to see it as his way of distancing in the marriage.

They were at a stage of the therapy in which they were doing much more of the work than they had initially. They had developed a fine sense of which interactions over the previous week were significant and knew how to develop them productively in the sessions. They were able to avoid most of the flagrant conflict at home that had disrupted life prior to therapy. And they were expertly following the development of the more abstract themes, such as intimacy, and were able to see the implications in everyday life.

In some ways, this makes my job easier. I am less frequently in the role of fireman, where I am controlling and eliminating brush fires in the form of tension and anxiety between them. But in other ways, my job is more difficult. What do I do to make myself useful? How do I help people who are increasingly sophisticated about their own emotional system but who are still saying that life is not right, and they want help? We are well past the stage where I can be useful by teaching them about triangles or by helping them to "communicate effectively." We are at a stage where we are dealing with difficult, abstract, and fundamental questions of intimacy.

There is no concise, catchy way of describing my role as therapist in this stage of the work. The spontaneous improvisation that is the most effective is a combination of classic therapeutic technique, awareness of my own personal beliefs about intimacy, and a comfort with knowing that I *don't know* what to do most of the time. Indeed, at one point I emphasized my own limits with Fred and Marie. They received the news that I was not omniscient and was frequently wondering just what I could do and what we would do together with good humor. They seemed to take even more responsibility for the work, while remaining strongly committed to continuing the process of therapy and making use of whatever input I had to offer.

One of the most frequently used class of interventions in this stage, if we can truly divide interventions into different classes, was to choose during the session which type of perspective, or which lens, would be the most useful for the situation. If Fred and Marie were focused on abstract ideas, which seemed to lose meaning for them, I would encourage the examination of everyday life. If they were agitated by everyday life and could not get any understanding of the situation, I might encourage a more objective and abstract perspective. Each perspective, or lens, has usefulness for different situations. I relied on my clinical judgment for decisions about what to focus on, from what perspective.

One continuously useful shift in perspective in the exploration of intimacy was that of the time frame. It was crucial to be able to understand the evolution of intimacy from the beginning of their relationship and not to become overly focused on the current lack of intimacy. Both of them needed to understand that they were more suspicious and guarded than usual because of the long and painful process of crisis and resolution.

> When I encouraged them in a couple session to review and discuss their impressions of intimacy from the beginning of their relationship, several significant themes emerged. Whereas both of them agreed that they seemed to have been most intimate at the very outset of their relationship, Fred admitted that even at that time he was aware of feeling less adequate than Marie. He searched for words that might capture his experience and thought that subservient, dependent, inadequate, and less powerful might suggest some of his feelings at that time.
>
> Marie was genuinely taken aback by this admission. She pointed out how she had been very happy during that time period and had intentionally worked at making Fred feel better about himself. She saw herself as reaching out to him, since he seemed a bit "shy," and always made it a point to defer to him in public.

As the conversation developed, Marie was able to see that the very need she was aware of, "to defer to Fred," was a signal of a disparity in power between them. Fred went on to clarify the idea that despite her good intentions, the pattern of her "reaching out" to him, since he was shy, established a pattern of her defining the type of relationship, and the type of intimacy, that would be typical of their relationship.

> He then had the courage to compare their relationship with his "other relationship." He said that he had learned in that relationship that there were styles of intimacy other than the style that predominated in their marriage. He found that he liked those other styles and would like them to become part of their marriage.
>
> With that background, Marie and Fred looked at ways they could work on the question of intimacy in real life over the next week. I reminded them that we didn't need to come up with the "right answer" regarding the form of interaction they should have. Rather, we could benefit from developing some type of experiment that might give us new information and ideas by way of their reactions to the experiment.

They agreed to take time during the week to discuss that old nemesis, money. We were all aware of the lack of resolution that plagued that topic, but anticipated a new perspective brought from this discussion. The dynamics of intimacy and power would likely be more overt, thus leading to a different emotional structure for the assigned conversation.

Their attempt to discuss money *did* work out differently. Fred enthusiastically expressed his satisfaction that Marie listened to him differently than she would have usually. Marie agreed and said that she had a very different experience of the power between them. She truly felt more equal to Fred. The complex entanglement of intimacy, power, and definition of self was becoming vividly transparent. It was clear that this track was vital to the dynamics that had maintained Fred's long-term affair.

We continued looking historically at their relationship, covering many of the mundane areas of life in the form of the various decisions necessary to carry on with the daily grind. Looking at them historically was, again, very complementary and helpful. In addition to this focus, there were two other major themes that offered fertile ground and clearly related to the overall question of intimacy and the overall level of satisfaction for both of them—the impact of the children on their relationship, and the impact of their respective families of origin.

The initial discussion of the subject of children was at least as tension-filled as was the introductory discussion of money in the early stages of therapy. Fred strongly emphasized his belief that their relationship suffered with the birth of their first child, Jennifer, and had never fully recovered after that. He saw Marie putting more time and energy into the children than she did into their marriage.

Marie was yet again somewhat taken aback by Fred's pronouncement. She was by now more accustomed to learning things about Fred that she never new, but ultimately she was quite confused by his analysis. She countered by saying that she had always seen him as being a good father and had thought that he, too, enjoyed having the children around.

Like the subject of money, and in keeping with what must by now be the obvious pattern of therapy in the more advanced stages of long-term work, the subject of children continued on for several sessions, through both the individual and couple sessions. Although it seems as if there just *couldn't* be that much to talk about, in fact seemingly insignificant daily interactions can effectively be plumbed for their complex dynamic implications, and longstanding historical patterns can be developed that organize series of seemingly unrelated incidents.

Although these patterns can be developed in several ways, it is always useful to return to such basics as triangles. I went to the board and drew a genogram of the family, and began developing different triangles on the board. Creating a triangle between Fred, Marie, and each one of the children (Figure 8.2) in turn yielded the valuable and apparently unseen trend that Marie was closer to the girls than was Fred. He, in turn, was closer to Andrew than he was to either of the girls. Marie, also, was more distant from Andrew than was Fred, and could at times, with the shifting of the triangles, be closer to the girls than she was to Fred. Although this is a classic and usually well-known pattern of gender coalitions in a family, it had been unseen or at least unacknowledged between Fred and Marie until it took on the visual reality of triangles on the chalkboard.

It is critical to keep in mind the point of departure here, the question of intimacy in the marriage. As central as the triangles are to the overall functioning of the family, there is more to be concerned

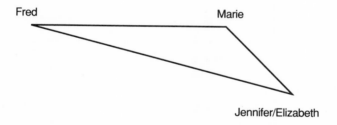

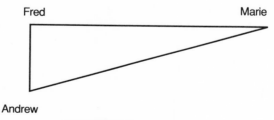

FIGURE 8.2

with than gender coalitions. The implications for the level and type of intimacy between Fred and Marie are powerful. It became very obvious that Marie did not see or experience the impact on the marriage in the same way as did Fred. As the exploration continued, it became clear that she was gratified and fulfilled with her relationships with the children in a way that put her in a more distant emotional position relative to Fred.

I was inclined to use the word *fusion* in my own mind. It seemed as though the fusion between her and the children operated in such a way that she took on a different type of closeness with Fred, one that seemed more operational and less romantic, for lack of better words. The warm type of emotional closeness, on the other hand, she was finding in her relationship with the children, and specifically the girls.

The development and understanding of these triangles and patterns of intimacy in the family as a whole added more depth and perspective to the problem of intimacy between Fred and Marie. They found themselves *feeling* different with each other through the weeks. It was an intangible that couldn't be identified with such obvious cues as less conflict, which they saw in the early stages of therapy, or a new capacity to discuss explosive topics, which they saw somewhat later in the therapy. The subjects were the same, but the type of connection between them, the intangible sense of intimacy, was becoming stronger.

The exploration of family of origin issues was quite similar to the exploration of the impact of the children. We drew triangles and talked about the coalitions and the implications of those coalitions. We talked about their perceptions of intimacy in their parents' relationships, and saw that both of them showed a tendency to try to replicate those relationships in their own marriage. Both of them saw marriages in which their mothers seemed to have stronger ties to the children than they did to their husbands. In Fred's case, he also remembered that his father, too, had a habit of long work hours. He unexpectedly remembered wondering as a young teenager whether his father was having an affair, because he remembered overhearing him on the phone talking "very nicely" to some woman.

Fred was willing to work on the idea that his father may have been involved with another woman. He even felt a bit curious that he should have forgotten about it until now. I was interested in the implications for Fred and his extramarital involvement, and wanted to instill the same curiosity in Fred. We worked on it in both his individual sessions and in the couple sessions.

The individual sessions, of course, afforded a more focused opportunity, since we could examine Fred's feelings, perceptions, and beliefs without taking the time to hear Marie's reactions. Not to say that there was anything to hide from Marie. Quite simply, if the couple sessions are going to be effective, there has to be some attention to group process. Although it is quite possible to work primarily with one person for the bulk of one session, it also works out better to get some minimal statement of reactions from the partner who is doing the listening.

As the exploration continued, Fred was able to consider previously unconscious ideas that it would be "OK" for him to be involved with another woman outside his marriage. It might even be expected! In considering that expectation, he looked at his perceptions of his father's expectations for him. He came to think that he, without any direct indication from his father, had believed that his father would have given approval and support to his extramarital activity.

Months Eighteen through Twenty-Four

The conclusion of the second year of therapy continued with many of the same themes as were developed above. Fred continued to think about the question of extramarital activities as a family pattern and decided to have a conversation with his father about the subject. I "coached" Fred prior to his discussion. We developed a strategy that was intended *not* to alienate his father. His father had already known that Fred had been having an affair. It was certainly no secret through the whole family. So Fred began the conversation with a reference to his problems, and the tension created by his affair. He proceeded to ask his father if he, his father, had ever had an affair, and how he had handled it.

> *His father was willing to discuss the situation, and he was open about verifying Fred's adolescent memories about his affair. The two of them looked at the problem of closeness in the marriage and at the impact of the affair on that closeness. His father also volunteered that his father, Fred's grandfather, had also had at least one affair, and probably more. Fred's father said that he understood how Fred could find himself involved in an affair, but it probably was creating a good bit of trouble for him and Marie.*

The effect of this conversation on Fred was difficult to describe. He clearly saw himself as part of a multigenerational pattern, which put an entirely new light on his individual behavior. The thought of Andrew, his son, finding himself in this position as an adult was perplexing and disconcerting. Despite the obvious relevance of this line of pursuit and the provocative nature of his discussion with his father, there was no clear cut and easily identifiable outcome to be seen at that time.

> Marie, meanwhile, was exploring patterns in her family. Along with the pattern of a strong coalition between mother and children and the corresponding lack of intimacy in the marriage, she, too, revealed that she believed that her father had been involved with another woman at one time. She was not sure and was not willing to discuss it with her father, even after seeing Fred's success with his father.

Whether or not Marie's father had an affair was only part of the importance of this line of thinking. The fact that she *believed* that to be true was significant in and of itself.

> I took the opportunity in an individual session with Marie, where she didn't have to be watching Fred out of the corner of her eye and defending herself, to provoke her and challenge her on the emotional implications of this belief. Marie cooperated by bringing up the subject of her father, and mentioning that she had been thinking about times as a teenager when she remembered being confused and angry about the possibility that her father was involved with another woman.
>
> "What kind of implications do you think that experience has for your relationship with Fred?" I wanted to establish a strong connection between her experience growing up and her marriage.
>
> "Only that I didn't ever want to be in that position myself. And now here I am!"

Marie's response was the basic, almost stock response in that situation. I didn't expect her to approve of the affair, either Fred's or her father's. At the same time, the potential for unconscious identification with the situation raises questions about Marie's unwitting and unconscious willingness to accept that emotional structure. I didn't assume that Marie *wanted* Fred to have an affair just because her father had one. I only assumed that the emotional balance would be familiar to her and an easy one to recapitulate.

"You know, the good thing about it is that at least you and Fred have set up a familiar situation for yourselves. You both know just how to act because that's how you were trained!" I said.

Since I said this with a smile, Marie knew I was intentionally provoking her. Our relationship was now close to two years old, so she knew me well, in some ways just as well as I knew her. With that, she took the provocation and was able to consider the implications of the multigenerational pressures on both of them.

We talked about the possibility that Fred's involvement with other women took the pressure off her to be close to him. We also considered the idea that Fred's involvement, to the extent that it may have been recapitulating her father's behavior, fit into an overall pattern in which she could relive her mother's role in ways she had not considered, and indeed did not want. We went on to consider the critical implications for intimacy between them. Marie was able to see how she contributed to the difficulty with intimacy by expecting certain styles and avoiding others.

The Struggle for Trust

As our work together concluded the second year and moved into the third year, life for Fred and Marie was noticeably better than it had been in a very long time. Both said that they would have to look to times very early in the relationship that could compare for the overall level of relaxation and lack of conflict. Given that level of progress, and the length of time in therapy, the question may arise as to the possibility of termination. This was a question I left up to them, and trusted their judgment. Basically, neither one of them felt so comfortable that they were sure of the long-term viability of their marriage.

They saw that things were much better than they had been. But they seemed to take turns identifying different problems that they feared could, ultimately, lead to the demise of the marriage. In many ways there seemed to be insignificant items in which they each seemed to "make a mountain out of a molehill." Fred, for instance, frequently complained that Marie was unable to help him when he needed help. Marie, at the time Fred needed help, was understandably tied up with her own business. Marie, on the other hand, would complain that Fred had not yet really confided in her. She still felt a distance between them and was afraid that Fred might not like her. Fred countered those types of accusations with reports of his latest efforts to "be nice" to her.

All of these nitpicking little exchanges suddenly could be deciphered as small parts of a broader, and more crucial dynamic between them—trust. It was revealed at the outset in the form of Marie's renewed concern that Fred was away from the house, and "working" too much. That, of course, triggered old feelings of fear that Fred was involved with someone else, perhaps Margaret. She revealed this to me in an individual session and asked whether she should confront Fred with her fears.

I remembered how I had coached her at the outset of the therapy to avoid confrontations with him, so she would avoid putting herself in the role of the pursuer. But this was a different time. Marie's fears were having a significant impact on her ability to be close to Fred. Since she didn't trust him, she was constantly fearful of getting close. I assumed that all of the work we had done prior to this would provide a context in which the question could be addressed differently than at the outset. So I encouraged her to confront Fred with her fears in our next scheduled couple's session.

Her confrontation yielded a startling and important dynamic. Fred did not exactly deny any involvement with another woman. Instead he emphasized how Marie always accuses him of being involved in an affair. From his point of view, he saw Marie continuing to avoid intimacy with him, and continuing not to understand the kind of things he saw as being important. Effectively, Fred was voicing his own mistrust of Marie. He did not trust that she was either willing or able to create the kind of relationship that he valued and needed.

The question of trust in the marriage now had a symmetry in definition that could, indeed, be lethal. Marie did not trust that Fred would eliminate other women from his life, and Fred did not trust that Marie was able to join with him in a relationship that met his needs.

This new definition of the question of trust in the relationship helped to make sense of all of the small complaints. We continued talking about it from every conceivable angle, including the familiar questions of money, household decisions, and sexuality in the marriage. Sex had, for the most part, been reasonably unaffected through most of the crisis. Now, however, they were finding themselves vulnerable to a level of mistrust that affected their ability to relate sexually. Neither one of them was interested in sex.

The Conclusion

By now it must be clear that any given crisis in long-term therapy usually has a way of working itself out. It took time, about another ten months, making the total time in therapy just over three years. But Fred and Marie *did* find ways of reestablishing trust between them. Fred never directly admitted to any recent involvements, but he began spending more time at home, and "working" less. Marie began listening to Fred and trying to understand what she had not been hearing from him in the past. Fred saw that and noted that she was succeeding where she previously had not.

Those were the observable changes that could be tracked. The more abstract dynamics that seemed to shift in this last stage of therapy I found most useful to define in terms of fusion and the definition of self in the relationship. The connection that had characterized their relationship in the past had been partially a function of mutual mistrust. It was not limited to affairs, although that was part of it. It was not a simple mistrust of insensitivity, though that too was part of it. In a more basic way, Fred and Marie mistrusted their own ability to be close to the other and still maintain their own identities.

As for the topics covered in that final stage of the therapy, they were essentially a subset of the topics that were present from the beginning. Fred was less focused on what he previously saw as Marie's inadequacies and instead was able to talk about his own reluctance to warm up to her. Marie was no longer preoccupied with her fear of Fred's involvement with other women, and she was able to focus on her own ability to be responsive to Fred and on her perception of his responsiveness to her.

Both of them had learned how to create a better balance in the power, thus eliminating most of the therapeutic focus on that idea. And they both continued to mull over the multigenerational implications of their predicament. Fred was intrigued with the notion that his involvement in affairs was possibly a way for him to identify with his father. Marie was frightened by the possibility that she may have colluded in the evolution of the affair as part of some mysterious process of recreating her own family.

The work on these dynamics proceeded in very much the same way as earlier in the therapy. They continued to take more of the initiative. I continued to offer ideas as to which perspective might add depth to the topic at hand and continued to provoke them when that seemed to be useful. As we neared the end of the work, the meetings decreased in frequency. Whereas we had been continuing a regular rotation of individual and couple sessions through the bulk of the work, we began to decrease the frequency of the individual sessions first, then the couple sessions. In the end, the couple sessions continued on an infrequent basis and there were no individual sessions.

EPILOGUE

It is continually astounding to see the striking similarities between the lives of one couple and another. By now, the notion of this being a "typical" case must be getting redundant and tedious. But it cannot be emphasized too strongly. As a reminder, Fred and Marie as they were specifically described here are fictional, as are Allen and Elaine.

But this description is the stuff of real life. With a surprisingly high frequency, the concerns in the lives of couples struggling with long-term affairs are the same, and the conversations in the therapy sessions are very similar. Even the episode of the inclusion of the lover in the course of therapy is an option that has been chosen by a number of couples in my own practice, without any type of prompting from me. I tried to capture my own reactions from my first outing with that strategy, to offer therapists who have never used that therapeutic technique a glimpse of one experience.

The idea of continuing therapy for slightly more than three years is, of course, grist for the debate over long- and short-term therapy, as was discussed in Chapter 7. It seems obvious to couples who continue for that duration, and obvious to me, that three years is not very long to disrupt patterns that have existed in the marriage for many years and have precedents dating back to both of the families of origin. Indeed, some couples in situations similar to Fred and Marie have continued in therapy longer than that.

In the brief therapy with Allen and Elaine, there was the distinct feeling of a lack of resolution of some of the dynamics. Likewise is there a possibility for a lack of resolution in long-term therapy. Although long-term therapy offers the opportunity to go into greater depth, it doesn't guarantee perfection. It would be more accurate to say that many of the original dynamics are modified permanently, whereas some of the others have only a satisfactory outcome. Yet others have a less-than-satisfactory conclusion.

Even at the conclusion of therapy, there was a sense that the level of intimacy between Fred and Marie was naggingly tenuous. At times they were able to establish a comfortable and effective rapport with each other, and at other times they were obviously more distant than either one of them wanted. But in the end, the strategy of triangling-in a lover to help balance out the equation had lost its effectiveness as an emotional solution.

CHAPTER 9

Affairs and the Social Context

Any attempt to define the connection between the broader social system and the more limited arena of a family emotional system, or an individual, is risky business. Questions of causality and influence become extraordinarily difficult. The temptation is to glance at that level of the system, acknowledge it with a "tip of the hat," and avoid a substantive examination. Just as it might be cleaner to develop a model of extramarital affairs that is built on intrapsychic factors and only generally acknowledge the impact of the family emotional system, so too would it be easier and cleaner to avoid the inclusion of the level of the social system. But that strategy leaves a rather significant gap in the model. Extramarital affairs, more than many other emotional dilemmas in the lives of individuals and families, interact in significant ways with the broader social context.

The complications of multidirectional causality are conspicuous in the examination of the societal dynamics of affairs. Although it is sometimes tempting to see forces within the broader social system "causing" events within the family, it is also tempting to see social process as being a reflection of, if not caused by, family emotional process. There are, of course, several different levels of social network beyond the family emotional system. The interaction between the family and the social system is more easily tracked with the more immediate network, which involves person-to-person relationships. The interaction of the family with the more impersonal and distant elements of the social system is correspondingly more difficult to establish and define.

THE IMMEDIATE SOCIAL NETWORK

Extramarital affairs belong to the group of symptoms that can trigger pronounced anxiety in the people closest to the situation. Other such symptoms include alcoholism and eating disorders. Close friends and neighbors, along with the extended family network, will frequently "take sides" regarding the meaning and appropriateness of the affair. The taking of sides generally has to do with their perceptions as to who is behaving more acceptably. Is the involved spouse doing what is unfortunate, perhaps, but understandable, because the noninvolved spouse is cold, hostile, and so forth? Or is the involved spouse "a bum or a tramp," because his or her behavior is betraying a kind and exemplary spouse and as such is inexcusable and immoral? Or is the affair simply "what's to be expected," or perhaps something seen as "innocent fun"?

These perceptions are, by definition, several steps removed from the immediate situation, poorly informed, sometimes distorted, and usually burdened by the feelings and general emotional makeup of the person offering the opinion. All of the well-known feelings about sexuality, intimacy, and emotional autonomy coalesce to create a highly charged opinion. Because of this emotional overlay, the opinions take on a life of their own, and they influence the overall balance in the emotional system of the individuals involved.

Peer Pressure and the Colluding Friend

One of the popular concepts related to teen-age alcohol usage is that of peer pressure. There is a belief that teen-age alcohol use is primarily instigated by the pressure that teens exert on each other. There may indeed be pressure from one teen to another. Peer pressure, however, is more effective on teens who have an emotional vulnerability that leaves them needing peer approval and needing the escape that alcohol provides. This vulnerability is created in the family and the emotional constellation that operates there.

The situation is quite similar with regard to extramarital affairs. There are times that people proclaim that an affair was prompted by a friend who offered encouragement. Here again, there may be a type of peer pressure that can have an effect, and perhaps even look like "the cause" of the involvement. But the peer pressure would not be effective unless there were the emotional vulnerability originating in the family.

Two different examples may help to illustrate this pressure. Tom came into treatment, anxious and upset, shortly after returning from an out-of-town convention. He had joined his long-time friend and business associate on a side trip to a bar, where the two of them had picked up women and spent the night with them. Tom's assertion was that he wouldn't have done it if he hadn't been with his friend and that he had felt obliged to "go along" with the events of the evening. As far as Tom was concerned, he had fallen prey to peer pressure and that was the reason for his transgression.

Alice presents a slightly different variation on this same theme. She came to treatment primarily because she was having trouble with her teen-age daughter, who was misbehaving in school and doing poorly in her grades. In the course of that treatment, Alice asked if she could have an individual appointment for herself. In that session she revealed that she was involved in an affair. She was becoming increasingly concerned about it, because she certainly did not want her husband to find out about it, and it was beginning to bother her in ways she couldn't exactly understand.

She saw herself as a victim of peer pressure. She had gone out for a casual dinner with a woman friend one night when their husbands were out of town on business. This friend then cajoled her into joining her in a visit to a singles' bar. The two of them, predictably, got "picked up" by two men. The casual pickups mushroomed into hot affairs. Both of the women initially seemed to demand that the other continue the involvement, because it continued the life of the foursome that had been established. Alice eventually grew very concerned about the arrangement, but she felt paralyzed and unable to extract herself from it.

Tom and Alice experienced peer pressure, but they were responsive to it because of their respective family situations. In Tom's case, Tom was later to discover unrecognized resentment toward his wife that related to her style of demanding his attention. He saw her as very insecure, and he believed that she looked to him for support, reassurance, and positive regard. Early in their relationship, he had thrived on her adoration of him and her self-deprecating manner. But he eventually became ambivalent about the very manner that had attracted him. He came to see that it gave him a false sense of importance.

The work in therapy with Tom quickly included his wife, Rose. The focus for Tom was to learn what had attracted him to Rose's neediness in the first place, and why he was vulnerable to moving away from it by way of an affair. The focus for Rose was to improve her self-image and diminish her neediness on Tom. Tom was surprised to learn that Rose felt that she needed him much less than she actually acted out. She had continued the act because she thought that Tom needed her to need him and was afraid that he might leave if she were to be more independent.

This process also went on to reveal Tom's own insecurities. He came to understand that he had been attracted to Rose's insecurities because it offered him a false sense of importance. The attraction of the affair was very much tied up in this need in him as well. He realized that he had been attracted to the fact that the woman he had been involved with saw him as very important. The combination of his own internal predispositions and the emotional balance of the marriage created an image that convincingly overshadowed the importance of peer pressure as a dynamic in his extramarital involvement.

Alice's case worked out in a similar way to Tom's. Alice's husband, Ben, had a job that demanded frequent travel. She felt lonely much of the time, but the situation was even more complicated by Ben's problem with alcohol. When Ben was home, he had a pattern of angry outbursts related to excessive alcohol use. His alcohol abuse came in isolated episodes and was not a continual problem. She was unable to identify any precipitating factors that seemed to relate to Ben's alcohol use. When Ben was included in the therapy, he talked about job pressures and his feeling that Alice was constantly dissatisfied with him and the standard of living he was providing.

The work of the therapy proceeded to explore Ben's alcohol use and angry outbursts. He discontinued using the alcohol and achieved control over his temper. Alice came to understand her need for attention, acceptance, and status. Her demands for more money or a better job had prompted Ben to accept the higher-paying travel job, which circled back to influence the emotional balance between them. She also came to understand that her need for acceptance kept her in the foursome with her friend and the two men. That need for acceptance was rooted in her family of origin. Alice, like Tom in the other case, discovered that the impact of peer pressure on her extramarital involvement was less important than she had originally thought.

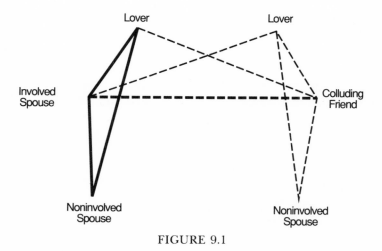

FIGURE 9.1

Tom and Alice represent a model of extramarital involvement that includes one more significant person in the emotional system. Whereas the isolated affair involves the triangle with the spouses and the lover, this type of involvement also includes the colluding friend. The four people (two spouses, friend, and lover) predicate the existence of several triangles between the four of them, as partially developed in Figure 9.1.

Just as the lover has a whole system of related triangles that were developed earlier, so too does the colluding friend. The number of triangles increases yet again if the triangles are developed into the area of the respective spouses, and so on. It is not uncommon for the two colluding friends to be friends with each other's spouse. Although those relationships, and the corresponding triangles, may have the more peripheral dynamic impact described here, they may have enough of an impact that some attention in the treatment would be indicated.

Sympathetic Friends

There are many situations where the friend is not actively involved and colluding in the extramarital activity, but she offers a sympathetic and responsive voice that can have an invisible and sometimes negative effect on the healing process. If this type of voice exists within the emotional system, it is necessary to identify it and neutral-ize its impact. With the involved spouse, for example, if the friend is supportive of the affair, there is the potential for this to add extra weight to the involvement that is unseen by the therapist. If the noninvolved spouse is confiding in someone who is prompting her to terminate the marriage, that also will have an impact on the course of treatment.

Thinking about the possibilities for triangles in the system offers a structure for the conceptualization of the system. Why, for example, might a person encourage the extramarital involvement of a friend? Think triangles. For example, there have been instances in which one man encouraged the extramarital involvement of his male friend because he was interested in the possibility of a relationship with the wife who would be "left behind." A quick survey of the possible triangles suggested the questions that revealed that dynamic. As this possibility emerged, the meaning of the support for the affair changed dramatically, as revealed by Figure 9.2.

A more common scenario involves a variation on the colluding friend format. The person with the sympathetic ear may not be fully colluding in the involvement, but she may have a need to live out an extramarital involvement vicariously. In this case, her own family situation is such that she feels the dissatisfaction but has not acted on the option of an outside relationship. The effect is a type of encour-agement for the outside relationship that defines it as an acceptable and understandable need to fulfill. If that type of opinion is being heralded, the involved spouse is caught in yet another triangle, which can have a direct impact on the process of therapy.

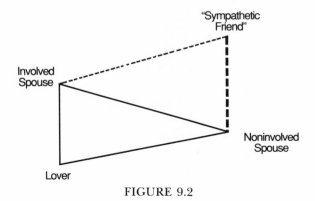

FIGURE 9.2

Sometimes the involved spouse can be confiding in a friend who is unsympathetic with the extramarital involvement and is supportive of the marriage. Frequently the involved spouse will continue candid conversations with this person because they have been life-long friends. Although the noninvolved spouse usually welcomes this type of influence, the dynamic impact of it is not entirely predictable. The involved spouse may be assaulted with an external expression of his own fears.

If the involved spouse hears the friend as pushing him to "put up with" the very problems he is trying to escape, it creates problems. It continues to emphasize the negative image of intimacy that must be altered if the marriage is to reconstitute with a new, healthy balance. It is then the job of the involved spouse, in conjunction with the therapist, to define the negative impact of the solution being offered by the friend and to minimize the impact of this voice in the system.

The type of voice that may influence the noninvolved spouse is slightly different. There is a popular emphasis placed on the notion of a retaliatory affair perpetrated by the "victim" of the affair, thus making the extramarital involvement symmetrical. This possibility seems to get more attention than my own clinical experience would support. The more common reaction is for the noninvolved spouse to seek out the emotional support of some close friend, often of the same sex, and to talk over strategies for handling the errant spouse. This, effectively, creates another triangle, another "therapist," and another source of emotional influence in the system.

The noninvolved spouse often seeks out someone to talk with who expresses an extreme opinion and reaction to the situation. Usually this extreme opinion represents almost a pure expression of one of the basic options for responding to the extramarital involvement. The two most predictable extremes are either to pursue vigorously the wandering spouse, in whatever way is imagined to work, or to act out intolerance, punishment, and even revenge. This extra voice in the system usually manifests itself in the individual sessions. The noninvolved spouse will, at some point in the session, question whether "it's a good idea to just tell the spouse to get out," or whether "it's a good idea to work harder at pleasing the spouse, because maybe there is something more that would help him decide to come back home."

Those types of ideas, of course, can come entirely from the

musings of the overwrought spouse who feels rejected and threatened by the revelation of the affair. But the possibility of the extra voice in the system should be considered and be addressed therapeutically. The sympathetic voice derives dynamic power by virtue of two interrelated dimensions:

1. It expresses one or both extremes of opinion related to the emotional distance needs in the couple—either to cut off or to fuse in an unhealthy enmeshment.
2. It establishes yet another operative triangle in the system. This triangle then implies the influence of the major triangles in the life of the individual who is the sympathetic ear.

The impact of this sympathetic friend usually can be minimized by an exploration of the dynamic meaning of the advice. If the opinion is revealed to be an extreme expression of one side of the dynamics, as in point number one, the client is better able to understand his own receptivity to the idea being rooted in his own internal impulses. Or if the client is less inclined to believe the friend, but is somewhat overwhelmed by the pressure experienced, understanding the possibilities for triangles in the other person's life establishes a level of detachment and objectivity that neutralizes the pressure.

The Gang

Moving a step beyond the one-on-one relationships of the colluding friend and the sympathetic ear, there is the immediate social network of the group of people who socialize together on a regular basis. Since so many extramarital affairs are born in this social context, whether it be in the work setting, a club setting, or neighborhood group, the dynamic interaction of this level of the system is potentially significant to the resolution of the crisis. And even if it is not central, it can present awkward situations.

The "awkwardness quotient," so to speak, is a function of who has access to what information and what type of opinions those people carry with them. Take, for example, a group of approximately fifteen to twenty people who have a work relationship with each

other. If they, in turn, know about an extramarital involvement between two of the group members, it has the potential to create a strain
in the group interaction. At times such as holiday celebrations, when
the work group is joined by the spouses, what is general knowledge
among the work group may be unknown among the spouses. Or it
may be known by everyone but the "victims," the noninvolved
spouses.

If a group of people know something significant about the emotional life of one person that that person doesn't know, there is a
significant discrepancy in power, given the connection between
knowledge and power. This will inevitably have an impact on the type
of relationships that evolve and the type of group acceptance the
noninvolved spouse will receive. Generally, this emerges as a treatment issue after the noninvolved spouse learns about the affair. Her
reaction, typically, is to feel shamed and embarrassed. The natural
desire is to avoid the group. The therapeutic approach to this type of
shame will be to stress the understanding of the systemic nature of the
affair and to stress the perception of the involved spouse as expressing an inadequacy in himself more directly than expressing a deficiency in the noninvolved spouse.

The noninvolved spouse is not the only person in the immediate
social group who is likely to be in an embarrassing position. Other
people in the system can be unwittingly caught up in the emotional
and practical consequences of the affair. Secretaries can be expected
to "cover" for the boss when the spouse calls and the boss is away with
the other person. Business partners can be frustrated when the extramarital activities preempt business responsibilities. These same
people may feel caught up in a web of conflicting loyalties, especially
if they have personal relationships with all three people in the
triangle.

Postaffair Relationships

One of the significant questions that is relevant to "the gang" will
be the status of the relationships after the termination of the affair.
This primarily concerns the relationship between the two people who
had the affair, but it can involve their respective relationships with
others in the group as well. If the group is an established group that
would be difficult to dismantle, such as a neighborhood or a work
group, there may be some pressure to keep the group intact, and not

expel either of the "offending" parties. This is likely to be an un-popular strategy with the noninvolved spouses, if they know about the affair. They are likely to be interested in banishing the person they see as the villain. There may, however, be constraints on the practical-ity of that solution if the two involved people occupy key positions in the work group, or if there are other circumstances that create ongo-ing opportunities for continued contact between the two involved parties.

The involved spouse may also express a strong desire to redefine the relationship with the "former lover" in such a way as to maintain the friendship and terminate the romantic element. This solution is actually possible, although it may not happen as quickly or easily as anticipated. Careful work on the emotional balance in the marriage, conscientious work on the dynamic meaning and importance of the relationship that was once an affair, and the full range of therapeutic intervention developed through this book can bring people to a point of truly redefining those relationships. But usually there is a need to distance themselves from each other until that process has been completed. For true success with this strategy, the emotional contract that was the foundation of the affair must be renegotiated to be one of a different order and type of intimacy.

There are other times when that type of resolution is impossible. In those situations, either the noninvolved or the involved spouse is unable to achieve the necessary emotional shift. The noninvolved spouse, for example, can be sufficiently threatened by the presence of the other person that she insists that all contact between the two people be eliminated. And on the involved spouse's side of the ledger, he can be unable to let go of the emotional intimacy with the other person that was the essence of the affair. It wouldn't be enough to simply discontinue sexual contact. The relationship must be totally terminated.

Depending on the circumstances involved, major disruptions in social networks can be experienced at the termination of an affair. Friendships that were important and central for many years can disintegrate. The reasoning is always understandable. There usually is an inability on everyone's part to carry out the necessary redefini-tion, acceptance, and forgiveness. Frequently, couples who have been a close foursome for many years will cease to have contact with each other as a result of the emotional involvement of the "right husband with the wrong wife."

BROADER SOCIAL NETWORK INFLUENCES

Once past the narrow confines of the immediate social network, the operations of the emotional system become murky to the point of being opaque. This is not to say that there is an absence of ideas about social systems. That, obviously, is the core of the study of sociology. The emphasis here, however, is on the workings of the emotional system of the couple struggling with an affair. Three primary questions arise. What elements of the broader social system have any relevance to the affair? What is the nature of the interconnections? What are the clinical implications of those connections?

The more abstract elements of the broad social system probably have the most relevance to the emotional system of the affair. Some of these can be seen as either emotional systems themselves, or as other levels of the same emotional system. Cultural and religious systems are two of the most obvious examples. A detailed examination of the intersection of the emotional system of the family with the values and emotional system of these broader systems would be pertinent to the understanding of affairs, but it is beyond the scope of this book. There are several other elements from the broader system that appear frequently in the therapy of affairs, including the mass media, the question of gender, the question of homosexual affairs, and social attitudes towards sexuality. These are much more limited in scope, but warrant a brief review.

The Mass Media

The turmoil of the initial crisis often prompts people to search out ideas to help them make sense of their experience. Beyond the need for meaning, there is potentially a hunger for guidance. Although the therapist is bound to be a major source in this effort, other sources will be found as well. Each of these sources represents different trends in the definition of the experience of an affair and different proscriptions for strategies.

Magazines are one of the most common venues. A month rarely goes by without some article addressing affairs. There are many months when articles about affairs occupy a disproportionate amount of space on the well-stocked magazine rack. Since magazines frequently are targeted at a narrower audience, the bias is likely to be more pronounced.

Magazines targeted at women, for example, frequently address articles to "women as victims" of the affairs. The attention-grabbing theme could have to do with surviving an affair of the husband, affair-proofing the marriage, or some formulation about the meaning of an affair. There seem to be fewer articles written to the audience who may be involved in affairs. It is even more unlikely to find articles aimed at the man or woman who may be in considerable turmoil as a result of the involvement. This could be seen as a perpetuation of the myth that the involved person is on some type of carefree vacation and needs no help. Or it could be an unwillingness to have the magazine be seen as colluding with some type of undesirable villain.

Every other mass communication medium encounters affairs in one way or another. Novels are built on affairs. Movies and stage plays frequently have affairs as either main plots and/or subplots. Musical lyrics often address affairs directly, and even more often address them indirectly in the form of allusions to rejection and unhappy love experiences. Television focuses on affairs from a variety of perspectives, including "straight" news reports, talk shows, situational dramas and comedies, and soap operas.

The attention to these in the therapy can be initiated by the client. Some mention is made of a recent encounter with a depiction of an affair in the media, followed by a brief report of the client's reactions. The emotional meaning that was personalized, as well as behavior that was implemented, can be tracked and compared to the systemic model. For example, if a noninvolved spouse came in with a renewed belief in being victimized as a result of reading an article, that perception, and the corresponding behavior, should be addressed in the therapy. On the other hand, it is possible that the encounter provided the client helpful insight regarding the situation. It is possible that the outside source helped to clarify points that had been a subject of the therapy but had not been integrated by the client.

In the vein of helpful input from the mass media, there are times when the therapist can initiate the integration of the mass media into the therapy. Retelling a scene from a movie that may be pertinent to a client's situation can prompt a more objective view of a traumatic, confusing situation. Suggesting reading material, as discussed in Chapter 5, can accomplish the same type of goal in a different way.

Women and Men: The Gender Question

The women's movement, including consciousness-raising groups, equal rights amendments, equal pay for equal work concerns, and a general celebration of womanhood, has been one of the more visible social movements of recent years. The men's movement has been but a shadow of the women's movement, though it has had many of the same agendas, such as celebrating manhood and sensitizing people to the demands that are gender-related. Both movements have provided a forum for the expression of ideas, needs, feelings, and grievances about a life experienced as bound up by gender membership.

It would be possible to "genderize" affairs. They could be defined as a form of self-expression and perhaps an inalienable right. They could be seen as an expression of the need to fight against the oppression of the opposite sex. From the woman's point of view, they could be defined as a form of coming of age, in which women, with the assistance of birth control technology, gain the sexual freedom heretofore enjoyed primarily by men. In doing so, they also gain equality in the emotional marketplace, gaining the right to enjoy multiple relationships, and attesting to their attractiveness just as men have been doing for years. A slight variation on this theme would be to capitalize on the right to develop relationships with other women, which may or may not be sexual.

From the man's point of view, they could be defined as the opportunity to search out relationships that offer the opportunity to relate to a sensitive, understanding woman. Or they could be defined as simple, harmless fun that does nothing to diminish the effective support and provider role they maintain in their primary relationships. The opportunity for man-to-man relationships would be the equivalent to the feminine relationships for women.

Yet another perspective on the gender question comes from Scarf (1987). She suggests, with some qualification, that men may be more likely to become involved in an affair because of a fear of intimacy and women may be more likely to become involved because of a hunger for intimacy. This type of bias is rather common, and it carries an overtone of a value judgment. If that presupposition is carried into the treatment, the therapy would clearly be skewed. This example highlights the need to clarify the assumptions about gender influences.

The position that emerges from this model of the emotional system is one that rejects gender bias. Both women and men are assumed to be capable of both wishes for and fears of intimacy. Both women and men are assumed to be capable of a full range of feelings. Both women and men are acknowledged to be capable of imperfection but to have the capacity to work toward a greater integration of self in their emotional lives.

It is quite impossible to "justify" affairs as some type of phenomenon founded on gender pressures, for either gender. The dynamics developed throughout the book offer a much richer image of the emotional foundations of affairs. Once these dynamics are understood, the emotional pain endemic to affairs becomes obvious. The notion of someone's "right" to have an affair quickly dissolves and is replaced by an understanding of the diverse emotional pressures that have culminated in the affair.

Although some concerns related to gender issues are valuable, it is impossible to assign gender dynamics precedence over the more fundamental themes developed throughout the book. The issues of self-definition, fusion, differentiation, emotional vulnerabilities, and so forth, simply are not the province of one gender over the other. They are the stuff of human existence.

The conclusion is that there is little to be gained from a major emphasis on gender-related concerns in the dynamic etiology of extramarital affairs. Affairs are not "a men's issue" or "a women's issue." Although there may be occasional superficial gender themes pertinent in any specific instance, the primary emotional structure, the core of the emotional system, greatly transcends these concerns. The gender-related dynamics are like interesting, but remote and transient background voices in the middle of a symphony with far more powerful main themes.

Homosexual Affairs

There are times when a man or woman in a heterosexual marriage becomes involved in a homosexual affair. This can precipitate extreme reactions. On the one hand, there can be an embarrassment and an understandable fear of sanction. On the other hand, there can be a self-righteous confidence and belief in the legitimacy of the experience. The justification is that "healthy" people can be attracted to people of the same sex as well as being attracted to people of the opposite sex. There is also the covert insinuation that people who are "able" to experience and act on both attractions may be in some way more sensitive and more emotionally viable than the mass of humanity that has "pathologically" suppressed homosexual impulses.

There may be some credence in the hypothesis that people, especially men, need to be able to allow themselves to feel and express positive feelings to others of the same sex. But it is impossible to forget the triangles and the corresponding emotional process. The emotional system of the affair transcends the element of sex. Clinical experience has shown that homosexual affairs are understandable with the same set of triangles that was developed earlier. As such, the question of the sexual choice can become a smoke screen for the fundamental problems with the intimacy in the life of the person involved. The imperative to develop relationships with both sexes must be balanced with the imperative to develop the full potential for intimacy in a mature, well-integrated, one-to-one, person-to-person relationship.

Sexual Ambivalence in Society

Sexual problems are commonly expected in the wake of an affair. There are some occasions when such problems may appear and can be treated with standard therapeutic techniques. They are not, however, a universal experience. What is far more typical is a call for a reassessment of the philosophical and emotional foundations of sexuality. This process is greatly complicated by general social attitudes.

The confusion between sexual and emotional needs that was noted in Chapter 1 is one small factor in a much broader confusion about sexuality in society. Affairs, by virtue of the sexual component, get swooped up in the general confusion. The confusion is centered around what is appropriate, with whom, and under what circumstances. The confusion stems not only from the differences in opinion between one person and another but from internal, personal confusion and ambivalence about sexuality. There is massive and widespread uncertainty about the degree to which sexuality is accepted as a personal experience and how it can be expressed.

The direct expression of affection between any two people usually has at least some overtones of sexuality. Some contact is more overtly sexualized, such as dancing. Other forms of expression, such as hugging and touching, are somewhat more ambiguous. There is marked ambivalence about this type of contact throughout society. In relationships outside the marriage, the ambivalence is partly related to a fear of the type of confusing emotional entanglements explored throughout this book. In the marriage, there are complications of intimacy and self-definition. In addition to these concerns, there are other problems that are pertinent to treatment.

There is confusion about the degree to which one may accept one's sexuality and express it as a part of "self." Certainly an individual's sexuality is a key ingredient coloring many of the nuances of interpersonal relationships. But contemporary western society has evolved in such a way that the prohibitions against expressing that sexual element are not only numerous but contradictory. If there are prohibitions against "owning" one's sexuality in the sense of expressing it in the context of daily life, then that can create a need to establish a clandestine life separate from daily life that will accept and tolerate the expression of sexuality.

There is confusion about how genuinely to feel and express the sexual energy that naturally exists between people and still maintain the hierarchy of relationships, that is, have the capacity to balance the emotional priority that one relationship has over another one. One common strategy for minimizing this conflict is to ignore or deny the attraction by going to extremes to de-sexualize relationships. Prohibitions against dancing with someone other than one's spouse, or against dancing at all, are an example of the extreme of this strategy. The more subtle prohibitions against touching also can be seen as attempts to minimize this conflict. But these sanctions bring liabilities. Not only is the natural element of sexual attraction suppressed, but the need for warm, nonexploitive human contact is unmet. People individually, and society as a whole, become progressively more isolated and suffer from a type of emotional malnutrition.

Extramarital affairs offer an intriguing glimpse into another area of sexuality, the complexities of sexual attraction. There is a common preoccupation with the relative sexual attractiveness of the three main characters. Whether the lover is seen as more or less attractive than the noninvolved spouse, and whether the involved spouse is sufficiently attractive to merit the others' interest, often become foci of discussions.

This interest in physical features reflects a misunderstanding of the process of physical attraction. Interpersonal attraction, though experienced as a physical attraction, and often attributed to certain physical features, is more pervasively a function of an emotional attraction, which includes an attraction to personality characteristics. Losing sight of this element of interpersonal attraction further contributes to the overall confusion about the meaning and impact of sexual attractiveness, and sexuality in general. There is a common desire to be attractive that can be felt as a fear of not being attractive. There is a desire to respond to others who are seen as attractive and fears about the repercussions of responding to that attraction.

SEXUAL MONOGAMY—EMOTIONAL MONOGAMY

One final theme to consider is the somewhat classic question about natural predispositions. More specifically, are human beings naturally monogamous, or is there really a natural need for variety that has been suppressed by social convention? This somewhat philosophical question can be an intellectualized attempt to gain control of the constellation of fears and desires that are intrinsic to the emotional system developed here. The fears include all of the more dynamic fears, such as isolation vs. enmeshment in a relationship, as well as rather mundane fears, such as the fear of a loss of sexual attractiveness. The desires cover the same range, including the desire to fulfill a primitive wish for a variety of physical sensations, as well as the desire to have a sense of closeness and rapport with another person.

These various fears and desires intersect at a point of confusion. They are joined there by philosophical beliefs about the need for individual freedom and self-expression. The result is experienced as a clash between the desire for self-fulfillment and the timeless expectations for a monogamous relationship. The conflict partially stems from the misconception that the impetus for a monogamous relationship is an imposed mandate rather than a natural inclination. There is a fear that no one relationship can fulfill all of an individual's needs. People continue to experience attractions to others and must presumably either deny those attractions or act in defiance of social convention.

The people in this book, beginning with Edward in the very first example, to Fred and Marie, Allen and Elaine, and all of the other people who made appearances, attest to a very strong pull toward emotional monogamy. The consequences of multiple loyalties are too painful. For most people most of the time, emotional monogamy translates into sexual monogamy. This is not a moralistic statement. It is not a proscriptive statement. It is not intended to restrict individual rights or freedoms. It is a reflection on human emotional functioning and the functioning of the emotional systems we live in.

For people who do feel a need for, or simply "end up in," coexisting relationships that are characterized by the emotional turmoil of the affairs seen in this book, that need can rarely be understood as anything other than a confused emotional response to emotional conflicts. The evidence illustrates that significant, or repetitive involvement in multiple relationships implies some variation on the range of systemic dynamics developed throughout this book. It does not suggest an emotional pattern that is based on healthy connections but one that is based on avoiding uncomfortable connections and reacting to conflicting emotional forces. If understanding that dynamic basis eliminates the need for the plurality, it does not represent a restriction of individual freedom so much as it represents a regaining of individual integration and mature self-definition.

Bibliography

Block, J. (1978). *The other man, the other woman.* New York: Grosset & Dunlap.

Boszormenyi-Nagy, I., & Spark, G. M. (1973). *Invisible loyalties: Reciprocity in intergenerational family therapy.* New York: Harper & Row.

Bowen, M. (1971). Principles and techniques of multiple family therapy. In *Family therapy in clinical practice* (pp. 241–258). New York: Jason Aronson, 1978.

Bowen, M. (1978). *Family therapy in clinical practice.* New York: Jason Aronson.

Brownfain, J. J. (1985). A study of the married bisexual male: Paradox and resolution. *Journal of Homosexuality, 11*(1–2).

Bugental, J. F. T. (1987). *The art of the psychotherapist.* New York: Norton.

Coleman, E. (1981). Bisexual and gay men in heterosexual marriage: Conflicts and resolutions in therapy. *Journal of Homosexuality, 7*(2–3).

Coleman, E. (1985). Integration of male bisexuality and marriage. *Journal of Homosexuality, 11*(1–2), 189–207.

Crane, R. D., Dollahite, D. C., Griffin, W., & Taylor, V. L. (1987). Diagnosing relationships with spatial distance: An empirical test of a clinical principle. *Journal of Marital and Family Therapy, 13*(3), 307–310.

Dell, P. F. (1982). Beyond homeostasis: Toward a concept of coherence. *Family Process, 21*(1), 21–42.

Dixon, D. (1985). Perceived sexual satisfaction and marital happiness of bisexual and heterosexual swinging husbands. *Journal of Homosexuality, 11*(1–2), 209–222.

Dixon, J. K. (1985). Sexuality and relationship changes in married females following the commencement of bisexual activity. *Journal of Homosexuality, 11*(1–2), 115–133.

Duhl, B. S. (1983). *From the inside out and other metaphors.* New York: Brunner/Mazel.

Duvall, E. M. (1977). *Marriage and family development* (5th ed.). Philadelphia: Lippincott.

Guerin, P. J., Fay, L. F., Burden, S. L., & Kautto, J. G. (1987). *The evaluation and treatment of marital conflict.* New York: Basic Books.

Haley, J. (1973). *Uncommon therapy.* New York: Ballantine Books.

Hite, S. (1984). *The Hite report on male sexuality.* New York: Knopf.

Hite, S. (1987). *Women & love: A cultural revolution in progress.* New York: Knopf.

Humphrey, F. G. (1985a). *Sexual dysfunction and/or enhancement interactions with extramarital affairs.* Paper presented at the Yale Sex Therapy Program, New Haven, CT.

Humphrey, F. G. (1985b, October). *Extramarital affairs and their treatment by AAMFT therapists.* Paper presented at the American Association for Marriage and Family Therapy annual conference, New York.

Humphrey, F. G. (1986, October). *Extramarital Affairs: A summary.* Paper presented at the American Association for Marriage and Family Therapy annual conference, Orlando, FL.

Humphrey, F. G. (1987). Treating extramarital sexual relationships. In G. Weeks & L. Hof (Eds.), *Integrating sex and marital therapy* (pp. 149–170). New York: Brunner/Mazel.

Humphrey, F. G., & Eldridge, S. (1984, October). *Unraveling and treating interlocking dynamics of sexual and marital complaints.* Paper presented at the American Association for Marriage and Family Therapy annual conference, San Francisco.

Humphrey, F. G., & Strong, F. (1976). *Treatment of extramarital sexual relationships as reported by clinical members of AAMFC.* Paper presented at the Northeastern AAMFC conference.

Karpel, M. A., & Strauss, E. S. (1983). *Family evaluation.* New York: Gardner Press.

Kinsey, A. C., Pomeroy, W. B., & Martin, C. E. (1948). *Sexual behavior in the human male.* Philadelphia: W. B. Saunders.

Kinsey, A. C., Pomeroy, W. B., & Martin, C. E. (1953). *Sexual behavior in the human female.* Philadelphia: W. B. Saunders.

Mahler, M. F. (1967). On human symbiosis and the viccissitudes of individuation. *Journal of the American Psychoanalytic Association, 15*(4), 740–763.

May, R. (1975). *The courage to create.* New York: Norton.

Meyers, L., & Leggitt, H. (1975). *Adultery and other private matters.* Chicago: Nelson-Hall.

Minuchin, S. (1974). *Families and family therapy.* Cambridge: Harvard University Press.

Moultrup, D. J. (1981). Towards an integrated model of family therapy. *Clinical Social Work Journal, 9*(2), 111–126.

Moultrup, D. J. (1985). Alone together. In A. S. Gurman (Ed.), *Casebook of marital therapy* (pp. 229–252). New York: Guilford Press.

Moultrup, D. J. (1986). Integration: a coming of age. *Contemporary Family Therapy, 8*(2), 157–167.

O'Neill, N. (1977). *The marriage premise.* New York: M. Evans.

O'Neill, N., & O'Neill, G. (1972). *Open marriage.* New York: Avon.

Paul, N. (1976) Cross confrontation. In P. Guerin (Ed.), *Family therapy, theory and practice* (pp. 520–529). New York: Gardner Press.

Pittman, F. (1987). *Turning points: Treating families in transition and crisis.* New York: Norton.

Pittman, F. (1989). *Private lies: Infidelity and the betrayal of intimacy.* New York: Norton.

Scarf, M. (1987). *Intimate partners: Patterns in love and marriage.* New York: Random House.

Selvini Palazzoli, M., Boscolo, L., Cecchin, G., & Prata, G. (1980). Hypothesizing–circularity–neutrality: Three guidelines for the conductor of the session. *Family Process, 19*(1), 3–12.

Sprenkle, D. H., & Weiss, D. L. (1978). Extramarital sexuality: Implications for marital therapists. *Journal of Sex and Marital Therapy, 4*(4), 279–291.

Stanton, M. D. (1981). An integrated structural/strategic approach to family therapy. *Journal of Marital and Family Therapy, 7*(4), 427–439.

Strean, H. (1980). *The extramarital affair.* New York: The Free Press.

Tennov, D. (1979). *Love and limerence.* New York: Stein & Day.

Thompson, A. P. (1982a). Extramarital relations: Counselling considerations and a developmental perspective. *Australian Journal of Family Therapy, 3,* 141–147.

Thompson, A. P. (1982b). Extramarital relations: gaining greater awareness. *Personnel and Guidance Journal 61,* 102–105.

Thompson, A. P. (1983). Extramarital sex: A review of the research literature. *Journal of Sex Research, 19,* 1–22.

Thompson, A. P. (1984a). Extramarital sexual crisis: Common themes and therapy implications. *Journal of Sex and Marital Therapy, 10,* 239–254.

Thompson, A. P. (1984b). Emotional and sexual components of extramarital relations. *Journal of Marriage and the Family, 46,* 35–42.

Thompson, A. P. (1987). Extramarital relations: Common questions. *Journal of Clinical Practice in Sexuality.*

Tomm, K. (1984). One perspective on the Milan systemic approach: Part I. Overview of development, theory, and practice. *Journal of Marital and Family Therapy, 10*(2), 113–126.

Walster, E., Traupmann, J., & Walster, G. W. (1978). Equity and extramarital sexuality. *Archives of Sexual Behavior, 7*(2), 127–141.

Weil, M. W. (1975). Extramarital relationships: A reappraisal. *Journal of Clinical Psychology, 31*(4), 723–725.

Index